Defining Medievalism(s)

Studies in Medievalism XVII

2009

Studies in Medievalism

Founded by Leslie J. Workman

Previously published volumes are listed at the back of this book

Defining Medievalism(s)

Edited by
Karl Fugelso

Studies in Medievalism XVII 2009

Cambridge
D. S. Brewer

© Studies in Medievalism 2009

First published 2009
D. S. Brewer, Cambridge

ISBN 978-1-84384-184-5

ISSN 0738-7164

D. S. Brewer is an imprint of Boydell & Brewer Ltd
PO Box 9, Woodbridge, Suffolk IP12 3DF, UK
and of Boydell & Brewer Inc.
668 Mt Hope Avenue, Rochester, NY 14620, USA
website: www.boydellandbrewer.com

A CIP catalogue record for this book is available
from the British Library

This publication is printed on acid-free paper

Typeset by Pru Harrison, Hacheston, Suffolk
Printed in Great Britain by
CPI Antony Rowe Ltd, Chippenham, Wiltshire

Studies in Medievalism

Studies in Medievalism provides an interdisciplinary medium of exchange for scholars in all fields, including the visual and other arts, concerned with any aspect of the post-medieval idea and study of the Middle Ages and the influence, both scholarly and popular, of this study on Western society after 1500.

Studies in Medievalism is published by Boydell & Brewer, Ltd., P.O. Box 9, Woodbridge, Suffolk IP12 3DF, UK; Boydell & Brewer, Inc., 668 Mt. Hope Avenue, Rochester, NY 14620, USA. Orders and inquiries about back issues should be addressed to Boydell & Brewer at the appropriate office.

For a copy of the style sheet and for inquiries about **Studies in Medievalism**, please contact the editor, Karl Fugelso, at the Dept. of Art and Art History, Towson University, 8000 York Rd, Towson, MD 21252–0001, USA, tel. 410–704–2805, fax 410–704–2810 ATTN: Fugelso, e-mail <kfugelso@towson.edu>. All submissions should be sent to him as e-mail attachments in Word.

Acknowledgments

The device on the title page comes from the title page of *Des Knaben Wunderhorn: Alte deutsche Lieder*, edited by L. Achim von Arnim and Clemens Brentano (Heidelberg and Frankfurt, 1806).

The epigraph is from an unpublished paper by Lord Acton, written about 1859 and printed in Herbert Butterfield, *Man on His Past* (Cambridge University Press, 1955), 212.

Studies in Medievalism

Volume XVII 2009

Two great principles divide the world, and contend for the mastery, antiquity and the middle ages. These are the two civilizations that have preceded us, the two elements of which ours is composed. All political as well as religious questions reduce themselves practically to this. This is the great dualism that runs through our society.

Lord Acton

Editorial Note

Every month my *SiM* mailbox yields at least one paper that has clearly lost its way. It was meant for *Speculum, October,* or perhaps *Psychology Today,* but it somehow wound up here, at a journal that may incorporate, but does not concentrate on, direct study of the Middle Ages, literary theory, or mental tendencies. I cannot always be sure who is to blame for these mix-ups, especially when the introductory letter is addressed to "Prof. Johnson," "Mr. Levey," or the ubiquitous "Whom It May Concern." But I suspect the problem usually begins with authors who are confused as to the definition of medievalism. I therefore thought it was high time to ask scholars who have long been associated with *SiM* to address the nature and parameters of our field.

Of course, owing to other commitments, and an admittedly short deadline, not all of the invitees were able to answer my call in time for this volume of *SiM.* And no two respondents seem to have interpreted my request in quite the same manner. But all of them have, I believe, answered in thoughtful and important ways. Kathleen Verduin gives a brief history of the founding of *Studies in Medievalism,* particularly as regards its approach to the field. Clare A. Simmons traces the roots of the term "medievalism" in nineteenth-century England and discusses the relevance of those origins to the development of the field. Nils Holger Petersen explores the modern borders of the field, especially as they relate to several fascinating case studies. Tom Shippey discusses the very real dangers in some uses of modern medievalism. Gwendolyn A. Morgan dwells on one of these dangers as she addresses the hypocrisies embedded in numerous academic approaches to the field. M. J. Toswell explores paradoxes in popular versions of medievalism. And Elizabeth Emery proposes measures to convey and perhaps expand the flexibility of our field, not least to avoid such hypocrisies and paradoxes.

As for my own contribution to this section, it does not directly tackle the history, etymology, theory, or implications of medievalism. But I hope it does give at least some idea of how *SiM* approaches the field. And if it does not, I hope its main points are evident from the sort of papers that come after the definitions of medievalism, for though not every article in this volume strictly adheres to the criteria I discuss in my essay, their authors generally pursue medievalism in ways long promoted by *SiM.* Emily Walker Heady discusses representations of King Alfred in two works by Charles

Dickens. Mark B. Spencer looks at how the Middle Ages are refracted through characters in Sigrid Undset's novel *Kristin Lavransdatter*. Gail Orgelfinger explores echoes of medieval bestiaries in J. K. Rowling's Harry Potter books. Douglas Ryan VanBenthuysen addresses medievalism as manifested in disparities between the printed and audio versions of Seamus Heaney's *Beowulf.* Thea Cervone analyzes how the playwright John Bale adapted medieval tropes to promote a Reformist agenda. Werner Wunderlich traces the roots of Händel's medievalism in *Rodelinda.* And Edward R. Haymes uncovers hitherto overlooked aspects of the *Nibelungenlied* in Wagner's *Ring of the Nibelung.*

Of course, the traditions of *SiM* permit many other approaches to the field. And, as I note at the end of my definition of medievalism, even overt departures from those conventions may find a home in future volumes of *SiM*. But I hope that the essays and articles in this volume will encourage potential contributors to carefully consider whether their papers qualify as medievalism and whether they substantially contribute to the field: whether they should in fact be sent to me or Mr. Levey.

The Founding and the Founder: Medievalism and the Legacy of Leslie J. Workman

Kathleen Verduin

Medievalism is the continuing process of creating the Middle Ages.
(Preface, *Studies in Medievalism* 8, 1996)

The archive is rich. I knew it, of course, having collaborated for nearly twenty years with the founding editor of *Studies in Medievalism*, Leslie J. Workman, as, in his preferred appellation, "Associate Editor and wife, not necessarily in that order": if there was any strain on our domestic circumstances, it was that as an inveterate historian he would throw nothing away. But sorting again through the thirty-odd banker's boxes now in the attic of the humanities building at Hope College, where I teach and where Leslie stalked the halls from our marriage in 1983 until the illness that ended his life in 2001, I am again convinced that there is a story worth telling here, and I am grateful that he preserved its documents. How does a discipline get established? What were the origins of Leslie's concept of "medievalism," and what did he mean by the word? How did his passion for the subject arise from his own education, his anomalous professional identity, his chronically precarious standing in the American academic world? This memoir – postponed until the interval between semesters and composed appropriately in the kind of frantic deadline-haste that always marked our work together (perhaps less work than collusion, I sometimes felt, but that was the fun of it) – makes a few preliminary stabs at answering those questions. Embedded in the vicissitudes of

Leslie's biography, the narrative is by turns proud and chagrined, rueful and loving: and I hope it will inspire some better historian than I to a fuller recounting at some future time.

I

Time is, in fact, a good place to start. Leslie was, I think, fascinated by time: he believed himself to have been the first to teach science fiction at the college level, and he had been personally acquainted with the pioneering science-fiction writer Arthur C. Clarke. If there was a significant landmark in his progress from religious faith to something I feel uncomfortable classifying as simple atheism, it was probably the writings of the futuristic theologian Teilhard de Chardin. As Leslie looked forward in time, of course, he more often looked back: I remember him telling me that as a boy he had been obsessed with solicitude for the Roman soldiers – how did they stay warm in northern climates, how did they care for their feet on long marches? – and a book he liked was *The Story of Man* (1954) by the anthropologist Carleton Coon. But his historian's sensibility was naturally rooted for him in his Englishness: born in London in 1927, he inherited the great age of English historiography (he was forever quoting the nineteenth-century scholar W. P. Ker's line "Ours is an age of history and science"), and, as he reminisced in an interview in the *Festschrift* Richard Utz and Tom Shippey edited for him in 1998, his birthplace, the London district of Hanwell, displayed monuments from several eras of the English past. His family traditions, and the ways they intersected history, were important to him as well; I will never forget how moved he was in 1993 when we visited, for the first time, the War Memorial in Edinburgh, where a yellowing typescript bore the name of an uncle, also named Leslie, who had fallen in the First World War. A Londoner, as I have said, Leslie nevertheless treasured memories of childhood visits to rural Somerset (the village was Brushford, near Exmoor), where a maternal uncle still served the county as a blacksmith.

Anecdotes suggest that Leslie was something of an individualist from early childhood: at the age of six he was slapped on the hand for ingeniously decorating the numerals his class was conning, and one of his teachers was overheard to pronounce, "The trouble with Workman is, when you expect him to answer back he looks at the ceiling, and when you expect him to look at the ceiling he answers back." Misfortune took the first of its swipes at Leslie when he was ten and his father died, of pneumonia and a bleeding ulcer; the boy, blond and blue-eyed and probably already manifesting a good deal of charm, returned to the Royal Russell School in London saddened and considerably poorer. His mother, vowing in the style of the age that she would never remarry, went to work announcing the trains at Paddington Station. Leslie experienced the Blitz – among my cherished possessions is a pencil portrait of him at twelve or so, sketched by his drawing master as the class huddled in an air-raid shelter – and he served in the Home Guard. Had the Second World War gone on any longer, he might have seen combat; as it was, his days in the British Army (1945–48) were passed in the Middle East, in Egypt and what is now Israel. He returned to matriculate at King's College of the University of London, where he received his B.A. with Honours in 1951: his studies were enlivened by a summer at the Borthwick Institute of Historical Research in York in 1950, at the same time that a flurry of post-war nationalism was reviving performance of the York Mysteries under Archbishop Purvis.

According to a conversation I had in 1996 with one of Leslie's university friends, the historian Peter Laven, historical studies at King's in the 1950s permitted only three areas of specialization: I have forgotten the first, but the others were the history of Venice, which Peter adopted, and the reign of Henry II, which Leslie took on. He would later describe himself as an English Constitutional historian, and certainly his endeavors at King's laid solid groundwork (was it there, I wonder, that he picked up two more favorite quotations, Sir Edward Coke's "Magna Carta is such a fellow as he will have no sovereign" and Tennyson's sonorous "A land of settled government, / A land of just and old renown, / Where Freedom slowly broadens down / From precedent to precedent"?). He then entered the civil service: opportunities for professional advancement in post-war England were limited. But I infer a coincident ambience of familial irritation: his mother had previously prevailed on him to forfeit a place at Oxford's Oriel College and study instead in London, where he could live cheaply at home. This was a concession he later bitterly regretted; he may have felt confined as well by the hovering presence of what was known in those days as a maiden aunt, succinctly captured in her nephew's memory as a lady who typically interposed herself between him and a bottle of beer with the chiding reproach, "Oh, Leslie, you *know* we never have it at *home!*" In any case, when American cousins visited in the early 1950s and suggested he start graduate study in the United States, Leslie apparently jumped at the prospect. He enrolled at Ohio State (where he politely submitted to an English fluency exam) in 1955, then transferred to Columbia two years later (delayed by an unexpected hospitalization for tuberculosis).

I wish I were better able, and had the time, to reconstruct Leslie's graduate years. The seminar paper he wrote on Jacob Burckhardt's *The Civilization of the Renaissance in Italy* (1860) has not come to light, though I am sure it is boxed somewhere; I know he read Wallace K. Ferguson's *The Renaissance in Historical Thought: Five Centuries of Interpretation* (1948), and the two titles suggest the germ of his growing interest in historical periodization. Among the few photographs I found in his desk was a funny one of him bowing before a banner emblazoned with the name of Arnold Toynbee (1889–1975), the primary historian of the rise and fall of civilizations, whom Leslie always credited as an influence. Leslie flourished at Columbia under luminary medievalists (more in literature, it seems, than in history) like the great Arthurian Roger Sherman Loomis and the Dante scholar Dino Bigongiari, and he professed to have been half in love with Laura Hibbard Loomis, by then a white-haired *grande dame* who liked to ensconce herself in a carved – nay, carven! – chair of ebony. New York itself was of course exciting, full of theatre and music and the new films of Ingmar Bergman. But the young Englishman was frustrated as well: among the correspondence I leafed through tearfully after his death was the carbon of a letter to a good friend, the historian and Columbia alumna Alice P. Kenney, where he railed against Columbia's endorsement of narrow specialization over attention to the grand over-arching historical patterns to which he was more attracted. Also plaguing him, regrettably, was the demon of procrastination he would battle all his life; his dissertation, on medieval sport, somehow never got done. An acid note from his Columbia advisor, whose name I forbear to dignify by inscription here, retorts to what was apparently Leslie's contrite resurfacing after long silence that he, the advisor, was "unable to imitate Our Lord and resuscitate the dead." When Leslie's brief career as a professor of history, first at Muhlenberg College and then at the Western College for Women in Oxford, Ohio (where to his credit he instigated an outdoor student production of the York

Cycle), unraveled to its terminus with the demise of the latter institution, the redoubtable Alice tried her best to console him (21 January 1971):

> You happened, unfortunately for you, to come to this country just at the time when Americans turned their backs on all kinds of commitments familiar to the English tradition – to institutions, to scholarship itself, to ideals in the Idealist sense, even to human beings in personal relations. This was particularly true, and particularly taught, at Columbia; you saved me from the consequences of learning what I was taught, and in the same breath showed me your own irreconcilable differences from them [...]. We are beginning to recognize our error, and I hope that a way can be found to make your experience of it redemptive, not only to yourself but to others. [...] [Y]ou must not give way completely to this hideous feeling of failure – though goodness knows you have more than reason. But the stubborn you that you are, who has "stopped crying myself to sleep and avoided drinking myself to sleep" – good for you, even that is accomplishing something, since you can say it – is, as usual, too English to know when you are licked, and so long as you keep fighting – well, I am Dutch enough to be thoroughly obstinate in another way, and I don't know when I'm licked either. [...] When you say "you could not make it" – and indeed this is not the first time you have said it to me – what is the *it* you are trying to make? If *it* is Columbia's idea of a Ph.D., or any other cog in our machines, of course not, for the good and sufficient reason that you were before you started a bigger *it* than they are [...].

Adversity often sounds a call to adventure. Alice was already fighting her own enemy, the disabling rheumatoid arthritis whose complications would take her life in the early 1980s; both in crisis, she and Leslie joined forces and secured a couple of NEH grants, which were of course a lot easier to land in those days. The collaboration was propitious: an Americanist by training (she made her mark with studies of her ancestors, the Hudson Valley Dutch), Alice complemented Leslie's expertise in English history and literature. More to the purpose, Leslie had by then taught undergraduate history courses long enough to realize, in some kind of Aha! moment, that the Middle Ages he was purveying at Western (where he was simultaneously observing, he admitted, "the Awful Anarchy of the American Adolescent Female") were largely a nineteenth-century construct, born of the "Awful Trinity" of British historians Stubbs, Maitland, and Round and betraying an entrenched Victorian bias at their roots. From this cluster of personal and professional events exploded, it seems, the nova of medievalism: Leslie himself dated its inception to 1974. Alice hooked him up with her connections at the Winterthur Museum in Delaware, and an extensive and prodigiously erudite essay jointly authored by Leslie and Alice, "Ruins, Romance, and Reality: Medievalism in Anglo-American Imagination and Taste, 1750–1840," appeared in the *Winterthur Portfolio* in 1975, lavishly illustrated. Interestingly, the word "medievalism," while prominent in the title, is conspicuously absent from the text, occurring, if I am not mistaken, only once: instead, the essay purports to re-examine the more familiar concept of the Gothic Revival. Medievalism is implicit, however, in the essay's promise to examine "the reciprocal influence of [...] fashionable Gothic genres and historical knowledge of the Middle Ages, particularly as fused in the overwhelmingly popular works of Sir Walter Scott, whose effect on his readers' visualization of the medieval past was incalculable." The wheels had started turning.

II

Leslie always (see, for example, "Medievalism in America") traced the establishment of medievalism as an academic subject to a single session at the Tenth International Congress on Medieval Studies at Western Michigan University (Kalamazoo) in May of 1976. The session, "The Idea of the Middle Ages in the Modern World," featured Leslie, Alice, and Peter Williams of Miami University; Alice Chandler, whose book *A Dream of Order: The Medieval Ideal in Nineteenth-Century English Literature* (1970) Leslie had hailed as a breakthrough, took the chair. Within a month Leslie was urging Otto Gründler, Director of the Medieval Institute at Western, to grant two sessions for the following year: "One of these sessions will have to be devoted to methodology. Since we are organizing virtually a new field of study of a uniquely interdisciplinary character, the need for this has already become a problem. At the same time the subject unfortunately lends itself to invalid generalizations and unconsidered methodology." Earlier, he had laid plans for a session at the Third Ohio Conference on Medieval Studies, set for October at John

Carroll University; on 19 April 1976 he wrote to the conference chair, Thomas Tomasic:

> It was good indeed to find a matching enthusiasm, but I must warn you that on the subject of medievalism my colleague Alice Kenney and I are not only enthusiasts but crusaders; and I seize this opportunity to explain to you what we are doing with this new field of study, at somewhat greater length than might seem necessary. […] Medievalism as a distinct area of study is attracting increasing attention; but those interested are drawn from history (medieval, American, European), literature in innumerable branches, religion, art and architecture, history, and some other disciplines. They are in both the academic and museum worlds, and each one is working virtually in isolation. No one person can keep even a cursory eye on all those fields, and collectively we do not really belong anywhere […]. [Medievalism] can be defined, too, as a form of intellectual history, including, however, the study of material culture and the relations between this and the history of ideas – which is not intellectual history as generally understood.

Citing his and Alice's "bridgehead in the museum world" – this referred to their reception at Winterthur – Leslie added:

> We decided recently that it was time to work the other side of the street, namely the medievalists; hence the session which I have organized for the Kalamazoo Conference – and next, hopefully, the Ohio Conference. What we are hoping to achieve, hopefully beginning at Kalamazoo, is some kind of continuing organization, a study group or conference, to draw together those interested in medievalism from widely scattered fields, probably a newsletter, and perhaps some continuing relationship with a conference like yours or the Kalamazoo one. The field is wide open and the need is becoming urgent.

The challenge, as Leslie evidently saw it, was somehow to inform a diverse group of scholars that they were in fact laboring in the same vineyard. "The trouble with medievalism," he told an early collaborator (12 September 1976), "is that it doesn't belong anywhere in the academic world, and people interested in it might come from almost any field – except perhaps microbiology. But I have found a home for it at two medieval conferences, and we do have, conversely, the fun of developing a methodology and so on for what is in effect a new kind of interdisciplinary subject." The year 1976–77 was clearly the *annus mirabilis*: in addition to the sessions at Kalamazoo and John Carroll, Leslie also organized two forums at the MMLA, both with a rack of distinguished commentators, and it was evidently here that he met the inimitable Veronica M. S. Kennedy, soon to be an enthusiastic associate. The momentum of these successes heartened Leslie to propose the formation of a quarterly journal, to be titled, simply, *Studies in Medievalism*. The rationale was largely hashed out, apparently, during a ride from the 1976 Kalamazoo Congress back to Oxford in the company of Britton Harwood, Miami University's resident medievalist: as Leslie recounts in the Utz-Shippey *Festschrift*, it was "something like a six-hour drive in the middle of the night, during which Brit took my mind apart, examined all the pieces critically and carefully, put them back together again and decided to give me his support [...]." An encouraging sign was the announcement that the 1979 Colloquium on Modern Literature at the University of West Virginia would emphasize "The Presence of the Middle Ages" (the program featured novelist John Gardner and also Bill Calin, who would become a stalwart supporter of Leslie's work). Certainly Leslie must have been gratified too by endorsements like the one he received from Rossell Hope Robbins (6 February 1978):

> My colleague in the English department here at Albany has verofaxed your note about the new journal, and may I wish you well in your project. Most scholars do not realize the concern of medievalists in the nineteenth century with the social and political movements of their times. It was not only a William Morris, the great non-exponent of medievalism, who led the May Day parade in London waving a red flag. Others too shared his sentiments. And we have the tradition of the later eighteenth century, and on through the romantics. It is a secondary and subsidiary stream, but I think one worth pursuing. May I wish you well.

Though Leslie no doubt balked at the assumption of an exclusively nineteenth-century reference and the "secondary and subsidiary" status, the attention of so distinguished a medievalist as Robbins promised the journal a favorable response. An impressive board of editors and advisors was assembled, and Leslie commissioned a massive bibliography. Bound in the conservative grey cover stock he favored, the journal's first issue, "Medievalism in England," was steered – indeed, "hustled" might be more apt – to production in 1979 with the help of Harwood and other friends at Miami. Leslie's editorial preface sets out his first formal attempt at definition, and he would frequently return to it:

> Ruskin apparently coined the word *medievalism* to characterize one of three periods of architecture, Classicism, Mediaevalism, Modernism. The term soon came to embrace "The system of belief and practice characteristic of the Middle Ages; medieval thought, religion, art, etc.," and "the study of these"; and by extension "the adoption of or devotion to medieval ideals or usages." These meanings in turn involved the use of medieval models as patterns of social action or artistic creation, didactic or otherwise, challenging the classical models which had dominated Europe from the fall of Rome through the eighteenth century.
>
> By the time that the *New English Dictionary* was published the first of these meanings was obsolescent: Thomas Hardy was perhaps the last to use the term consistently in this sense. This, in any case, is the province of medieval scholarship. *Studies in Medievalism* is concerned with the remaining meanings, the study of the scholarship which has created the Middle Ages we know, ideals and models derived from the Middle Ages, and the relations between them. In terms of these things medievalism could only begin, not simply when the Middle Ages had ended, whenever that may have been, but when the Middle Ages were perceived to have been something in the past, something it was necessary to revive or desirable to imitate.

The preface also intimates what would later become a major definitional battle, the traditional absorption of medievalism as such by the larger and better known (yet, to Leslie, inherently dubious) construct of Romanticism:

> The perception of medievalism has been obscured by confusion between medievalism and romanticism, by confusion between revival and survival, and by the fact that since 1914 we no longer look to the past for models. [...] *Studies in Medievalism* has consequently been established in the conviction that it is time to begin the inter-disciplinary study of medievalism as a comprehensive

phenomenon, analogous to classicism or romanticism. Is it, like these, a term almost too general to be definable, or is it like *Classicism* or *Romanticism*, one susceptible to analysis and definition, a field apt for endless controversy? Should we speak of medievalism or medievalisms? Are there common denominators in Spenser and Scott, Hugo and Hardy, Cervantes and Rossetti, Walpole and Wagner, Twain and T. H. White? It is, perhaps, too early to answer most of the questions: it is certainly time to ask them.

The tone here is judiciously moderate, but the surrounding correspondence documents Leslie's exhilaration, the rush not simply of a new venture but of a faltering career infused suddenly with vitality. One senses the exuberance of it all in letters, for example to an editorial associate: "Tempted though I am to begin *in medias res*, since most of my ideas are on epic scale, I shall begin at the beginning, for which I have the authority of *Alice in Wonderland* [...]" (8 December 1976). Or later (26 May 1979):

> On criticism I adhere rather to the view that C. S. Lewis ("Plenty of fact, reasoning as brief and clear as English sunshine, and no personal comment at all") picked up from Arnold – "The great art of criticism is to get oneself out of the way and let humanity decide" [...]. Portrait of a Die Hard [...] well, somebody has to hold the line. [...] I have to admit a reactionary (no doubt) suspicion that a certain bland and deadly conformity which I find in scholarly articles is the result, though not the intent, of the American cultivation (cult is an unkind word) of expository prose – this just tends to happen when you are obliged to try and reduce things to rules.

The letter is signed "Edward Hyde," with the teasing note, "Dr. Jekyll will be in touch in due course."

Yet this was also a time when everything else in Leslie's life was looking (you should pardon it) damned dismal. As he told Alice Chandler (25 September 1975), "When the Western College folded beneath me I made the rather dramatic decision to stay here in the village (it is a little like Cranford if you look at it 'with a sort of mental squint') and write, and so far have not regretted it." But remaining in Oxford rigidly circumscribed his options: he was in fact keeping himself a few degrees above the poverty level by renting out rooms and cleaning the local supermarket, and later he would be digging trenches for the Oxford Natural Gas Company (an interval he would nevertheless remember with affection for the gentle Appalachian men with whom he worked). Miami University, now the only academic game in town, failed to pick up his bid for part-time employment, and a brief stint with the local library's new research collection disintegrated in record time. Unfortunately too, medievalism as an innovative concept was hardly meeting the kind of open-armed approval Leslie may have expected. In June of 1978 he sent a long memo to the Medieval Institute at Western in a quixotic expectation of institutional support: "Medievalism – the post-medieval study of the Middle Ages and the use of that study in a variety of contexts, from economic and social theory to fantasy and poetry – has been a powerful cultural force from the sixteenth century to the present," he asserted, and it implied "the relation of scholarship to the various arts, the relation of what is now frequently called 'elitist' to popular (including folk) culture and the relations of any society to the past, in terms of seeking inspiration or models. It involves not least the relations of those who work in universities and those who work in museums." The same document admits, however, that "The editor's conviction that it" – medievalism – "is a major phenomenon analogous in scope and potential interest to Romanticism is not shared by all his colleagues," and indeed "those who work in museums" were not seeing the light either: Leslie's applications for a Winterthur fellowship in 1978 and 1979 were both turned down, with a terse handwritten annotation to the second proposal, "You certainly can apply as often as you wish, but after 2 tries I can't be optimistic." Although an approving TEAMS reviewer would observe in 1981 that "[t]eachers of medieval subjects will find *Studies in Medievalism* both a stimulus for tying together literary trends and ideas as well as a forum for understanding medieval scholarship," the Medieval Institute remained apparently impervious to Leslie's exercised insistence (5 December 1978) that "Medievalism is a big subject, bigger than Romanticism, and at the moment we have it all. I have a very solid board of editors, most of them with at least one good book to their credit, all young and moving fast"; Miami declined further support on the grounds that *Studies in Medievalism* was not a strictly institutional enterprise. In 1981 the English Department at the University of

Akron agreed to pick up the journal and actually saw several issues into production, but the arrangement ultimately collapsed. *Studies in Medievalism* drifted into limbo, a journal in search of a home.

III

As things turned out, the home was mine. Leslie and I met, briefly, on the last day of the Medieval Congress in 1980: I, a still relatively young Assistant Professor who specialized in American literature but dabbled in medieval studies, found myself at the same breakfast table with him and was duly swept away by his wit, charm, and erudition (imagine a big broad-shouldered Englishman joking, flirting, tossing out historical references, and quoting the poems of Ezra Pound all at the same time). I secured his plenary address, "Pagan Classicism and Christian Medievalism," for a conference on Christianity and classical culture we organized at Hope in 1982, and this introduced him to the campus (where, to my dismay, a few people took him for my father). In 1983, to our mutual astonishment, we found ourselves married, and the fortunes of *Studies in Medievalism* burrowed their way into my personal as well as professional activities. It was, of course, exciting to attend together a conference on medievalism at the Scarborough campus of the University of Toronto in 1984, within a year of our wedding, and even more the conference on Medievalism in America, organized by Paul Szarmach and Bernard Rosenthal at SUNY-Binghamton the same year. I was aware, however, that these hopeful signs of cultural ripeness also made Leslie nervous: his "little ewe lamb" of medievalism, as he called it in the biblical discourse of his youth (see II Samuel 12:3), was clearly susceptible to expropriation. Fortunately, this somehow never happened; eventually Hope College granted Leslie an office and me a computer, and together we initiated the annual International Conference on Medievalism in 1986, during my first sabbatical semester. I am proud to say that in 1985 the journal came close to adoption by the University of Chicago Press – "What we have to offer at the moment," Leslie asserted in his proposal, "is a virtual monopoly of a proven field. The publisher who joins with us will enjoy an unbeatable lead in a market which competition, when it comes, will only strengthen" – but we were turned away at the gates by the flaming sword of Chicago's Marketing Department, who ruled that the subject had no existing audience.

Studies in Medievalism was finally adopted, to great rejoicing and in company of a jeroboam of champagne, by the English publisher Boydell & Brewer in 1990, with the provision that it be reconceived as an annual volume.

Leslie's struggle to launch, or relaunch, his series in those years constitutes a testimony to what he called his "sheer bloody stubbornness" and deserves further study in its own right: but of more interest is his developing understanding of the scope and meaning of the academic subject he was laboring to establish. Crucial to his thinking was the differentiation between medievalism and classicism posed in his first editorial: with the second issue of Volume III (Fall 1990), *Studies in Medievalism* adopted its continuing epigraph from Lord Acton:

> Two great principles divide the world, and contend for the mastery, antiquity and the middle ages. These are the two civilizations that have preceded us, the two elements of which ours is composed. All political as well as religious questions resolve themselves practically to this. This is the great dualism that runs through our society.

Leslie had found the quotation in an anthology edited by Herbert Butterfield, *Man On His Past* (1955). The larger "other" was still Romanticism, and Leslie would continue for the next decade to define medievalism by way of this double polarity. Thanks to a cache of letters recently sent to me by his boyhood friend Geoffrey Read, it is evident that "classicism" and "romanticism" had long been festering in Leslie's mind, as in this letter from Egypt in 1948 (22 June):

> It's time someone devoted a book to those abused and abusive terms "classical" and "Romantic" – so many definitions, essays, opinions – a conclusive treatise is now necessary. [...] Say rather that Classicism is the art of a group, a common inspiration, Romanticism essentially the art of an individual, *in* a group maybe.

Leslie's plenary addresses for the first two International Conferences on Medievalism, both at the University of Notre Dame, provided early forums; there was also his invitation to compose an entry on medievalism for the *Arthurian Encyclopedia* in 1986, where he reverted to Ruskin, adding, "The term rapidly came to be employed not only for the study of the Middle Ages, which had been going on since the sixteenth century, but in particular for the use of medieval inspiration or models for almost every aspect of modern life." His offer of a similar piece for the *Spenser Encyclopedia* was refused, however, on the grounds that medievalism was "just a Victorian fantasy," a dismissal that fortuitously unfurled something of a serviceable battle flag. By March of 1989 ("St. David's Day," as he dated it in deference to Welsh antecedents on the maternal side), Leslie was able to assess a decade of advances and setbacks in an internal document titled "Studies in Medievalism: Progress and Potential": at the outset of the enterprise, he noted, there had been:

> great confusion about the term *medievalism* itself, and the confusing term "neo-medievalism" also enjoyed some circulation: *Studies in Medievalism* can claim to have restored utility to the term *medievalism*. [...] The journal has successfully countered a contemporary trend to trivialize medievalism as a quaint Victorian fantasy or consign it to societies for creative anachronism.

He also noted:

> In 1974 I concluded that a general field embracing the several manifestations of medievalism would not only throw new light on each of them, but would raise more fundamental questions about the general phenomenon and make it possible to subject medievalism to a more philosophical and theoretical scrutiny. A journal was clearly needed. In focusing on both the historiographical and imaginative recreation of the Middle Ages, *Studies in Medievalism* would call attention to method and premises, and to the cultural context in which art and scholarship interact. [...] However, it was also clear that carving out a new field in the academic landscape posed problems very different from those of simply offering a new journal in a recognized field. In 1979, when the journal began publication, medievalism simply did not exist as an academic specialty, and the word itself provoked only confusion. The very term had to be established, bibliographical research had to be initiated, and it was necessary to create not simply a market but a network of scholars and resources. [...] In short, medievalism demanded institutionalization, the creation of an academic infrastructure which in other fields could be taken for granted.

The note about the confusion surrounding the word "medi-evalism" is an understatement; again and again we were obliged to return submitted manuscripts on *Beowulf* or Chaucer, and our desig-nation of "medievalism" as the journal's official subject resulted in similarly regular returns of its *Directory of Periodicals* questionnaires by the obviously baffled MLA. By the late 1980s, however, the campaign had gained unsuspecting reinforcement in the rising trend toward deconstruction and reception study: the "present climate of criticism," Leslie continued in the "situation report" quoted above, "has turned attention to heuristic and epistemological problems, reminding histo-rians that the past is something we create." At some point in the decade, Leslie met at Kalamazoo Ulrich Müller, a professor of *Germanistik* at the University of Salzburg, who introduced us to the concurrent movement of *Mittelalter-Rezeption* and proposed to our delight a joint conference – with the memorable words, "I think I can get the government to give us a castle." The conference took place in 1990, as the Berlin Wall crumbled, at Burg Kaprun in the Austrian Alps. I think that Leslie's plenary address for the occasion, "Modern Medievalism in England and America," remains one of his most succinct expressions. Again, he set out to detach medievalism from Romanticism ("Romanticism might seek inspiration in the Middle Ages, but had no necessary connection with the Middle Ages") and ally it with classicism: "If I am right in asserting that medievalism and Romanticism are different kinds of study, it follows that Romanticism is not a suitable analogue or pattern for the study of medievalism, and we might ask what is. I suggest that an obvious answer is classicism, to which both Romanticism and medievalism are antitheses. The terms *classicism* and *romanticism* are polarities of the human mind; *classicism* and *medievalism* are polarities of the European past." The occasion permitted personal retrospection as well, particularly with regard to the "realization" of the Middle Ages:

> For me, it started with Dorothy Sayers' translation of the *Inferno* in 1949; Dante as not simply the greatest Christian poet but very much a human being, a humorist in all senses of the term. Another date was the production of the *Play of Daniel* in the Cloisters in New York in 1952 or 1953, and a great breakthrough was Nevill Coghill's modernized Penguin *Canterbury Tales* in 1970, which very soon appeared on the London stage.

He cited also the "cultural revolt of the 1960s," the search for alternative lifestyles that led inevitably to models of a pre-industrial society.

This address invokes incidentally a new passion, the fiction of Robertson Davies; it contains also Leslie's first public reference, at least so far as I am aware, to the emergence of the so-called "New Medievalism," a development he liked to describe in private correspondence as (*sic*) "abhominable." His animus toward this irruption was largely aimed at its confident appropriation of the word he had fought so long to define, and he would articulate this in his review (in a 1997 issue of *Arthuriana*) of R. Howard Bloch and Stephen G. Nichols' *Medievalism and the Modernist Temper*:

> Unfortunately I feel obliged to focus my attention here on the disturbing and apparently random misuse of the term *medievalism*. The first sentence of this book refers to "something exciting going on in medieval studies." The next sentence, however, turns to "the study of medieval literature and culture," which is a very different matter indeed. These "signs," which clearly involve much more than the "New Medievalism," include appointments at major universities, renewed interest among graduate students, the founding of scholarly journals, and special issues of established journals. An interesting omission is the one journal devoted to medievalism. For the New Medievalism, I am obliged to turn back to the volume by that name. "As a term, 'new medievalism' denotes a revisionist movement in romance medieval studies [...] a disposition to interrogate and reformulate assumptions about the discipline of medieval studies broadly conceived" (1). One thing must be made absolutely clear at once: the English term *medievalism* does not and never has referred to *medieval studies*.

Whatever suppressed resentment might be manifest here was of course amplified by our sense of inferior privilege. But a champion was already riding into the academic lists. It was in May of 1990 that the phone in our kitchen rang, Leslie kicked aside the cats and answered it, and then froze in a posture of paralyzed astonishment, finally stammering, "Well, bless my soul." The caller was the eminent if controversial medievalist Norman Cantor, who had noticed an ad for *Studies in Medievalism* that appeared courtesy of the Conference of Editors of Learned Journals in the *Times Literary Supplement*. Cantor was then at work on *Inventing the Middle Ages: The Lives, Works, and*

Ideas of the Great Medievalists of the Twentieth Century. As Cantor wrote to Leslie on 1 June 1990 (in a letter typed with characteristically magnificent ineptitude, much inked over with corrections):

> My book will, I hope, stimulate the subject of 20th century medievalism. It will also arouse much controversy. I hope you will be on my side, but in any case I congratulate you on what you have accomplished in the past decade or so. You are on the right track, and I hope your efforts are suitably recognized and rewarded.

Cantor's study set out to deconstruct, if you like, the careers of twentieth-century medievalists, confirming the tendentious, arbitrary, and culturally-inflected character of medieval studies *per se*. This was obviously much appreciated on our side, and on the appearance of Cantor's book in 1991 Leslie immediately set about organizing a bank of related sessions for the 1992 Kalamazoo Congress, "Medievalism and Medieval Studies." The first of the three sessions, unfortunately the only one for which a transcript exists, was ornamented by Tom Shippey, whom we had met a year earlier at Kalamazoo and whose authoritative work on Old English literature and J. R. R. Tolkien had long commended our admiration; Rich De Prospo, who finally supplied our crying need for a theorist; and Paul Szarmach, then still director of the Center for Medieval and Early Renaissance Studies at SUNY-Binghamton. Paul and Leslie had similarly sorrowful stories to tell of highhanded snubbing from medievalists, Leslie because of a rejected MLA session and Paul through two failed proposals for an NEH institute on medievalism in America he had put together with Bernard Rosenthal. Cantor delighted us by unexpectedly showing up (and later taking us to dinner). Always a self-appointed *agent provocateur* in the academic establishment, Cantor wrote Leslie a few months later (10 August) with regard to Leslie's perceived "air of disappointment" at the impact of the sessions:

> The fact of the matter is that most professional medievalists are not going to support actively what you are doing – it is too activist, for one thing. Secondly, the more "medievalism" is studied the more their own work will be judged from that perspective and they fear it will be found wanting, as it will. [...] The fact is that there is still a well of inspiration out there in the general culture. My book has tapped into it, while sneaking under the wire, more or less, of

academic respectability. Whether you and your wife realize it or not, you are doing something more bold; you are challenging the bastion of medievalist academia by conjuring up a general cultural movement. All power to you.

IV

I think of the 1990s as the decade when *Studies in Medievalism* came into its own: I do know that it was at the 1992 Conference, at the University of South Florida, that Leslie was referred to in the program as "the Founder," which struck him as hilarious and which his friends and I milked for all it was worth in gestures of mock-obeisance. At the risk of betraying his memory, though, I think whatever successes we enjoyed need to be seen against the backdrop of Leslie's persistent self-doubt and self-recrimination. I remember with heartache the late summer afternoon when Dr. Cantor called to invite Leslie to review *Inventing the Middle Ages* for the *Times Literary Supplement*: the prospect seemed to awe Leslie, to signal his entry into the world of English authority and privilege. It was starting to storm, and I joined him on the front porch where he was sitting with a gin and tonic and watching the lightning. In the drama of the setting (and perhaps a little affected by the gin), he looked at me and said soberly, "Kathleen, I am going to tell you something about myself. I am very intelligent, and I've thrown it all away." In fact, of course (though the review was ultimately aborted), he was beginning to salvage his career and achieve his long-deferred reputation. Kaprun was the first of our International Conferences on Medievalism to be held in Europe, to be followed by ones in Leeds in 1993 and in Canterbury in 1997; thanks to our friendship with Nils Holger Petersen of the University of Copenhagen we enjoyed two trips to Denmark, one of them for a performance of Nils Holger's lovely liturgical opera *A Vigil for Thomas Becket*, which had been featured at the Canterbury Conference. Volumes of *Studies in Medievalism* were appearing in succession, the Conference was thriving, our Kalamazoo program continued year after year, we mounted seven nearly consecutive Special Sessions at the MLA, Leslie reviewed the Ruskin–Norton correspondence for the *New England Quarterly*, and he was receiving invitations for public addresses. Our clientele was by now truly international. At Kalamazoo we had met Toshiyuki Takamiya of Keio University in Tokyo, a Cambridge-educated medievalist whose interests had shifted toward the nine-teenth century. Professor Takamiya attended our Conference at the University of Delaware in 1991 and subsequently asked Leslie to edit a special double issue of the Japanese English-language journal *Poetica*.

The *Poetica* collection, titled *Medievalism and Romanticism 1750–1850*, provided Leslie an arena in which to pit, as he put it, "the David of medievalism against the Goliath of Romanticism," and the project was exciting but daunting. His own introductory essay, "Medi-evalism and Romanticism," runs to forty-four pages and drags a bibli-ography of seventy-eight items; he labored over it, tried the patience of his Japanese publishers, and had to interrupt its composition in February of 1995 when, on the last day of the ACMRS conference at Arizona State (happily devoted that year to "Reinventing the Middle Ages and the Renaissance"), he suffered a mild but frightening stroke. Looked at critically, the essay lacks the smooth coherence its matter deserved. Yet it remains a massively exhaustive dismantling of Roman-ticism, a searching illumination of the academic forces that erected it and of its original inseparability from, and ultimate devouring of, medievalism:

> Medievalism and Romanticism are both comparatively recent terms in scholarship. The establishment of Romanticism cannot without ambiguity be dated much before 1930, or of medievalism before 1970. At the same time, both have a prehistory dating back to the middle of the eighteenth century. The failure to recognize this historical perspective, to cling to an unreal picture of its own scholarly past, is one of the problems of Romanticism today. [...] The problem with medievalism is clearly very different. It is not a period term at all, but an open-ended theme running through postmedieval Europe, a concept which we have barely begun to work in the manner suggested by Acton. [...]
>
> Medievalism and Romanticism are thus not comparable phenomena. Romanticism is a definable movement, occurring at a particular time and within certain parameters; medievalism has been a polarity of European society since the end of the Middle Ages. Its emergence in the mid-nineteenth century as a more or less definable tendency in the arts is a function or product of the new nineteenth-century history, and it is notable that a new kind of classicism began to appear at the same time.

Another milestone was the Special Session at the 1995 MLA, "Medievalism, New Medievalism, Medieval Studies: Contested Territory or Common Ground?" As the title suggests, the project was blatantly territorial: as Leslie asserted in his own position paper, "It is axiomatic that every generation has to write its own history of the past, and this is especially true in the case of the Middle Ages. It follows that medievalism, the study of the process, is a necessary part of the study of the Middle Ages." Leslie's plenary address, "The Future of Medievalism," offered broader scope and a ten-year retrospective at the 1995 International Conference at Worcester, Massachusetts (an event memorable for what we believed to be the first-ever performance of Robert Southey's *Wat Tyler*). Predicating his remarks on what he termed "an axiom dredged up from freshman history [...] the Past is not there," Leslie appealed to C. S. Lewis's *De Descriptione Temporum* and its "invaluable series of definitions, starting with the total content of time past and working down to so much of it as is recoverable, as has been recovered, is known to historians, and finally, is known to students and believed to be known by the man in the street." This prompted yet another attempt at definition: "But the Middle Ages quite simply has no objective correlative. This a truth which has been pretty generally overlooked. [...] It follows quite simply that medieval historiography, the study of the successive recreation of the Middle Ages by different generations, *is* the Middle Ages. And this of course is medievalism." With his preface to *Medievalism in Europe II, Studies in Medievalism* VIII (1996), Leslie finally reached a serene clarity that merited the placement of this sentence as epigraph to the present essay: "Medievalism is the continuing process of creating the Middle Ages."

There were other ventures, now aimed at installing medievalism in the classroom: in 1996 and 1998, with the help of Clare Simmons and David Metzger, we held two four-week summer institutes on medievalism at the University of York in England, distributing draft versions of an anthology. The institutes realized Leslie's long-time dream, inspired no doubt by his memories of the Borthwick experience. But his ambitions were admittedly reeling out of control: if ever a man's reach exceeded his grasp, it was probably in Leslie's increasingly Faustian compulsion somehow to have it all while there was still time. We were editing the *Studies in Medievalism* series, organizing our annual Conference, trying to sustain our program at Kalamazoo and move as well into the new International Medieval Congress at Leeds, fumbling with a complementary series of conference papers, ensnaring monographs (we had sponsored Janet Grayson's edition of Jessie Weston's *Romance of Perlesvaus* in 1988), trying to write. The bats that began mysteriously to invade our home's upper story seemed to me, I remember, an emblem of some ominous ("onimous," as Leslie perversely pronounced it) entropy. Leslie had always said he would never abandon the enterprise until it could fly by itself. Fortunately the wings were sprouting. By 1998, Tom Shippey had succeeded Leslie as editor, Gwendolyn Morgan had courageously taken on the enormous burden of conference organization, and Richard Utz was active everywhere on the operation's behalf. Richard and Tom then crowned the efforts of the last quarter-century by compiling a *Festschrift, Medievalism in the Modern World: Essays in Honour of Leslie Workman*, the first in the series Making the Middle Ages overseen by, among others, Geraldine Barnes of the University of Sydney, whom we had met in 1995 at the conference at Arizona State. As he entered his eighth decade, Leslie could look back on his achievements with something like satisfaction.

Surveyed from my present perspective, the history of *Studies in Medievalism* seems to me indeed rather heroic. I quote from Britton Harwood's kind note to the *Festschrift*:

> It is a special pleasure to pay tribute to Leslie Workman. Because I was teaching in Oxford, Ohio, when he established *Studies in Medievalism*, I was a first-hand witness to the tenacity and resourcefulness with which he focused international attention on defining medievalism and investigating its avatars. With his wide learning, an urbane irony, and always an unpretentious willingness to set his hand to any necessary task, Leslie organized meetings and published a journal without any of the usual academic perquisites and support. So far as medievalism exists today as a subject of academic inquiry in its own right, his has been the seminal effort.

Always the historian, even (indeed, more and more) of his own life, Leslie enjoyed placing things in historical perspective as well. When German-born Otto Gründler retired from the directorship of the Medieval Institute, Leslie wrote in gratitude (3 May 1995):

It is a great pleasure to us to recall that the birth of modern medievalism, which Norman Cantor has described as "a remarkable
achievement," occurred at the International Congress on Medieval
Studies just twenty years ago. [...] Much of this, in our view, is
due to the smoothly running organization and to the friendly and
informal atmosphere which you have somehow managed to maintain at the Congress, despite its growing numbers. I recall that you
and I are the same age, that we were both soldiers of a sort, in
different uniforms, in a war that seems as remote as that of the
Greeks and the Trojans, and so there is much that we have never
needed to say to each other.

And he was clearly feeling mortality: the stroke had jarred him,
and he almost died from a blood clot in 1997, just as we were about to
fly to Canterbury for the Conference. He described the incident a
month or so later to Bill Calin (28 August 1997):

Fortunately [...] a cardiologist who had just joined the faculty at
Holland Hospital that very day, with a big reputation from
Chicago, was among those present and diagnosed a pulmonary
embolism: the way I hear it, about an hour before I was about to
say farewell forever. If I had really missed my own deathbed in this
frivolous fashion I should have been really pissed off. Anyway, the
Grim Reaper took his shot and missed.

Free of *Studies in Medievalism* and its satellite activities, he was
turning his attention to the last project, *The Idea of the Middle Ages:
History and Imagination*, a consummate history of medievalism – the
Big Book, as he called it. The structure would have to be chronological, he explained to Ulrich Müller (12 February 1999), because "one
of my theses is that medievalism has political as well as cultural implications, which is to say that it exists and develops in time." In the fall
of 1999, after a wonderful summer trip to the Lake District following
the Leeds Congress, we made another transatlantic flight to a conference organized by Nils Holger Petersen. Awash with pleasure at the
event, Leslie wrote in November of that year to Richard Utz:

Let me tell you about the Christianity and the Arts conference in
Copenhagen. It was a great trip for me because here were all these
scholars from Europe and America who did not want anything
from me, like publishing their papers and stuff, but did want to

congratulate me on the achievement of *Studies in Medievalism*. A copy of the festschrift was there to reinforce the lesson and aroused considerable interest, for which I thank you yet again. [...] I was part of the opening panel and also unexpectedly part of the concluding panel, "Perspectives," which dealt with the future. I was not prepared for this at all, but I was able to revive a thirty-year-dormant knowledge of historical theory (principally Toynbee) and of science fiction, mainly represented by my old acquaintance Arthur C. Clarke. [...] In short, the Copenhagen experience revived my interest in medievalism and what I still have to say, and I look forward to a productive year of quiet scholarship and a return to Copenhagen. I am planning a big presentation for next year's conference, which I think will be as it were my last public appearance.

Six months later he woke up with chest pains and was carted (by me) off to the hospital, where we scheduled the cardiac surgery whose complications (accompanied, I am now convinced, by medical error) brought about his death after ten months of suffering.

V

I now assay a summation. In Leslie's mind, it seems to me (and I proceed gingerly here, because there were strata of his mind I never came to know), *medievalism* was first of all historically based: it required a broad and comprehensive knowledge of history and of multiple historical traditions (the pervasiveness of medievalism in America, for instance, continued to arrest him). He was always fretting that so many of the papers we were offered were too cautious – "nice little papers on Tennyson," as he sometimes grumbled – and that so few of them addressed theories of history and of historical research; another of his favorite quotations – and he had a box of them, carefully set down by hand – was from the American historian Morris Cohen, "History is an imaginative reconstruction of the past, scientific in its determination, artistic in its formulation." He argued always for the immense cultural importance of medievalism as applicable both to survivals and revivals of medieval culture; "neo-medievalism," suggestive of intentional (and hence usually fatuous) efforts at regeneration, was a coinage he abhorred, since it tacitly limited the broader range of implications on which he insisted.

Instead, medievalism involved any engagement with the Middle Ages, conscious or unconscious, from the lunatic fringe of medievalist kitsch to the most solemn scholarship and from approximately 1500 to the present and beyond; and it broached consistently the question of why the "Middle Ages," the *medium aevum* bracketed off by sixteenth-century humanists, had to be invented at all. Medievalism might be present across the spectrum of culture: art, architecture, literature, historiography, music, theatre, dance, religion, economics, politics, costume, material artifacts, and probably more. "Classicism" was an acceptable analogue, and here the Acton dictum remained paramount; at some point Leslie initiated correspondence with the Institute for the Study of the Classical Tradition at Boston University, hoping for fruitful dialogue. I suspect he would have been greatly intrigued, had he lived to see it, by John Ganim's *Medievalism and Orientalism* (2005). "Romanticism," whatever that word might mean, was always to be challenged, especially because it had so long obscured awareness of medievalism as a separable, and farther-reaching, phenomenon; Leslie often pointed out that "medieval" and "romantic" had at the outset been essentially interchangeable, a view he corroborated by appeal to Mme. de Staël's *De l'Allemagne* and the critic Henry Beers's statement as late as 1899, "Romanticism, then, in the sense in which I shall commonly employ the word, means the reproduction in modern art or literature, of the life and thought of the Middle Ages."

I feel fairly confident in laying out these principles, yet by themselves they seem too abstract, even sterile – as the pristine scholarly references to articles in *Studies in Medievalism* I now come across from time to time seem so little related to the welter of anxiety in which our volumes were inevitably produced. To tell the truth, Leslie's twenty-five-year enterprise was probably crossed at some point by nearly all the Seven Deadly Sins, Sloth not the least; and it involved a cast of academic characters who ranged dramatically from self-seeking and venal to generous, loyal, blessed. Contingency had its part as well: Leslie emerged on the academic stage at a moment when there was probably a "medievalism-shaped place" on it, as he liked to envision "an Arthur-shaped place" in early Britain, but he may still be credited with seizing the potential of the subject; too stubborn, as Alice Kenney had predicted, to know when he was licked, he persevered against formidable obstacles, including a few of his own making (he quoted lines from the ballad "Fight on, fight on, said Sir Andrew Barton" so often that I had them engraved on his headstone). Like the best poetry, the most authentic scholarship is ultimately based, as Yeats has it, in "the foul rag and bone shop of the heart," in the scholar's humanity, and certainly Leslie had plenty of that. I believe that for Leslie medievalism was deeply personal, arising almost organically from who he was. His admiration for Sir Walter Scott, for instance, was genuine and unabashed, and so enduring that when his Social Security checks started coming in he wasted no time assembling his collection of Scott first editions; he often (I take it here from his essay "To Castle Dangerous") quoted the historian G. M. Trevelyan's assessment of Scott's salutary influence on historiography, "The difference between Gibbon and Macaulay is a measure of the influence of Scott." But in a larger sense medievalism was for him nostalgic, in his bones: it called up the profound reverence for the English past that, as a self-exile, he probably cultivated more tenderly. The renewed sense of pride in English tradition sharpened by two world wars no doubt left its imprint on him; though he never mentioned it, he must have experienced the Festival of Britain, the great celebration of British culture staged in London in 1951, and he loved best the music of Ralph Vaughan Williams, so much of which draws on native themes. I have always liked something Leslie said in a review of Carolyn Hares-Stryker's *Anthology of Pre-Raphaelite Writings*:

> Within the memory of living man, that is, in the period immediately after the Second World War, one could buy a Pre-Raphaelite painting for five pounds in any junk shop in London. [...] Later again, the proposal of the Tate Gallery to empty its basements of the vast Chantry Bequest of Victorian painting led to an excited correspondence in the London Sunday papers, and William Morris's Red House in a London suburb came up for sale. (I thought we should buy it, but my mother thought not.)

I would like to think too, though, that for Leslie medievalism offered yet another avenue to his contemplation of the future. In his plenary address "The Future of Medievalism," he predicted that if the project of medievalism succeeded the result would be "that we shall have informed and changed the field of medieval studies. In this process of course we would virtually lose our separate identity." But even this was too modest an objective, and he closed with the following observation:

> The opening day of our Conference in Austria in 1990 coincided with the reunification of the two German republics, and I argued that this event epitomized not simply the end of the Cold War, but hopefully also the end of the period of world wars and hopefully the end in fact of the whole balance of power and nation-state system which began, like medievalism, with the end of the Middle Ages. If this is true and we are indeed embarking on a new age, we shall certainly need an understanding of the past age, which is medievalism. Hopefully some words of Sri Jawaharlal Nehru, by which I am haunted, may turn out to be prophetic: "Politics and religion are obsolete; the time has come for science and spirituality."

Prudently Googling the Nehru quotation just in case Leslie had it wrong, I find that it was a favorite of Arthur C. Clarke, and this was no doubt where Leslie discovered it in the first place. All forays into the past are arguably also about the future, as I think Leslie was well aware. Meanwhile, as he liked to say, "there is clearly a very great deal to do."

WORKS CITED

Unpublished correspondence and other writings by Leslie J. Workman cited in this essay remain, of course, in my personal possession. His editorials and prefaces to volumes of *Studies in Medievalism* are readily available in libraries; other published works are listed below. For a complete bibliography, see Richard J. Utz, "Medievalism in the Making: A Bibliography of Leslie J. Workman," *The Year's Work in Medievalism* 15 (2001): 127–31.

"The Future of Medievalism," Plenary Address at the Tenth International Conference on Medievalism, Higgins Armory, Worcester, Massachusetts, September 1995, James Gallant, ed., *The Year's Work in Medievalism* 10 (Holland, MI, 1999): 7–18.

"Medievalism," in Norris J. Lacy, ed., *The Arthurian Encyclopedia* (New York: Garland, 1986), 387–91.

"Medievalism and Romanticism," *Medievalism and Romanticism 1750–1850*, ed. Leslie J. Workman, *Poetica* 39–40 (1994): 1–44.

"Medievalism in America: The First Decade," in Jürgen Kühnel, Hans-Dieter Mück, Ursula Müller, Ulrich Müller, ed., *Mittelalter-Rezeption* III (Göppingen: Kümmerle, 1988), 143–46.

"Medievalism, New Medievalism, Medieval Studies: Contested Territory or Common Ground?" A Special Session at the1995 Convention of the Modern Language Association, *The Year's Work in Medievalism* 10: 223–38.

"Modern Medievalism in England and America," Plenary Address at the Fifth Annual General Conference on Medievalism, Burg Kaprun, Austria, October 1990, Ulrich Müller and Kathleen Verduin, ed., *Mittelalter-Rezeption* V / *Year's Work in Medievalism* 5 (Göppingen: Kümmerle, 1996): 1–23.

" 'My First Real Tutor': John Ruskin and Charles Eliot Norton," review of *The Correspondence of John Ruskin and Charles Eliot Norton*, ed. John Lewis Bradley and Ian Ousby, *New England Quarterly* 62.4 (December 1989): 572–86.

Review of *An Anthology of Pre-Raphaelite Writings*, ed. Carolyn Hares-Stryker, *Prolepsis: The Tübingen Review of English Studies* 15.1 (1998). <http://www.uni-tuebingen.de/uni/nes/prolepsis/98_2_wor.html>.

Review of *Medievalism and the Modernist Temper*, ed. R. Howard Bloch and Stephen G. Nichols, *Arthuriana* 7.1 (1997): 159–60.

"Ruins, Romance, and Reality: Medievalism in Anglo-American Imagination and Taste, 1750–1840" (with Alice P. Kenney), *Winterthur Portfolio* 10 (1975): 131–64.

"Speaking of Medievalism: An Interview with Leslie Workman," conducted by Richard J. Utz, in Richard J. Utz and Tom Shippey, ed., *Medievalism in the Modern World: Essays in Honour of Leslie Workman*, Making the Middle Ages I (Turnhout: Brepols, 1998): 433–50.

"To Castle Dangerous: The Influence of Scott," in Naomi Reed Kline, ed., *Castles: An Enduring Fantasy* (New Rochelle, NY: Caratzas, 1985), 45–50.

Medievalism: Its Linguistic History in Nineteenth-Century Britain

Clare A. Simmons

In Mary Elizabeth Braddon's 1865 potboiler *Sir Jasper's Tenant*, the Sir Jasper of the title is a widowed baronet with an especial fondness for the art of William Etty, the early Victorian artist best known for his sensuous studies of nudes, both women and men.[1] True to his idol's tastes, Sir Jasper has an eye for the voluptuous charms of a lady visitor who happens to be an evil twin in disguise, but he also likes the brooding manliness of his equally disguised tenant, George Pauncefort. Attempting to persuade George to spend Christmas with him, Sir Jasper promises him, "No country families, no would-be medievalism, – boars' heads with lemons in their mouths, rejoicing retainers, fiddlers in the music gallery, and so on; none of your Christmas-in-the-olden-time absurdities."[2] What Sir Jasper means is that Christmas will not be in the "Old English style" as famously witnessed (or possibly fabricated) by Washington Irving in his visit to "Bracebridge Hall" about 1818 and as revived by Victorians longing for the supposed old days of medieval jollity.[3] My interest here, though, is in Sir Jasper's use of the word "medievalism", which is very much in accordance with its modern usage as implying a respect for or revival of the practices and values of the Middle Ages.

The word itself was only a few years old, seemingly emerging about the time of the Great Exhibition of 1851 and being used in print by John Ruskin in the early 1850s as part of an apology for Pre-Raphaelite art.[4] Sir Jasper, then, can contemptuously use the word "medievalism", which was not in the English vocabulary a few years earlier. Yet critics who have used Ruskin's coining as decisive proof that medievalism is a Victorian rather than an earlier phenomenon probably do not realize how recent the English word "medieval" is itself, or even that the phrase "middle ages" was limited in its use as a historical category until the nineteenth century. "Medieval," derived from the Latin *medium aevum*, was a synonym for the Middle Ages, the Renaissance way of explaining the middle period between ancient learning and civilization – the classical period – and their own revival of learning. I would suggest that the English word "medieval" is a Romantic-era invention that reflects a new attitude to the past. I here trace what is known of the history of the word "medieval," and suggest that the reasons why, when historians had at least fairly comfortably managed without it, nineteenth-century Britain found a need for the term are themselves medievalist.[5]

The word "medieval" was readily available to the British public certainly by 1851, when the Great Exhibition included Pugin's "Mediaeval Court." We find it increasingly used during the 1840s – for example, by the indefatigable antiquarian editor Thomas Wright in his 1844 edition of *St. Brandan*, which is subtitled "A Medieval Legend of the Sea." I should point out, by the way, that from the outset, some writers spelled the word "mediaeval" and others "medieval": Ruskin, for example, spells it with the dipthong, Wright without, and the printer of the Tauschnitz edition of *Sir Jasper's Tenant* likes it both ways. To move back further, Sir Francis Palgrave was among the earliest users of the word: the phrase "mediaeval period," for example, appears in his *Truths and Fictions of the Middle Ages: The Merchant and the Friar*, published the year of Queen Victorian's accession (1837). Clearly showing the term's Latin original, R. T. Hampson used the word not just in his Latin title but in his text in *Medii Aevi Kalendarium; or Dates, Charters and Customs of the Middle Ages* in 1841; in his review of the work for *The Quarterly Review*, Palgrave employs the word "medieval" several times.[6]

At least in the phrase "mediaeval aera," then, the word was in widespread usage by the later 1830s. The earliest known usage of "mediaeval" is only a few years earlier. In 1827, *The Gentleman's Magazine* published a communication dated 29 November from "S. Tymms" with the title "Antient Peg-Tankards." Samuel Tymms was the name of a father and son involved in antiquarian writing in the eighteenth and nineteenth centuries. Since the better-known Samuel Tymms the Younger, who was to write *The Family Topographer: A Compendious Account of the Antient and Present State of the Counties of*

England, was only nineteen in 1827, it is probable that Samuel
Tymms the Elder has the distinction of being the earliest writer in
English listed by the current edition of the *Oxford English Dictionary*
to use the word "mediaeval." Tymms wrote of the decoration of a
peg-tankard, "Similar churches to this occur in the sculptural representations of the mediaeval aera."[7] While Tymms may have been the
first to use the word in print, very possibly, the word was already
circulating among antiquarians, and there may be earlier instances still
to be found. Why in 1827 did the word "medieval" become a neces-
sity?

As Romantic-era nationalism prompted a new interest in the
indigenous past not as a source of embarrassment but as part of Britain's heritage, writers simply needed more words to describe the medieval period. Many works up to this time, interestingly enough, do not
so much as use the phrase "middle ages." *Mangnall's Historical and
Miscellaneous Questions*, a widely used grade-school textbook printed
from 1800 onwards, avoids "middle ages," referring to the entire
period between the fall of Rome and the fifteenth-century "revival of
learning" as "a night of darkness."[8] Legal historians such as David
Hume, in his *History of England*, tend to talk of the "feudal period";
an electronic search of Hume's *History of England, From the Invasion of
Julius Caesar to the Accession of Henry VII* (1762) identifies fifty-three
uses of the word "feudal" and no uses of the term "Middle Ages" –
indeed, the phrase "of the middle age" occurs only once.[9] Henry
Hallam, in his *View of the State of Europe during the Middle Ages*,
placed "middle ages" in the title of his 1818 work but, again, still
seems to have preferred the phrase "the feudal period." Occasionally,
one finds the phrase "middle age" used as an adjective, but the only
adjective used in reference to the period as a whole is "gothic." What
was probably holding medieval studies back was the association of the
Middle Ages with Roman Catholicism. We can see as late as the 1820s
an anxiety about the medieval period as somehow a blot on true
Englishness. The myth of the Norman Yoke – that England had a free
constitution before the invasion of William the Conqueror brought
feudalism – is enmeshed with the ideas that the English Church was a
national institution in ancient times and that the coming of the
Normans brought it under the Church of Rome. For example, Robert
Southey's 1824 *Book of the Church* has a similar sense of England's
Anglican destiny as does John Foxe's Elizabethan *Book of Martyrs*: of

the Middle Ages, a phrase that he avoids in his work, Southey writes, "dark ages we call them and dark they were" (1:343). Although William Blake wrote in his Marginalia "and not talk of dark ages or of any ages, ages are all equal," in this as in many things, Blake was the exception rather than the rule. To avoid the phrase "Middle Ages," then, or only to use it where the meaning is clearly pejorative, could be seen as a patriotic duty.

Similarly, Washington Irving, probably sensitive to the negative connotations for his American readers, also avoids the phrase "Middle Ages," preferring less historically specific phrases such as "olden times" and "days of yore," or occasionally, "the age of chivalry." For example, contemplating a Crusader's tomb in Westminster Abbey, Geoffrey Crayon muses:

> There is something extremely picturesque in the tombs of these adventurers, decorated as they are with rude armorial bearings and gothic sculpture. They comport with the antiquated chapels in which they are generally found; and in considering them, the imagination is apt to kindle with the legendary associations, the romantic fiction, the chivalrous pomp and pageantry, which poetry has spread over the wars for the sepulchre of Christ. They are the relics of times utterly gone by [...].[10]

Irving's approach is interesting because he makes the English past palatable by not clearly distinguishing between practices derived from medieval and Elizabethan times, as if "ancient" for him as an American is a relatively straightforward idea. Even more calculated thinking may have gone into John Lingard's careful limitation of his use of the phrase "middle ages" in his 1819 *History of England*. As the first avowed English Catholic to write the history of his country, Lingard seems to want to avoid characterizing the Middle Ages as a whole and, although he does not quite go to the extremes of Helen W. Pierson, who in 1883 wrote a *History of Eng-land in Words of One Syllable*, he does go to lengths to avoid "middle ages": I found it once in his 1500-page work, although I am prepared to admit that I may have blinked somewhere. Yet at the time of Roman Catholic emancipation, England was beginning to come to terms with its medieval past as a valid part of its heritage, rather than as an aberration. The "middle ages" enforced distance and difference in a way that its Latinized version "medieval" did not do as clearly, and was for some authors a more acceptable choice.

At the same time, another Romantic-era phenomenon affected views of the Middle Ages: namely, the notion of the spirit of an age. Self-evidently, historians had always found ways to divide up their discussion of the past. Political histories of England used the simple division of monarchies. Eighteenth-century antiquarians tended to divide the English past into neat categories of British, Roman, Saxon, Norman, and Early English (the answer, I believe, to Fred Robinson's question of why English uniquely refers to the Middle Ages, not to the Middle Age). By the 1800s, we see attempts to characterize the Middle Ages as a phenomenon, not merely as a number of years. A work that deserves more attention is Robert Henry's *History of Great Britain Written on a New Plan*, completed in the 1790s and frequently reprinted. Henry's "new plan" was to divide the early history of Britain (as a Scot, he discussed Scotland too) by "periods" rather than monarchies, and to look at developments in each period under a regularized set of categories: for example, political and constitutional, religion, arts, and learning, as well as manners and customs. For Henry, the phrase "middle ages" is immensely useful, because it imparts a character to the period as a whole.

An even more frequent user of "middle ages" was Charles Mills, who wrote histories of the Crusades and of chivalry. Mills's *History of Chivalry, Or, Knighthood and its Times*, published in 1825, is a work sadly in need of the word "medieval". His sense of the Romantic-era development of enthusiasm for the Middle Ages is quite revealing:

> Attention to the subjects of the middle ages of Europe has for many years been growing among us. It was first excited by Warton's history of our national verse, and Percy's edition of the Relics of ancient English Poetry. The romances of chivalry, both in prose and metre, and the numberless works on the Troubadours, and every other description of literature during the middle ages which have been published within the last few years, have sustained the interest. The poems of Scott convinced the world that the chivalric times of Europe can strike the moral imagination as powerfully and pleasingly in respect of character, passion, and picturesqueness of effect, as the heroic ages of Greece; and even

very recently the glories of chivalry have been sung by a poetess whom Ariosto himself would have been delighted to honour.[11]

Mills pays tribute to Sir Walter Scott as a scholar of the Middle Ages in his poetry and his essays on "Chivalry" and "Romance," which were highly influential works contributed to the first edition of the *Encyclopaedia Britannica* and featuring the term "middle ages" without apology. Both Mills and Scott make a clear distinction between "middle ages" and "Gothic." I am not going to go into detail here about how the word "Gothic" was very much overworked by the 1820s, becoming more and more an aesthetic rather than a historical category until Ruskin defined "Gothic" as a style and "medieval" as a state of mind. I will just say that Mills and Scott use the word "Gothic" to describe tribespeoples of the centuries immediately after the fall of Rome, and "chivalric" as the only adjective they have for the High Middle Ages beyond the phrase "of the middle ages." I will quote one sentence from Scott's "Essay on Chivalry" to show his desperate need of the word "medieval", although, failing that, a careful editor might have helped. Describing the Crusades, Scott writes:

> The harebrained and adventurous character of these enterprises, not less than the promised pardons, indulgences, and remissions of the Church, rendered them dear to the warriors of the middle ages; the idea of re-establishing the Christian religion in the Holy Land, and wresting the tomb of Christ from infidels, made kings, princes, and nobles, blind to its hazards; and they rushed, army after army, to Palestine, in the true spirit of Chivalry, whose faithful professors felt themselves rather called upon to undertake an adventure, from the peculiar dangers which surrounded it, and the numbers who had fallen in previous attempts. (528)

In contrast, while Mills pays tribute to Scott the poet and historian, he rejects the historical authority of the Author of Waverley (apparently, as late as 1825, some people had not worked out that Scott and the Author of Waverley were one and the same), who happened to have questioned Mills's interpretation of a medieval romance about Richard the Lion-Heart and, worse, had misspelled Mills's name.[12] The Waverley novels were probably already exerting influence in creation of a sense of historical period, but their role would become more clearly defined as a contribution to the

development of medievalism after Scott acknowledged them and especially after the Magnum Opus editions added historical annotations.

The final alternative for the word "medieval" that I have not yet
discussed is, of course, "romantic." Leslie Workman has argued that,
for England at least, Romanticism is medievalism,[13] and there remains
still more to be done on pondering the affinities Romantic-era writers
felt with the medieval past. "Romantic," in the sense of partaking of
the qualities of medieval romance, that is, depicting a world of more
heroic figures, grander actions, and more marvelous occurrences than
those that limit the reader's own, remains a term commonly found in
Romantic-era accounts of the Middle Ages, and is unquestionably a
crucial reason why the Romantics found the Middle Ages more to
their taste than eighteenth-century rationalists had done. But here lies
the final paradox for Romantic-era history. A romance is by definition
a made-up story, yet part of the romantic appeal of medieval history is
that it is true. According to those medievalists who attempted to
recuperate the Middle Ages – figures such as Kenelm Digby, the
members of the Young England movement, and A. N. W. Pugin –
there really was a time when human beings would sacrifice all for religion or for love or for honor, when those who sought power always
lived on the brink of danger, and where society was in many respects
governed by the cycles of nature. Too real to be romance, too
romantic to be dismissed as the murky Dark Ages or prosaic Middle
Ages, it needed to be medieval and to pave the way for the medievalism of the High Victorian period.

NOTES

1. William Etty (1787–1849) was a Royal Academician who continued
to attend the Life Class, working from nude models, his entire life.

2. Mary Elizabeth Braddon, *Sir Jasper's Tenant*, 3 vols. (London:
Maxwell, 1865), 1:69.

3. See *The Sketch-Book of Geoffrey Crayon* (1820) and *Bracebridge Hall*.

4. See my introduction to *Medievalism and the Quest for the "Real"
Middle Ages* (London: Frank Cass, 2001), 1.

5. In "Medieval, The Middle Ages," *Speculum* 59:4 (October 1984):
745–56, Fred C. Robinson traces some of the background of these terms in
English usage; his focus is, however, mainly on the connotations of the terms
rather than the contexts of their early use.

6. See *The Quarterly Review* 71 (1841): 379–91.

7. *Gentleman's Magazine* 97:2 (1827): 490.

8. *Mangnall's Historical and Miscellaneous Questions*, 86.

9. David Hume, *History of England from the Invasion of Julius Caesar to the Accession of Henry VII*, 2 vols. (London: A. Millar, 1762), 1:236. As Fred C. Robinson remarks in his survey of the use of the term "medieval," English's adoption of a plural term – "middle ages" – is peculiar, and not all early users of the word agreed that the ages should be multiple.

10. "Westminster Abbey," in *The Sketch-Book of Geoffrey Crayon, Gent* (1819– 20), 151.

11. This is a reference to L. E. L.'s *The Troubadour*. Charles Mills, *History of Chivalry, Or, Knighthood and its Times*, 2 vols. (London: Longman, Hurst, Rees, Orme, Brown, and Green, 1825), introduction.

12. "In the composition of his tales, the author of Waverley has seldom shown much respect for historical keeping […] if he seriously designed to unite the province of the historian with that of the novelist, he has chosen a very unlucky expedient for his own reputation; and thus, in either case, he has wantonly led his readers into error, and brought against others a charge of ignorance, which must recoil more deservedly on himself" (Mills, xviii–xix).

13. See Leslie Workman's Introduction to *Poetica* 39–40 (1993).

Medievalism and Medieval Reception: A Terminological Question

Nils Holger Petersen

In this paper I would like to address a question that is absolutely central to the definition of "medievalism": namely, should this term be used for everything that derives from the Middle Ages, or should it be reserved for post-medieval interest in the revival of phenomena belonging to the period or notion of the Middle Ages? The importance of this question has been underscored by its great relevance to many of the conferences and publications sponsored by *Studies in Medievalism* over the years. Moreover, I am convinced that in limiting the possibility of conclusively theorizing about or mapping medievalism, the ambiguity addressed by this question has significantly hampered scholarly interest in the field. I therefore believe we must tackle this question directly and stake our position(s) in relationship to it.

Of course, I have no illusion that I can give anything near a definitive answer to it, but I would like to contribute to the debate on it by taking up Leslie Workman's classic position that medievalism is the continued construction of the Middle Ages. In one of his editorial introductions, which also observes that the term "The Middle Ages" was a Renaissance humanist creation that has "been elaborated and reinforced from different perspectives from the sixteenth century to the present," Workman wrote: "[...] medieval historiography, the study of the successive recreation of the Middle Ages by different generations, *is* the Middle Ages. And this of course is medievalism."[1] Furthermore, referring to scholarly historical writing as well as what is traditionally considered to be part of artistic reception in such media as literature, the visual arts, film, music, and even political discourses and actions, Workman maintained: "[...] the *study* of the Middle Ages on the one hand, and the *use* of the Middle Ages in everything from fantasy to social reform on the other, are two sides of the same coin."[2] This constructivist approach to history in general – an approach that is very much in line with attempts such as those by Hayden White to overcome traditional borders between the artistic and the scholarly in historiography[3] – and to medievalism in particular is a wonderful point of departure for defining the field of medievalism. It is clearly an inclusive approach, yet it revolves around at least a reflection of something received as "medieval" or the "Middle Ages." Moreover, it is based on contemporary historical practice rather than the chronology of particular phenomena. What is looked upon as medieval is, indeed, medieval.

All problems are not solved, however. As so often in the case of reception history, we have to face the question of subjectivity or individualism as a challenge to the notion of the general relevance or usefulness of academic ventures. The most obvious solution – again, as in reception history – is to talk about communities of understanding, which, in our case, center on Western academic sensibilities that echo the wider academic communities to which we belong. But this approach is somewhat circular, in that we are back at defining medievalism as that which is done and discussed in the communities interested in medievalism. Moreover, it elides the difficulty of overcoming an ambiguity or lack of communicability that I and, I believe, many others who feel at home in the medievalism community encounter when we try to communicate our understanding of medievalism beyond the community that defines and shapes it. Thus, in the end, our medievalism community is not that well-rounded.

We should, therefore, perhaps take a little time to discuss the borders of medievalism, as is driven home by a short article from Mette Birkedal Bruun, a colleague of mine at the Centre for the Study of the Cultural Heritage of Medieval Rituals. In "A Case in which a Revitalization of Something Medieval Turned out not to be Medievalism," Mette Bruun distinguishes between, on the one hand, the uses of medieval ideas, practices, concepts, or texts that are marked by a historical distance from the phenomenon in question, and, on the other hand, the uses of those that are not.[4] The case she takes up is a discussion in the late seventeenth century between two French monastic figures, Armand-Jean de Rancé (1626–1700) and Jean

Mabillon (1632–1707). Whereas Rancé is known for his Cistercian reform at La Trappe, which he presented in his *De la sainteté et des devoirs de la vie monastique* (1683) as a "Cistercian genealogy ranging from the Old Testament prophets, via the apostles, [...] onwards to the *Rule of Benedict* and the Medieval Cistercians," and which led to the strict Trappist branch of Cistercianism, the Benedictine (Maurist) monk Mabillon is acclaimed as one of the leading scholars in the critical editorial efforts of the Maurists, and is particularly celebrated for participating in the critical editions of the oeuvre of Bernard of Clairvaux. Mette Bruun points out that for Rancé, academic study was "alien to the spiritual purpose of the monk," whereas Mabillon maintained that "study had always been a crucial part of the monastic curriculum." By way of conclusion, she writes:

> [...] Rancé's project appears to be almost contra-temporal. To Mabillon, similarly, Bernard's message was spiritually compulsive. He was, however, also aware that the Bernadine texts were steeped in another time and handed down through various links and transmissions. To Mabillon, Bernard's historical distance is constantly present. The Maurist is a monk, but he is also a historian; and in his approach to Bernard, he is very much both. In Rancé's view, history is a discipline that belongs way out of the monastic focus [...]. His revitalization of Bernard is not a revitalization of the medieval monk, but of a set of ideals synchronically present.[5]

The question here, then, seems to be whether the idea of historical distance is indeed – or should be – an inherent part of the concept of medievalism. I shall now try to address this question mainly by way of another example – Venetian liturgy at San Marco in the eighteenth century.

In a forthcoming article I discuss certain features of the liturgy in San Marco, Venice, as preserved in liturgical books of the eighteenth century.[6] I base my argument mainly on a 1716 book, *Officium Hebdomadae Sanctae Secundum consuetudinem Ducalis Ecclesiae S. Marci Venetiarum*, which is preserved in the Biblioteca Nazionale Marciana, Venice.[7] To be sure, all Catholic liturgy up to the Second Vatican Council can be said to be "medieval" in some way, preserving to a large extent the structure, text, and even music of medieval offices. However, in San Marco, particular celebrations for Good Friday and Easter Sunday are preserved that – generally speaking –

were no longer practiced after the Council of Trent (1545–63). For example, texts printed by Walther Lipphardt in his volumes of sources for the so-called dramatic Easter ceremonies demonstrate how the liturgy for Holy Week and Easter in the eighteenth century contained both the *depositio* (burial) of the host and the *visitatio sepulchri*, most probably until the fall of the Republic in 1797.[8]

I shall avoid going into liturgical technicalities and minutiae, since I intend to focus not on the details of how this liturgy was performed but on how certain traditional medieval practices were broadly appropriated by this liturgy during the eighteenth century. Elsewhere, I have discussed these ceremonies and their Venetian transformations in the sixteenth century, something further discussed with many more liturgico-musical details by Susan Rankin.[9] The main focus of my discussion was primarily the appropriation of medieval liturgical traditions in which the host – the *corpus Christi* as instituted during a previous Mass (not on Good Friday) – was ceremonially buried after the *Veneration of the Cross* (with the *improperia*) in the afternoon of Good Friday to be represented as resurrected on Easter morning at a so-called *visitatio sepulchri* ceremony. In San Marco such ceremonies were combined from the sixteenth century on with ducal processions in a way that makes explicit the divine dependence on Christ of the ducal office and that serves as one of many ways to enliven the Venetian myth of *la serenissima* for participants and onlookers alike.

In the *Officium Hebdomadae*, this sixteenth-century tradition is strictly followed. At the same time, arrangements for the liturgical procedures for the Good Friday deposition of the host are found that deviate – in small details – from the sixteenth-century liturgy: traditionally, the so-called *improperia*, a staged dialogue between the crucified Christ and his congregation in which the latter is reproached for having crucified its Savior, was combined with the *Trishagion*, the penitential glorification of Christ, "Holy God, holy and mighty, holy and immortal, have mercy on us," sung in both Latin and Greek. In the *Officium Hebdomadae*, the *improperia* appears detached from the *Trishagion* and was repeatedly used during the procession to the sepulchre where the *doge* at the end sealed the grave in which the host would remain until Easter morning. This rearrangement may seem to underline the penitential atmosphere of the deposition ritual but otherwise does not appear as having in any way radically changed the perceived meaning of the ritual.

In the context of my earlier question, this seeming lack of a marked re-interpretation of the ritual is, in my view, what is interesting about this example. The mentioned change may, as far as I know, have been made at any point during the seventeenth or early eighteenth century and shows first of all that the medieval procedure continued to be thought of as meaningful enough to be practiced and even to be worked on to make it function as well as possible. It was, obviously, not just done again as it "always" had been but was appropriated and updated, edited as it were, although, at least from what I can see, without any particular new interpretation. Thus, what we have here is another example of a medieval appropriation made not with a conscious idea of historical distance, not as a revitalization of a distant medieval ceremony, but rather as something seemingly felt as a synchronically relevant present tradition. One might describe the difference as between a "modern" re-appropriation of a medieval ceremony, as in the revivals of so-called liturgical dramas in the twentieth and twenty-first centuries, and the simple feeling of "belonging to the medieval" while living in the eighteenth century, or at least feeling as if, in that particular respect, one "belongs to the medieval." The question we must deal with, then, is whether what they did in San Marco in the early eighteenth century is something we should think of as medievalism, or something not of interest to the "medievalism" community (cf. Mette Bruun's distinction above).

Of course, the question involves the issue of intentionality. Should Rancé and those who "edited" the medieval deposition ceremony be considered as having felt in some respect – concerning the traditions they perpetuated – that that they lived onwards in a medieval world? As Mette Bruun points out, Rancé's reforms were not necessarily in accordance with a "Bernardian spirit" as they were to such a high degree informed by Rancé's own seventeenth-century context. In a similar way, the "same" ritual in the eighteenth century would have had a different cultural impact than in the Middle Ages (and the sixteenth century). In the eighteenth century it must have been seen as ancient, standing out for its sublime grandeur and solemnity as such a concept of "the sublime" gradually came to the fore. But what are we considering in terms of medievalism? The intention by which something was "recreated" or "represented" or just preserved, or the perception of the phenomenon in question at the time? If it is perception, then all of the problems of determining intentionality are compounded by the challenges of determining how the past has been seen across vast historical distances and different degrees of historical consciousness than our own.

For the sake of clarity, or perhaps for the sake of fruitful confusion, let me ask what we should make of Mozart's use of medieval liturgical traditions. For his *commendatore* in *Don Giovanni*, Mozart used liturgical features that were undoubtedly well-known from his Salzburg experiences as a liturgical musician and composer but were, even so, of medieval origin and clearly used as a signifier of "the Other." In other instances, he quoted medieval chant in liturgical music (for instance, in his *Requiem Mass*). We do not know the exact intentions behind these moves. They may be based on a lack of distance (in the sense of Mette Bruun's example), especially since such quotations are few and smoothly integrated into the musical web, but they may also be read as a way of incorporating signs of the transcendent. I shall not pursue this discussion here, but merely ask: does the relevance of Mozart's use of medieval components for the "medievalism community" depend on the answer to such a question?

In a recent article, another colleague from the Copenhagen Centre, Eyolf Østrem, has argued that the personal history of an author cannot be completely separated from his or her academic construction of history. Østrem illustrates this point by intermingling a personal account of encountering medieval music during his youth with a scholarly discussion about historiography and about the idea and practice of medieval music, a discussion that emphasizes two fundamentally different aspects of the construction of medieval music as it has been practiced in the Early Music movement: 1) the scholarly striving towards authenticity, and 2) the creative "interior" aspect of personal dreams of a different world imagined in medieval music:

> [...] the integration between individual, existence, and history makes it impossible to separate the one from the other, so that the question whether this is a personal history or a history about the early eighties, becomes fairly meaningless; the histories, the way they are represented, become a web of references, where the appropriation of the Middle Ages in a personal project, the loss of the innocent gaze upon existence in the early adult age [...], and the fundamentally historical character of language, slide over and into each other.[10]

In Østrem's personal recollections from his childhood of encountering the "old" through his father's writing of Gothic letters in the snow at Eastertide, these drawings become interchangeable with the idea of the "medieval," since both signified the very old to him at that time. And in the recognition of that mixture comes not only acknowledgment of the borders between the historical and the personal but also an invitation to explore the results of their interaction.

Of course, there may not be a direct and complete correlation between, on the one hand, the implications of Østrem's discussion about how personal and academic domains overlap and, on the other hand, the answer(s) to questions about how the individual – and, therefore, in the end, also personal – intentions of medievalist practices intersect with the general reception of those practices. But in relationship to the question with which I began this paper, I would argue that medievalism should not be restricted to features in which a historical consciousness is explicitly at work, primarily because all practices are received in a culture where manifold attitudes will be or have been at work. Thus, regardless of the intentions or the consciousness behind a particular practice or artifact, it will form part of a general reception in which it may play a part as an element in the construction or recreation of the Middle Ages. Certainly, the eighteenth-century San Marco liturgy and, broadly speaking, pre-1960s Catholic liturgy as a whole – and even Mozart's music – contribute to such a continued construction of the Middle Ages and thereby make the question of when the Middle Ages ended obsolete. It did not end, which is precisely the point of the quotations I gave above from Leslie Workman; it is recreated over and over again, always being made into something new, whether this is the Gothic letters drawn by ski poles in Eyolf Østrem's account of his childhood, a strict Trappist practice devised by Rancé, or the convincing integration of liturgical recitative and chant into Mozart's music. The only alternative I see would be to actually have to define when the Middle Ages ended, a historiographic project partly without end and partly at odds with the history of the concept itself.

NOTES

1. Leslie J. Workman, "The Future of Medievalism," in James Gallant, ed., *Medievalism: The Year's Work for 1995* (Holland, MI: Studies in Medievalism, 1999): 7–18 (12).

2. Workman, "The Future of Medievalism," 12.

3. See Hayden White, *Tropics of Discourse: Essays in Cultural Criticism* (Baltimore, MD: The Johns Hopkins University Press, 1978), especially Chap. 1: "The Burden of History" (27–50).

4. Mette Birkedal Bruun, "A Case in which a Revitalization of Something Medieval Turned out not to be Medievalism," in *Universitas: The University of Northern Iowa Journal of Research, Scholarship, and Creative Activity* 2/1 (2006), an Internet journal accessible at <http://universitas.grad.uni.edu>.

5. Bruun, "A Case," conclusion.

6. Nils Holger Petersen, "A Note on the 'Medieval' Passion Liturgy in San Marco, Venice, in the Eighteenth Century," in Alexander Andrée and Erika Kihlman, ed., *Hortus Troporum: Florilegium in honorem Gunillae Iversen* (Stockholm, forthcoming).

7. *Officium Hebdomadae Sanctae Secundum consuetudinem Ducalis Ecclesiae S. Marci Venetiarum: A Dominica Palmarum usque ad diem Paschae inclusive ad antiquum ritum et integritatem restitutum* (Venice: Typis Ioseph Prodocimi, 1716), kept under the shelfmark 171 D 199 in the Biblioteca Nazionale Marciana.

8. Walther Lipphardt, ed., *Lateinische Osterfeiern und Osterspiele*, 9 vols. (Berlin: Walter de Gruyter, 1975–90), 2:593–607 (nos. 429, 429a, and 430). See also the commentary on pages 347–50 in volume 7. Since the editions of Lipphardt, however, many more Venetian ceremonies have come to light. See also Giulio Cattin, *Musica e Liturgia a San Marco: testi e melodie per la liturgia delle ore dal XII al XVII secolo*, 4 vols. (Venice: Edizioni Fondazione Levi, 1990–92), 1:89 and 3:50–51; and Edward Muir, *Civic Ritual in Renaissance Venice* (Princeton: Princeton University Press, 1981), 219–21.

9. Nils Holger Petersen, "Il Doge and the Liturgical Drama in late Medieval Venice," *The Early Drama and Music Review* 18 (1995): 8–24; and Susan Rankin, "From Liturgical Ceremony to Public Ritual: 'Quem queritis' at St. Mark's, Venice," in Giulio Cattin, ed., *Da Bisanzio a San Marco: Musica e Liturgia* (Venice: Società Editrice il Mulino, 1997), 137–79 (and appendix, 180–91).

10. Eyolf Østrem, "Interiority and Authenticity: A Glossed Medieval History about Music and the Taste for Apples," in *Universitas: The University*

of Northern Iowa Journal of Research, Scholarship, and Creative Activity 2/1 (2006), an Internet journal accessible at <http://universitas.grad.uni.edu>. See also an earlier version in Norwegian: Eyolf Østrem, "Inderlighet og autentisitet: En glossert middelalderhistorie om musikk og smaken for epler," in *Passepartout 25* 13 (2005): 30–42.

Medievalisms and Why They Matter

Tom Shippey

According to the *Oxford English Dictionary*, "mediaevalism" is "The system of belief and practice characteristic of the Middle Ages [...] the adoption of or devotion to mediaeval ideals or usages; *occas.* An instance of this." This wording is found in the first edition of 1933, though it must have been composed considerably earlier, with supporting quotations running from 1853 to 1890. The editors of the second edition of 1989, however, saw no reason to adapt or expand the old definition, which thus remains standard and in a sense author-itative. The *OED* sense of the word, moreover, remains perfectly familiar: when a very recent book on C. S. Lewis refers to Lewis's "medievalism" (modern spelling), his "devotion to medieval ideals and usages" is exactly what is meant.[1] However, in recent years, and very largely as a result of the initiatives of Leslie Workman,[2] a second sense has become current, which I would define – trying as far as I can to imitate the *OED*'s magisterial style – as "Any post-medieval attempt to re-imagine the Middle Ages, or some aspect of the Middle Ages, for the modern world, in any of many different media; especially in academic usage, the study of the development and significance of such attempts." This is what is meant by the title of this journal, *Studies in Medievalism*.

The trouble with such a definition is that, in its effort to be comprehensive, it lacks clarity; and, as the history of submissions to this journal still too often shows, it lacks general acceptance and recognition even within the academic world. That situation is certainly changing, but even the most cursory glance at publications within "medievalism (sense 2)" shows why a comprehensive definition does not say very much. Medievalism in this sense is an enormous field, still largely unsurveyed, and even the most ambitious books about it do not look much like one another. Thus, Michael Alexander's *Medievalism: the Middle Ages in Modern England* (2007) is a study of literary medievalism within one particular country: it takes the reader from Scott through Coleridge and Keats, Tennyson and Morris, Eliot and Pound and the Inklings, with sections also on Victorian sages like Ruskin and Carlyle, on the paintings of the Pre-Raphaelite Brotherhood, and on the architecture of Pugin: a field quite sufficiently large for any volume. But if one then turns to Joep Leerssen's *National Thought in Europe* (2006), one sees that it too is quite avowedly a study of medievalism, has an even broader range, but still barely mentions any of the names that dominate Alexander's account. Leerssen's central figure is Jacob Grimm, whose centrality was at one point both literal and symbolic: at the "National Assembly" convened at Frankfurt in 1848 to discuss the future of *Deutschland* (at that point still only an idea, not a political entity), a special seat was reserved for Grimm, set apart from those of all the other delegates, and in the exact mid-point of the Assembly facing the Speaker. Its position was a tribute to Grimm's enormous feat of "cultural consciousness raising" expressed in his linguistic works such as the *Deutsche Grammatik* (1819 onwards), and his *Deutsche Mythologie* (first edition 1835) – the former considering above all pre-modern and indeed pre-medieval forms of the Germanic languages, the latter determinedly attempting to "re-imagine" a mythology no longer existent (except perhaps in forms such as fairy-tale) in the modern world. Grimm's impact on the history, politics, and map of modern Europe remains incalculable; but it was based on his version of what one might call "philological medievalism."

Already one is dealing with medievalisms, plural rather than singular, and there are many others, perhaps surveyed most comprehensively by Veronica Ortenberg's *In Search of the Holy Grail: the Quest for the Middle Ages* (2006). Architecture: the House of Commons, though we have got used to it, was when first built a kind of deliberately medieval Disneyland. Public ceremonial: Leerssen points out that the whole drive of this, during the nineteenth century and beyond, was to connect with the (recently rediscovered) past, from the deliberate invention or requisitioning of national anthems to the building of ceremonial golden coaches for the British and Dutch royal families. E. J. Hobsbawm and Terence Ranger's collection on

The Invention of Tradition (1983) has made that idea familiar, but the contributors to it characteristically underrated the medievalizing impulse behind such inventions. Then there is "musical medievalism," a topic well covered in recent issues of *Studies in Medievalism*, though I pick out here, for the way in which it connects several of the themes just mentioned, only Werner Wunderlich's study of the truly bizarre adaptation of Mozart's opera *La Clemenza di Tito* to a libretto about the Agilulfing dynasty of medieval Bavaria, designed once again to connect the nineteenth-century ruling dynasty with its legendary past.[3] With four films based on *Beowulf* released within the last ten years, one can hardly forget the enormous field of "movie medievalism," well surveyed by Kevin Harty's *The Reel Middle Ages* (1999), and now again by Nickolas Haydock's *Movie Medievalism: the Imaginary Middle Ages* (2008), a work which took off from his 2002 article in *Studies in Medievalism*.[4] But vast as it is, movie medievalism forms only a small proportion of what one has to call "popular medievalism," which takes in books, especially the best-selling genre of heroic fantasy derived essentially from Tolkien, "the English Grimm," as well as comics, graphic novels, and probably much else not yet appropriated in any way by academic scholarship – though, NB, it invariably, if at many removes, *derives* from academic scholarship. One such mode just coming into view is "touristic medievalism," or "the Heritage industry," often marked by strange anachronisms.[5] And one can imagine "iconic medievalism": as Andrew Wawn has pointed out, everyone in the Western world knows what "a Viking" looks like, and indeed how he is supposed to behave, but the clichés of skull-drinking and berserk-frothing, which have long been rejected and resented by academic scholars, nevertheless derive from a long and powerful process of academic rediscovery and popularization, which one can follow in Wawn's closely focused study of *The Vikings and the Victorians: Inventing the Old North in Nineteenth-Century Britain* (2000). Ronald Hutton has done something very similar in his provocatively titled *Witches, Druids and King Arthur* (2002), flanked by his wider study *The Triumph of the Moon: A History of Modern Pagan Witchcraft* (1999) and a narrower one, *The Druids* (2007).

It would be possible to continue, but already the subject goes beyond any one person's competence even to survey. "Medievalism" is a very broad field, much less capable of definition than, for instance, "modernism." One is tempted to say that a better term would be "medievalisms [plural]", and that a natural academic approach is to single out just one of them. But at the same time one has to remember that, though its many manifestations may develop separately, they are all capable at any point of interacting, and have always done so. A very appropriate mode of academic study, then, is the collective anthology, with single theme but varied perspectives, and this is what has guided/is guiding one enterprise in which I take personal interest, and which I – to some extent for personal reasons – regard as of especial importance for the modern world, and even for modern geo-politics.

This has shown itself so far in two edited collections co-published by Brepols, in Belgium, and Medieval and Renaissance Texts and Studies (MRTS), from Arizona State University in Tempe. The first of these was my *The Shadow-walkers: Jacob Grimm's Mythology of the Monstrous* (2005), a study of the materials covered in Grimm's *Deutsche Mythologie* (mentioned above), updated and with some reference to their (many) modern transformations. I am honored to report that the second volume, edited by Andrew Wawn and others, was a festschrift produced for me, titled *Constructing Nations, Reconstructing Myth* (2007), with contributions from several nations showing how the "Grimmian revolution" has had both literary and practical effects across the world. I hope a third volume will appear, which will derive from a sequence of panels on the topic "Forging the Nation(al Epic)" presented at the 2006 and 2007 Kalamazoo conferences, and at the 2007 Leeds conference. The word "forging" in the phrase above is deliberately ambiguous, as is the double grammatical object of "nation" and "epic." One aspect of "philological medievalism" – often at the same time "literary" and "nationalistic" – was the urge felt by national, sub-national, regional, or ethnic groups in Europe, from the eighteenth century on, to anchor their often-disputed or denied existence in some ancient text of suitable grandeur: and if no such text existed, then to make one, or sometimes appropriate one.

The great model was James Macpherson's "Ossian" fragments, which created a Europe-wide sensation, asserted the value of the culture of the Gaelic-speaking Highlands of Scotland – then still in the process of active suppression after Culloden Moor (1746), the last battle of the century-long British civil wars – and started an immediate wrangle – "Produce your manuscripts!" – over their authenticity. Did Macpherson "forge" them? The issue is not yet settled, and turns on what one means by "forgery."[6] Meanwhile, the most successful example of nation- and epic-creation must be Elias Lönnroth's *Kalevala*, first published in 1835–36. Here there were no manuscripts, for Lönnroth derived his material from oral sources. Like Macpherson, Lönnroth believed that what he had were fragments of an ancient epic, now dismembered, which he then "forged" into a connected whole. But, unlike Macpherson, Lönnroth was extremely scrupulous in recording exactly what he had and had not done; and while Macpherson succeeded in creating much of the now-familiar Highlander image, Lönnroth went beyond him, arguably, in creating the national and linguistic identity of modern Finland from what had been Swedish and Russian territory.[7]

Curiously and conversely, while Lönnroth, under the influence of one theory of epic composition, was putting together an epic from fragments, German-speaking scholars, under the influence of *Lieder-theorie*, were busily disintegrating rediscovered national epics, pre-eminently the medieval German romances *Nibelungenlied* and *Kudrun* and the Anglo-Saxon *Beowulf*, back into what they believed to be their original forms, sometimes (I would argue) in the service of a kind of linguistic regionalism: the native tongue of several prominent German scholars was not *Hochdeutsch* but *Plattdeutsch*, and though no Low German epic has survived, such merely factual considerations never stopped a true philologist. There are several cases of scholars rewriting works into the language they *should* have been recorded in – or "forging" work and language together. The most certain case here must be the (once more regionally oriented) Frisian *Oera Linda-boek*. Goffe Jensma's definitive study *De Gemaskerde God* (2004) leaves no doubt that the work was deliberately "forged," in all senses, by a consortium including the philologist Eelco Verwijs, though with results entirely different from what was intended. Much more contro-versially, Edward L. Keenan's book *Josef Dobrovsky and the Origins of the Igor' Tale* has argued that the Russian "Lay of Prince Igor," a defining text for Russian identity, is a forgery perpetrated by Dobrovsky, another early philologist: here the story is that there *was* a manuscript, discovered in the 1790s but destroyed during the French attack on Moscow in 1812. Keenan's claim has been strongly contested, but very similar arguments surround still-extant manu-scripts in Czech. And then there is the Estonian answer to the *Kalevala*, the *Kalevipoëg*, and the whole world of Celtic rediscovery, including the works of Edward Williams, alias "Iolo Morganwg," currently being sifted by Mary-Ann Constantine of Aberystwyth, and the Breton *Barsaz Breiz* published in 1846 by Théodore de la Villemarqué, once again on the basis (he said) of oral ballads no longer rediscoverable.

All these, and many more, form part of the history of literary, linguistic, national, and in-ambition-national medievalism, something best perceived, as Professor Leerssen has remarked, both as a network and as a "non-stop multi-media cult."[8] It remains for me to add that in my opinion (not widely shared) this is not something safely distanced, an affair of books and libraries and scholars. There is a medievalism still at work in the world, and it is a dangerous one: which is why scholars, having set the bomb ticking, have a duty not to distance themselves from any possible explosion.

I begin my final argument with what will seem a trivial case. As an Englishman, brought up for some years in Scotland and resident there for several more, I could not help noticing the souring of the Anglo-Scottish relationship over the last fifty years, which has shown itself in the demands first for Scottish devolution and then for independence; in the very pronounced resultant upsurge in specifically English national feeling, which now so worries senior British politicians;[9] and, not least, in the abandonment of the oldest annual international sporting fixture in the world, the England–Scotland football match. (In 1989, after more than 100 years of fairly amicable competition, the police said they could no longer be responsible for keeping the peace. The countries have since played each other, as in 1996 and 1999, only when drawn against each other in European qualifying games: there are no more "friendlies.") This souring has many causes, but was certainly exacerbated by the very popular movie directed by and starring Mel Gibson, *Braveheart* (1995). The film is a historical travesty, as many have observed, and its racism and homophobia, if directed against any group other than the regularly-in-Hollywood-vilified English, would surely have prevented its release, but if the United Kingdom does break up, as some predict, it will have played a significant part. This may not matter – English opinion, when canvassed, is on the whole indifferent to the prospect – and the institutions of the European Union, designed to prevent war among European states, may well be able to cope with such a separation: there are recent encouraging precedents in Eastern Europe.

When I first remarked on this phenomenon, however, at a conference in 2001, Professor William Calin, whose opinion I respect, told me I was making too much of it. There are nevertheless two things which continue to give me pause, both of them again born of personal experience. One derives from what we must now call "the former Yugoslavia." I attended a conference at Zagreb in 1986, and spent much of the summer of 1988 on the Croatian island of Pag. The 1986 conference was attended by Croats and Serbs, Bosnians and Albanians, all chaffing each other in much the way that the English and the Scots used to. Pag in 1988 was a tourist resort well on the way to becoming a Yugoslavian Riviera. Just a few years later, however, it had become the hinge of Croatia, and the causeway off the southern end of the island was the only road-link between the north and the potentially very valuable long coastal strip down to Split and Dubrovnik: it was surrounded by anti-tank and anti-aircraft batteries. As for the conference attendees of 1986, all the ones I knew have disappeared.[10] My other experience was a strictly academic one, caused by reading through the vast scholarly literature about *Beowulf* written in nineteenth-century Germany. Here one could not fail to notice how philological discovery became nationalistic assertion and eventually – the greatest tragedy of the twentieth century – racist and then genocidal polemic. I have traced this in some detail elsewhere, ending my account with the strangely symbolic figure of Walter Berendsohn (1884–1984), totally committed as a scholar to the medievalist Germanicizing project, totally unaware that it would eventually expel him from position, nation, and – very nearly – life, for being Jewish.[11] A contributing factor to the Yugoslav break-up was certainly the medievalizing memory of the Battle of Kosovo (1389), as much a fiction, it seems, as *Braveheart*,[12] while the Nazi ideology derived much of its popular appeal from a fictional medieval world brought into being by scholars and by poets. Joep Leerssen has pointed out that it was Feldmarschall von Gneisenau, Gebhard Leberecht von Blücher's chief of staff, not commonly regarded as a sentimentalist, who declared, "The security of the [Prussian] throne is founded on poetry."[13] Poetry, one might say, like the Middle High German *Nibelungenlied*, a German icon for the Napoleonic Wars.

Nor are the German, Yugoslav, and British cases the most currently unsettling ones. It seems unlikely that the American directors of the present Gulf wars ever had any real intention of refighting the medieval Crusades, but for a time "Crusades" formed part of their rhetoric, and this was certainly picked up and resented in the Islamic world.[14] Arguably, moreover, the total lack of future planning revealed since 2003 sprang from a "medievalist" root. Movies like *Braveheart*, again, or more recently Jerry Zucker's *First Knight* (1995) and Antoine Fuqua's *King Arthur* (2004), operate on the proposition that the troubles of this world are caused by wicked oppressors: remove the oppressors, liberate the people, and all will be well.[15] There is no need for future planning, as the only problem will be, not restoring the electricity supply, winning popular acceptance, or maintaining public order, but simply sweeping up the triumphal rose petals. It would be sad to think that the highest levels of public policy have been determined, however unconsciously, by a historical awareness derived from medievalizing movies: but in America the movie world and the political world are increasingly closely connected, and the movie world (not, fortunately, medievalist aspects of it) has been shown to have had real-world political effects.[16]

As Professor Calin said, I hope correctly, I may be making too much of these uneasy parallels, and the nationalist medievalizing of the nineteenth and twentieth centuries in Europe may now be over – though there are now far more nations in Europe than there were twenty years ago, all with an identity to create and defend, and Europe is not the only continent where nations have a medieval past waiting to be discovered and used. There are, as said at the start of this piece, many medievalisms in the world, and some of them are as safe as William Morris wallpaper: but not all of them. Here, as much as anywhere in the academic world, scholars have a duty to trace connections, to expose errors, and above all to make their voices heard inside and outside the academy.

NOTES

1. Michael Ward, *Planet Narnia: The Seven Heavens in the Imagination of C. S. Lewis* (London: Oxford University Press, 2008), 19.

2. For a brief account of the history of these, see the "Introduction" to Richard Utz and Tom Shippey, ed., *Medievalism in the Modern World: Essays in Honour of Leslie Workman* (Turnhout: Brepols, 1998), 2–6.

3. Werner Wunderlich, "Medieval Mozart: *König Garibald* and *La*

Clemenza di Tito," in Tom Shippey and Martin Arnold, ed., *Appropriating the Middle Ages: Scholarship, Politics, Fraud, Studies in Medievalism* 11 (2001): 113–43.

4. Nickolas Haydock, "Arthurian Melodrama, Chaucerian Spectacle, and the Waywardness of Cinematic Pastiche," in Tom Shippey and Martin Arnold, ed., *Film and Fiction: Reviewing the Middle Ages, Studies in Medievalism* 12 (2002): 5–38.

5. As pointed out by Steve Watson, "Touring the Medieval: Tourism, Heritage and Medievalism in Northumbria," in Shippey and Arnold, ed., *Appropriating the Middle Ages*, 239–61.

6. See Stefan Hall, "James Macpherson's *Ossian*: Forging Ancient Highland Identity for Scotland," in Andrew Wawn, Graham Johnson, and John Walter, ed., *Constructing Nations, Reconstructing Myth: Essays in Honour of T. A. Shippey* (Turnhout: Brepols, 2007), 3–26.

7. See Keith Battarbee, "The Forest Writes Back: the *Ausbau* of Finnish from Peasant Vernacular to Modernity," in Wawn et al., ed., *Constructing Nations*, 71–96.

8. The first remark made in conversation; for the phrase quoted, see Joep Leerssen, *National Thought in Europe: A Cultural History* (Amsterdam: Amsterdam University Press, 2006), 203.

9. Cynics, of whom I am one, observe that since such a disproportionate number of them are Scots, the last thing they want is to be returned to the smaller pastures of Edinburgh or Kirkcaldy.

10. I would add that the entirely peaceful disagreement between myself and Professor Calin, in 2001, ended with a Serbian lady in the audience bursting into tears.

11. See Tom Shippey and Andreas Haarder, *Beowulf: The Critical Heritage* (London and New York: Routledge, 1998), 69–71.

12. See Noel Malcolm, *Kosovo: A Short History* (New York: New York University Press, 1998), esp. chap. 4, "The Battle and the Myth."

13. Leerssen, *National Thought*, 118.

14. See Abdulhay Yahyah Zalloum, *Oil Crusades: America through Arab Eyes* (London and Ann Arbor, MI: Pluto Press, 2007). Nickolas Haydock is preparing an edited collection on *Hollywood and the Holy Land*, to be published by McFarland. The kind of connection I am suggesting is argued much more forcibly by Bruce Holsinger, *Neomedievalism, Neoconservatism, and the War on Terror* (Chicago: Prickly Paradigm Press, 2007).

15. The scriptwriter of *King Arthur* agreed that the movie had parallels with Vietnam, but denied any connection with Baghdad on the grounds that the script was in existence before the invasion of 2003. See, however, Tom Shippey, "Fuqua's *King Arthur*: More Myth-making in America," *Exemplaria* 19/2 (2007): 310–26.

16. For which see H. Bruce Franklin, *MIA: Mythmaking in America* (New York: Lawrence Hill, 1992). The article cited above echoes Franklin's title deliberately.

Medievalism, Authority, and the Academy

Gwendolyn A. Morgan

Despite denoting one of the fastest growing approaches of academic inquiry within a number of fields, the term "medievalism" remains somewhat slippery. It may describe the use of medieval themes, stories, characters, or even styles in the fiction, art, or film in any period following the close of the Middle Ages. Politically, it frequently denotes the recreation or refashioning of historical figures or events to justify the ideologies or national identities of a subsequent age. It has been applied to the adoption and adaptation of medieval philosophies to illuminate the issues of a later time. It may even describe the revival of early medical or other scientific practices. One thing, however, that underlies all such endeavors, is the reliance on the medieval past to lend authority to contemporary thought. Consider, for example, that the Tudors rested their claim to the English throne partly on an invented lineage leading back to the fabled King Arthur, even going so far as to manufacture and "discover" his Round Table. Or, on a more modern note, consider that most New Age Wicca adherents believe they are reviving an ancient Celtic spirituality somehow secretly kept alive for 1500 years, despite the fact that the very name of their cult derives not from early Welsh but from Anglo-Saxon and that much of their supposedly arcane knowledge has no documented existence prior to the nineteenth century. Yet, in the popular imagination, to be rooted in the medieval is to have unquestioned tradition and authority, to be legitimized. In *Travels in Hyperreality*, Umberto Eco discusses the phenomenon in Freudian terms:

[…] all the problems of the Western world emerged in the Middle Ages: modern languages, merchant cities, capitalistic economy, […] the nation state, […] the struggle between the poor and the rich, the concept of heresy or ideological deviation, even our con-temporary notions of love, […] the conflict between church and state, trade unions, […] the technological transformation of labor […]. Thus, looking at the Middle Ages means looking at our infancy.[1]

To this end, Eco continues, we have invented multiple, wildly different versions of the medieval period, described as his "Ten Little Middle Ages," which allow us to explain and justify the issues facing us and the beliefs we hold in the twentieth and twenty-first centuries. Moreover, the Middle Ages have been and continue to be deliberately manipulated and appropriated by those in various positions of influence to further their agendas, be those Nazi ideology, feminism, various nationalistic movements, theories of art, or religious systems, producing a view palatable to the general population. This latter practice provides the material for Norman Cantor's *Inventing the Middle Ages*[2] and the numerous studies that follow his lead. Still others, such as Ronald Hutton, in *Witches, Druids and King Arthur*, or Michael Cramer, in his recent examination of the Society for Creative Anachronism,[3] celebrate the medievalism in popular culture as a positive, creative force allowing for the development of effective responses to contemporary problems and ideologies. That the connection to the Middle Ages claimed for such manifestations of medievalism is all but completely fictional is, in the view of its practitioners, inconsequential.

The possible approaches and particular fields available for the study of medievalism are thus abundant, and all reflect our continued need (identified by Eco) to pay our psychic debts in medieval currency. The created medieval past is our justification for the present, our invented authority. Our penchant for appealing to it echoes closely the medieval poets citing real and invented classical authorities for their own art, and thus represents a double practice of medievalism. However, whether scholars "pooh-pooh" popular misconceptions and adaptations or appreciate conscious manipulations of our medieval past, they tend to exude superiority in not having been taken in by them. Yet, the academy itself also practices medievalism, and to the same end: to gain authority for scholarly paradigms and ideological positions by asserting their origins in the golden Middle Ages. It is this phenomenon I wish to examine here, for, I would argue, what appears to be self-deception among academics is closely akin to the medievalism practiced in popular culture.

Medievalism in the academy may be illuminated by the theory expounded by Thomas Kuhn in *The Structure of Scientific Revolutions*.[4] According to Kuhn, an ideological "paradigm" is established as the basis for scientific "knowledge" in any particular discipline, a paradigm that encompasses the perception of the world, the pedagogy used to describe and teach it, and the methodology that extends this knowledge in the examination of the previously unexplained. Under such a paradigm, intellectuals will force-fit all observation into the accepted view and dismiss as anomaly or insufficiently explored any "facts" that do not fit it. For example, according to contemporary physics, a bumblebee cannot possibly fly, a theoretical difficulty that, my colleagues in the field insist, does not mean our paradigm is wrong, merely that we do not fully understand it. However, as Kuhn explains, when the accumulation of such anomalies reaches a critical point, the paradigm crumbles under its own weight of tacked-on disclaimers and caveats, and a new one must be developed from or in contrast to the old, and with it new perceptions, pedagogies, and methodologies. Such, says Kuhn, is the ongoing, cyclical process that drives scientific inquiry.

If we adapt Kuhn's theory to the various areas of medieval studies, this means we similarly subscribe to a particular *academic* paradigm for viewing and interpreting the Middle Ages, refashioning new knowledge and events in an effort to force-fit them into it; in effect, changing reality to support theory. I would argue that this paradigm has two distinct purposes and, consequently, two particular manifestations. The first follows Kuhn's exposé of scientific thought directly, interpreting factual discoveries to fit a pre-established view of the period. The discovery of the so-called Lindow Man in a peat bog in the mid-1980s provides an amusing case in point.

Found by peat-cutters in Lindow Moss, Cheshire, a man's upper body was carbon-dated back to the first century. Once this was accepted, the Lindow man was used to confirm a belief in Celtic human sacrifice attested by hostile contemporary Greco-Roman authors recording the Roman conquest of Britain. As Ronald Hutton relates the incident:

The man was naked, and appeared to have suffered a triple death of the sort which features in early Irish literature; his skull had been fractured by a blow and his throat cut with a sharp blade, while he had been strangled with a cord which was still around his neck.[5]

The discovery spawned a number of academic books from respectable presses, touting the Lindow Man as a new window into ancient Celtic spirituality. It was, therefore, as Hutton notes, "extremely embarrassing" when, in 1998, a professional pathologist was commissioned by the BBC to examine the body. He determined that no strangulation had occurred and that the cord around the neck was most likely to have been a necklace; that the gash in the neck was accidental, resulting from the peat-cutters' activities; and that the cause of death was a blow to the head. Moreover, the first-century dating of the body was "a piece of guesswork after three different laboratories had come up with three widely divergent results," the chemical make-up of peat bogs already having been proven to render carbon dating utterly ineffective.[6] The BBC scientists concluded that the victim was just as likely (or more so) to have been the victim of a modern mugging as of an ancient Celtic practice.

The Lindow Man affair indicates Kuhn's theory of academic paradigms to be fully operational in two academic communities: the scientific (holding to carbon-dating despite its short-comings) and, more to the present point, the humanities (in their recreation of the Middle Ages). Previous and subsequent study of Roman historical writings about the Celts has proven their unreliability, and other than those writings there is absolutely no evidence that the Celts practiced human sacrifice, as Hutton has proved conclusively in *Pagan Religions of the Ancient British Isles*. Likewise, Peter Berresford Ellis[7] relates a number of slanderous classical accounts about Celtic women, such as that they were so fierce and unfeminine that they participated in combat while suckling their infants or that they severed the genitals of fallen enemies. Hutton, Ellis, and other eminent historians repeatedly emphasize that a primary purpose of such classical "histories" was to justify the brutal Roman conquest as necessary to "civilize" dangerous barbarians, and that to this end classical writers invented any number of atrocities that they then attributed to Britain's early inhabitants. Nonetheless, when Lindow Man was discovered, scholars rejected the

mundane explanation (mundane, because it is most likely) and enthusiastically embraced classical pseudo-history and ancient literature,
along with unreliable scientific method, to justify their belief in what
Eco calls the "Barbaric Middle Ages." Kuhn's theory, clearly, applies
to more fields of knowledge than the scientific.

Perhaps more interesting is the second flavor of academic medievalism. In this, we approach our actual identity and status as
members of the academy, justifying our call for greater appreciation
and compensation and criticizing our treatment at the hands of
governing bodies and the public alike, based on our own fictionalized
medieval past. Yet, somehow, authors of various studies advocating
this presumed precedent seem totally unaware of this self-deception.[8]
Already involved in examining the medievalism of popular culture –
especially in the last two or three decades – members of the academy
have developed corollary interest in all things medieval, not merely in
the humanities but also in psychology, philosophy, theology, the
history of science, and even medicine. Such investigation has, indeed,
borne important fruit. Along the way, however, we have fallen prey to
introducing false medievalism into our examination of the state of the
profession. Nowhere is this more apparent than in our rebellion
against the model of the so-called "corporate university."

Rooted in capitalistic ideology, a new view of the university
appeared in the mid-twentieth century, a view characterized by two
main issues: first, that the main purpose of higher education is to train
students for their future careers in a manner that optimizes their
economic success and, second, that such education is a commodity to
be sold, and thus the university, as the producer and retailer of that
commodity, should operate as a business, maintaining self-sufficiency
reflected on a type of profit-and-loss statement. This obviously had a
profound impact on program offerings, in which courses in traditional
study of a subject took a back seat to those producing clearly recogniz-
able business skills. For example, English professors were flooded with
writing courses, while their colleagues in Art found that the emphasis
in their courses was transferred to commercial illustration, advertising,
and mainstream television and film. Other disciplines suffered similar
shifts. Additionally, under the guise of increasing professorial "produc-
tivity," enrollment caps and course loads have continued to climb
while we produce graduates in assembly-line fashion: do the time, get
the degree. Sadly, despite the "publish or perish" and service demands

of the profession, the general perception of academic salaries focuses solely on that student production, and professors were therefore viewed as under-worked and overpaid. Consequently, compensation has generally failed to keep pace with inflation. More work, fewer dollars, decline in intellectual inquiry: the mounting crisis led to a spate of books bewailing the state of the profession, appearing from the mid-eighties onward. Their cry for reform, no matter how valid, nonetheless turned to the Middle Ages for credibility.

The traditions and idealism of the modern academy have always been medieval in tone. Academic regalia – cap and gown styles distinguishing the discipline and degree, colors identifying particular institutions – developed in the Middle Ages and remain linked to them in appearance. Graduation ceremonies are characterized by solemn processionals and classical music, and the enactment of rituals a millennium old. Diplomas (mine is actually in Latin) attest that degrees are awarded "together with all the rights, privileges, and honors appertaining thereto." This provision, too, dates back to the Middle Ages, when teaching faculties presumably *did* have exclusive rights and honors, along with attendant respect and prestige within the community. As today's academy rises in protest against their devaluation by the corporate university, they nostalgically point to this proud medieval heritage as a justification for their complaints.

Day Late, Dollar Short[9] provides a cross section of the academy's medievalism in their cry for improved conditions and compensation typical of much of what is out there. A collection of essays purporting jointly to expose the sharp decline in academic conditions and standards, the book's contributors vary widely in philosophical approach and political ideology. Nonetheless, the essays share two common premises: first, that a "post-theory generation of scholars" entering the profession after the great theory wars of the 1960s and '70s has negatively changed the face of the profession; and, second, that the public call for "accountability" (i.e., profitability) has resulted in the corporate university model. The former asserts that post-theory academics, facing a rapidly shrinking job market, were forced to subscribe to the once-radical theories of their professors, now institutionalized and hence no longer radical. As a result, the new generation had no room for intellectual freedom, partly because the Theorists sat on the hiring and tenure committees and partly because the extremist nature of the now-accepted ideologies left little room for novelty: after all, if one accepts the absence of meaning and the reduction of the Signified to the Signifier, how much further can one go? Such intellectual enslavement, combined with the increasing trend to use graduate students for the all-important service courses, provided a hostile environment for the post-theorist faculty, limiting them (so *Day Late, Dollar Short* contributors argue) to regurgitation at worst or hyper-specialization and extended application of Theory at best. Finally, theory courses proliferated, further reducing offerings concentrating on the object of study itself. Between corporate university and all-powerful Theorists, academic freedom and privilege shrinks to almost nothing. Added to this are complaints of insufficient travel funding and library resources; the looming abolition of the tenure system; the reduction of employment opportunities resulting from growing use of adjunct and graduate student instructors; and the "dumbing down" of curricula to retain poorly prepared students who view higher education only as technical training for the job market.

Most scholars who argue there has been a reduction in academic power and prestige look only as far back as the 1960s and '70s to find professorial utopia and suggest that this era was the end of a long history of privilege established in the Middle Ages, "an age [...] dynamic and swiftly changing: an age where knowledge was sought and valued; where great universities were born and learning fostered."[10] In *Day Late, Dollar Short*, Barbara Reisling, for example, asserts that corporate-university proponents view tenure as "the inherited privilege of an ancient regime, ripe for the shaking,"[11] while Crystal Bartovich argues that maintaining the trappings of that regime, "*devoid of their original content*, is what keeps academics from wholesale revolt against current conditions" (my emphasis).[12] Other recent studies, including William Reading's *The University in Ruins*[13] and Stanley Aronwitz and William DiFazio's *The Jobless Future: Sci-Tech and the Dogma of Work*,[14] look to the same era for the beginning of decline. Still others retreat further into the past. Satya Mohanty finds the academy's decline rooted in the eighteenth century,[15] while Robert Scholes returns to the late Renaissance period.[16] All agree, however, that in the golden (if misty) Middle Ages, education, learning, and seeking knowledge for its own sake were revered, as were the institutions that fostered such.

The argument, however, is by no means new. As if the proliferation of such studies over two and a half decades was not enough to suggest the idealized medieval academy and recent decline in it as established belief, one might return to the nineteenth-century laments of Charles Sanders Peirce that the universities of his day served only to uphold the business and social status quo and thereby discouraged true intellectual dissension and exploration.[17] A decade earlier, the journal *The Contemporary Review*, a pioneering effort in establishing the medieval period as worthy of study, published articles using the medieval university as a model for debate on the same issues, lauding it as a paragon of learning and intellectual freedom. Thus, despite our own *academic* investigation of the issue reaching back over a century and a half, our medievalism causes us to ignore its perennial nature and see the problems of our own age as new and unique. The question, then, becomes, when *did* the academy not suffer from the same complaints?

Despite general consensus, the answer most emphatically does *not* lie in the Middle Ages. The medieval university, whence hooding ceremonies and the grandiose phrases appearing on our diplomas originated, shared the very same woes as its counterparts from the sixteenth century to contemporary times. In *English University Life in the Middle Ages*,[18] Alan Cobban provides an intensive study of the schools at Oxford and Cambridge from the twelfth through the sixteenth centuries. The picture that emerges is frighteningly familiar: high student drop-out rates, untenured lectureships, marginal economic rewards: indeed, medieval teaching Masters received relatively *lower* salaries than those accorded professors today. Poor funding existed for libraries and other facilities, and monies accorded the humanities came in a distant second to law. Graduate fellows (today's teaching assistants and adjuncts) taught utility courses for starvation wages, indeed were frequently required to do so as part of their course of graduate study. This latter point, however, stemmed more from a problem in retaining faculty than a desire to exploit, for, aside from job security and wages, medieval Masters had a number of complaints.

Because universities relied so heavily on private benefactors, much professorial "free" time was spent praying for their souls. Also heavily dependent on student fees, Masters were forced to participate in popularity contests with their lectures; Cambridge, for example, allowed students two weeks to sample them before committing to a particular Master. We might see this today transmuted into the practice of student course- and professor-evaluation. Pressures from both student and benefactors, not to mention the Church hierarchy, which controlled and regulated the universities in medieval times, limited what was taught and how subjects were approached. Thus, the supposed intellectual freedom we credit to the medieval academy was substantially qualified and undercut. Nonetheless, despite his own findings, Cobban goes on to describe today's universities as significantly declined from the medieval:

> Curricular and other professional concerns were generally settled by the self-regulation of the masters' guild. The academic regime and the examination criteria were internal matters that were not subject to external validation. The masters' guild did not experience the humiliation of having to produce banal and disingenuous mission statements or of having thrust upon it the inappropriate verbiage of a mercantile society, to name only two of the albatrosses that so depress modern British universities. Regent masters were free to pursue lines of intellectual inquiry that were independent of the siren call of crude market forces.[19]

This statement is remarkable for two reasons. First, apparently Cobban is oblivious to the contradictions in his own evaluation, not only those summarized before this complaint but his further discovery that the ecclesiastical councils, directly and through the masters' guild, exerted substantial control on subjects and intellectual approaches. Indeed, according to Jeffrey Burton Russell, "freedom of thought" was a concept utterly foreign to the Middle Ages.[20]

Second, Cobban's assertion quoted above also reveals the true impetus for part of his study – the same discontent with the situation in the contemporary academy as is found in books overtly criticizing the state of the profession drives – and colors his own investigation into his perceived academic utopia. Additional criticisms of the present management of higher education liberally sprinkle his study, jarring conspicuously with his mounting enumeration of the medieval academy's woes: prohibitively expensive books, faculty obligations to oversee student morals and behavior, the exclusion of women from education, and so forth. As regards the supposed respect and prestige commanded by the university, Cobban devotes an entire chapter to the relations between "town and gown." His conclusions evince the populace's bitter resentment of the privileged legal position of students and masters (governed by ecclesiastic, and later guild, courts), which outweighed any awe of learning. Moreover, successful masters, like the students who left without achieving a degree, chose to pursue careers outside the academy, where better pay and greater job security awaited. In other words, the university was merely a springboard to more lucrative and expansive opportunities, even though such were almost always service positions and offered little in the way of social advancement. Thus does the first significant study of the university's medieval heritage explode the myth of the academic golden age, offering in its place a bitter and sober picture of intellectual control and poor professional conditions. Yet at the same time, thus also does the first significant study perpetrate the myth, fallen prey to the paradigm of medievalism that dominates theories of the academy: Cobban contradicts his own findings as he mounts a diatribe against the administration of today's institutions, citing a medieval ideal as precedent.

All in all, the academy has no medieval golden past from which it has declined. Instead, the affluence growing out of the post-war economic boom finally filtered down to the academy and combined with increased enrollments (fed by the boom) to allow a brief period in which there were more academic jobs than Ph.D. graduates. The competition for bodies, obviously, affected salaries, course loads, sabbaticals, research grants, and other perks. The golden age of academe lay not in the Middle Ages but in an anomalous decade or two produced by a unique combination of circumstances. Yet theorists on the state of the profession, despite their own findings, refuse to admit the fanciful nature of their beliefs. Just as historians and various scholars in the humanities *chose* to believe Lindow Man was an ancient Druid prince, so do we as a profession *choose* to believe in our version of the medieval academy. What remains to be seen is what sets us apart from other practitioners of medievalism.

I would submit that academic medievalism is the most complex form, as well as the least justified. When popular culture un (or sub) consciously uses the Middle Ages as a filter to understand contemporary dilemmas, express desires, and justify beliefs, they respond to one of the many "little Middle Ages" already established, adopting and extending it as their purpose requires. Few in the general populace – indeed, few in the academy – have any significant knowledge of medieval culture, living conditions, practices, or spirituality. Such knowledge as may exist with regard to the medieval period tends to be limited to those specializing in it, in one or another academic field.

On the other hand, conscious medievalism practiced by various power groups to further their agendas is at least not self-delusion: little sets it apart (ethically, at least) from the myriad other techniques of chauvinism, be they mud-slinging, false reporting, theological imperative, peer pressure, or brain-washing. However, whether the impulse to medievalism is deliberate or unconscious, both groups of practitioners manipulate perceptions to address contemporary needs, one from ignorance, the other from an understanding of psychic advertising. With academic medievalism, we have both conditions existing simultaneously.

The two major facets of our jobs – research and teaching – require that we learn and extend the base of knowledge in our discipline, and that we impart an understanding of it to those dependent upon us as experts. Yet, although our very research tells us that many of our paradigms for describing the Middle Ages are faulty, we nevertheless invent another Lindow Man, another monolithic Age of Faith describing a period of religious uproar and revolution, a simplified Tripartite Society that denies any female social power or the existence of a Middle Class. We understand the medievalism of others, and prove it, and theorize about it, yet we practice it with the blithe unconsciousness of *Lord of the Rings* fans, continuing to insist that Middle-earth did indeed exist. Thus, we are both expert and ingénue, manipulator and manipulated, deluder and deluded, and our subject-victims are ourselves. The intellectual acrobatics necessary to accomplish this are astounding; their explanation lies beyond the scope of the present essay and certainly requires someone with a different expertise than mine. However, it may here be enough to note that, among what Tom Shippey has termed "dangerous medievalisms," surely academic medievalism – inventing an authority to support our theories, using those theories to prove our invention, ultimately using both to perpetrate visions of the Middle Ages for others to employ in their particular self-justifications – is the most dangerous of all. While certainly, as Hutton and Cramer have argued, medievalism can be a positive force, it can also be turned to negative, even disastrous ends; one need only recall the medievalism essential to Nazi ideology to perceive the latter. Because of the inherent authority the Middle Ages hold in the Western psyche, those of us who have chosen the period as our focus hold, in a sense, a Holy Grail: the source of whatever the beholder most needs, most desires. It is an awesome social power. Yet it must be wielded with care, and at the heart of responsible action lies an understanding of the truth. If we continue to delude ourselves, whether with regard to our position as academics or with our presentation of the medieval period to others so that they may do with it what they will, the truth will never emerge, and we must be held at least partly guilty for whatever evil is perpetrated in its name.

NOTES

1. Umberto Eco, *Travels in Hyppereality*, trans. William Weaver (New York: Harcourt Brace, 1986), 64–65.
2. Norman Cantor, *Inventing the Middle Ages* (New York: William Morrow, 1991).
3. Michael Cramer, "Psychedelic Medievalism," in Gwendolyn A. Morgan, ed., *The Year's Work in Medievalism 2005–2006* (Eugene, OR: Wipf and Stock, 2007): 117–27.
4. Thomas Kuhn, *The Structure of Scientific Revolutions* (Chicago: University of Chicago Press, 1970).
5. Ronald Hutton, "The New Druids," in Gwendolyn A. Morgan, ed., *The Year's Work in Medievalism* (Bozeman, MT: Studies in Medievalism, 1999): 7–22 (9).
6. Hutton, "The New Druids," 10.
7. Peter Berresford Ellis, *Celtic Women* (London: Constable and Co., 1995).
8. Parts of the following discussion have appeared in my book, *The Invention of False Medieval Authorities as a Literary Device in Popular Fiction* (Lewiston, NY: Edwin Mellen, 2006), 97–106.
9. Peter Herman, ed., *Day Late, Dollar Short* (Albany: State University of New York Press, 2000).
10. The quote is from Michael Crichton's Postscript to his novel *Timeline* (New York: Alfred A. Knopf, 1999), 437. While Crichton is not himself an academic, he is perceived as a highbrow author closely associated with the academy and embraced by intellectual readers inside and outside of it. Hence, his perceptions are part and parcel with it.
11. Barbara Reisling, "Contextualizing Contexts: Culture Studies, Theory, and the Profession – Past and Present," in *Day Late, Dollar Short*, 175–98 (189).
12. Crystal Bartovich, "To Boldly Go Where No MLA Has Gone Before," in *Day Late, Dollar Short*, 77–94 (82).

13. William Reading, *The University in Ruins* (Cambridge, MA: Harvard University Press, 1996).

14. Stanley Aronwitz and William DiFazio, *The Jobless Future: Sci-Tech and the Dogma of Work* (Minneapolis: University of Minnesota Press, 1994).

15. Satya Mohanty, *Literary Theory and the Claims of History* (Ithaca, NY: Cornell University Press, 1994).

16. Robert Scholes, *The Rise and Fall of English* (New Haven, CT: Yale University Press, 1998).

17. For Peirce's arguments and those presented in *The Contemporary Review*, I am indebted to Scott Buchanan's "*The Contemporary Review* and Its Contributors," presented at the 37th International Congress on Medieval Studies at Kalamazoo, Michigan, May 2002.

18. Alan Cobban, *English University Life in the Middle Ages* (Columbus: Ohio State University Press, 1999).

19. Cobban, *English University Life*, 64.

20. Jeffrey Burton Russel, *Dissent and Order in the Middle Ages: The Search for Legitimate Authority* (New York: Twayne, 1992).

The Tropes of Medievalism

M. J. Toswell

Lexicographers identify two principal modes of establishing the meaning of headwords, both of which are generally used in each dictionary entry: denotation and connotation. The former attempts a precise indication of meaning, beginning with a genus word and then providing differentiae that distinguish the term from others in the same class, often using a matrix to establish elements of contrast that make the definition steadily more precise. Connotation, on the other hand, provides synonyms and paraphrases, but works by providing examples of usage, arranged diachronically or analytically according to the logical developments of the word and its occurrences. A good definition will provide both denotative and connotative information, and in a historical or academic dictionary the definition will also note which usages of the headword are standard or accepted and which are unusual, perhaps extensions from the standard usages or idiomatic, even idiolectal, collocations.[1] The term "medievalism" offers particular difficulties and confusions, given that its etymologically inspired meaning might be "study about the Middle Ages," both in English and in some other European languages. Although scholars who study the Middle Ages and who style themselves medievalists occasionally consider themselves to be engaging in medievalism – particularly when they stray into the historiography of their field – nonetheless that interpretation is universally rejected by the scholars who engage in the study of medievalism, and that rejection has achieved some measure of general acceptance in humanistic scholarship.[2] There remain those who study the Middle Ages who do at times further confuse the issue by the use of such collocations as "new medievalism(s)," which appears to mean new approaches to the study of the medieval period (and particularly approaches using new theoretical paradigms). These are nevertheless red herrings, although they do provide evidence that the field of medievalism, while no longer in its infancy, may not yet have moved out of its childhood, since it cannot quite yet claim its terrain without argument. However, just what the parameters of that terrain are remain uncertain.

Michael Alexander in a recent book avoids a clear definition of "medievalism," describing it as "a word which gestures towards an unwieldy province of cultural history which comprises both the Middle Ages and what has been made of them."[3] The imprecise image of gesturing, of pointing in a relatively general direction, of bundling together both the Middle Ages and the idea of their recreation or remaking in more recent centuries: these are the usual parameters of the definition of medievalism. As attempts at denotation, such approaches hardly even establish a genus, because medievalism is both a scholarly field of study and a nostalgic impulse to rework or recreate or gesture towards the Middle Ages, sometimes in a careful and precise way but mostly making use of some standard images and motifs that evoke the medieval. Often, medievalism is described as the consideration of the Middle Ages as an aesthetic object, a representation of what might have been. (Incidentally, the Middle Ages under discussion by way of the term "medievalism" denote only the Western, more specifically the European and North American, approach to the years 500–1500.) Already distant in time, the Middle Ages through this approach are made yet more distant in space and in mode, turned into a kind of dramatic scene that can be produced and re-enacted and directed by a range of scholars and enthusiasts. Clearly, then, the approach by way of denotation is not entirely successful, and is doomed to arguments over the genus as much as the differentiae. Connotation, as with many other abstract nouns of this ilk, may be the solution. I want to investigate very briefly here two examples of how the Middle Ages seem to be made into aesthetic objects through the use of standard images and motifs, or tropes. Investigating the tropes that inhere in the representation or recreation of the Middle Ages may prove to be a useful approach to thinking about the definition of "medievalism" by way of its connotations, rather than trying to establish steadily more precise descriptive terms.

The tropes of medievalism, of which there are a congeries (knights; heroes; swords; vast landscapes with castles and forests and mountains; handmade artifacts; treasure-hunting; quests; witches and warlocks; various representations of the Other, including giants, elves, dwarves, and so on; flowery speechifying to make declarations about honor and justice; medieval weaponry and armor; magic), offer ways in which someone engaged in recreating the Middle Ages can do so with a kind of useful shorthand, or can engage in extensive and deliberate research so as to reach for authenticity. One such trope is the dragon, a mythical being of awesome power and aggression that Cirlot's *Dictionary of Symbols* describes as "a fabulous animal and a universal, symbolic figure found in the majority of the cultures in the world."[4] Recreations of the Middle Ages tend to involve dragons, from Spenser to Tolkien, from J. K. Rowling to *Dungeons and Dragons* to the *World of Warcraft* to dragon gargoyles and dragon-headed canes. Joyce Lionarons offers one point of view on the trope of the dragon today, proposing that the modern fascination with the dragon has a specific purpose – "the dragon may once again serve as a potent reminder of the ultimate danger involved in unending, reciprocal human violence, the threat of human annihilation."[5] She thereby connects the role of the dragon today with its traditional role as the monster in medieval literature. This is an important and profoundly political, even somewhat apocalyptic, conclusion about the role of dragons in the twenty-first century. David E. Jones concludes his book *An Instinct for Dragons* with the opposite argument: the dragon has decayed and slept, and has now largely been destroyed, killed by the culture wearing armor and carrying a sword:

> The curious feature of the dragon's demise is that even in fantasy it unifies the human community. Once the unification resulted from the fear of the beast, and now we enjoy our final conquest over it by using its name and image in sports teams, in children's folktales, movie monster manifestations, and the shoddy plaster statues of cute, absolutely non-threatening and whimsical creatures found in all tourist haunts.[6]

Both Lionarons and Jones elucidate elements of the modern trope of the dragon – but neither one in these conclusions accurately depicts the modern avatar of the medieval dragon. The dragon has certainly been tamed, commodified, digested, and made a part of everyday life – as Jones appears to conclude. Its very ubiquity has denuded it of the significance it had in surviving medieval texts. However, the dragon is now also imbued with other significance, including – some might argue – a return to the medieval belief in its existence. That existence, however, is no longer fraught with apocalyptic significance evoking the Book of Revelation or the destruction of a nation and its people – which Lionarons wants to suggest. Rather, the trope of the once-mighty and all-powerful fear-inducing monster that was the dragon is both domestic and divine, tame yet alluring, friendly yet dangerous – and somehow real.

Three examples of modern representations of the dragon may clarify this point. *Dragons: A Fantasy Made Real* is a documentary made in 2004 by Discovery for the Disney Channel and produced by Kevin Mohs with Neil Gaiman as creative consultant. Narrated by Patrick Stewart, this apparently scientific documentary makes great use of computer-graphic interface (CGI) animation to tell the life story of a particular dragon in the Carpathian mountains. The film anthropomorphizes the dragon throughout, resembling in its life story of the young male a nature documentary with its breathless, in-the-moment recounting of each episode filmed as if it were live and happening. New Age books also subscribe to this breathless realism, perhaps better described in these works as an incipient belief. Ash "LeopardDancer" DeKirk, in *Dragonlore*, produces a gazetteer of dragon tales and sightings from around the world, including in board games and film, with a segue into three creative pieces about dragons.[7] The foreword, by Oberon Zell of the Grey School of Wizardry, notes that dinosaurs existed and were like dragons. Thus, since alligators, crocodiles, various kinds of large snakes and lizards including the Komodo dragon and the iguana exist, perhaps dragons do too. The book pursues this elision of the real and existing fauna of the world with the fantastic and nonexistent dragon, throughout opening the possibility that dragons exist. According to D. J. Conway, in *Dancing with Dragons*, dragons are even more: a part of everyday life and living on the astral plane, from which the dragons contact our physical plane if they so choose.[8] Conway makes the witchcraft implied in DeKirk's book real by providing detailed instructions as to how to contact dragons on the astral plane, engage in various rituals with them, and accomplish particular goals with their aid. We have here the Middle Ages spiritually remade (not just aesthetically), taking dragons as familiar spirits and allotting to them the roles that angels or patron saints once played for Christian believers. A strange medievalism indeed.

Dragons today, then, are a set of beings that can be given a scientific veneer, a taxonomy, and a biology that are outlandish but appear plausible, a family tree going back to the Egyptian *Book of the Dead*, the Book of Job in the Old Testament and Judaic tradition, and even the notion of dinosaurs. At the same time they share a familiarity and an immediacy in the modern day that allow them to become an Other that can be supernatural, although not quite divine. Dragons no longer appear to figure the Other as a monster that must be destroyed in order to achieve redemption. They do, still, reflect a yearning for some entity large and powerful and separate from us, one that will take over, take power, and take charge.

In other words, two somewhat paradoxical conceptions of dragons exist in the present day. First, dragons in their many and varied incarnations in modern texts have become an empty signifier, devoid of all semiosis. The trope of the dragon exists everywhere and nowhere, and it includes cats, serpents, eagles, spirits, servants, and companions. Second, dragons exist but have been humanized, denatured, made accessible and domestic without having been wholly declawed. Humans can catch a ride on dragons in a plethora of fantasy tales, or communicate with them, and recognize their needs as fitting on Maslow's hierarchy. Dragons are a trope of medievalism now so everyday as to have lost all but the outward trappings of the medieval representation and significance of the *draco*.

At what might appear to be the opposite end of the spectrum, indeed of several spectra, is what could be called the trope of realism. A strong sense of authenticity, of the attempt to recreate the "real" Middle Ages, inheres in many medievalisms. There are various reasons for this urge towards the authentic, and the urge itself might be the reason why some scholars argue that medievalism is always and inherently a scholarly impulse – not just in the sense of studying those who produce medievalism, but in the sense that those who nowadays produce medievalist texts endeavor mightily to construct themselves as true scholars. One sub-category of this trope of realism is the trope of living white males recreating medieval times. Usually, they explicitly do so in order to tell interesting stories and to revisit historical moments, but it seems that almost invariably they do so in order to permit themselves greater latitude in agency and representation than is permitted in contemporary culture. For example, Melvyn Bragg in *Credo* writes the story of St. Bega, who – if she existed – survives today in the place-name St. Bee's in Cumbria. Because Bragg establishes his story in seventh-century north England, he can write a sweeping novel about dynasties, about a nation, about a panoramic view of Britain and its doings, with his focus a king's daughter, a strong and individualistic protagonist. Bega spends much of her time running a kind of underground railway for followers of Celtic Christianity, and refuses again and again – because of her vocation to God – to marry the prince of Rheged, Padric, who is the hero of the tale. In this latter respect Bega is modelled on St. Ethelthryth – but Bragg cannot wholly ignore the fact that Ethelthryth's refusal to consummate either of her two marriages was so extraordinarily unlikely as to be worth Bede's notice. There remains, then, a continuing tension between Bragg's modern conception of a woman as someone who chooses her own destiny and the medieval construction of the female who does so as exceptional. Bega is thus a modern female figure transplanted into an early medieval context, but surrounded by carefully crafted details and historically accurate material.[9]

Almost unbounded numbers of similar cases exist. In the ancillary material to the DVD of *Beowulf and Grendel*, Gerard Butler speaks at great length about the care with which his opening scene was shot, with him dragging himself in through a mud flat from a three-day swim in the ocean – his anguish and misery, he suggests, were absolutely genuine and required no acting. Realism is a focus and a goal, and the extra actor in all the scenes is the landscape, shot richly with panoramic slow scans. The film, however, reconstructs the story of *Beowulf*, humanizing the monster Grendel and providing him with both a father and a solid reason for revenge against the Danes. The screenplay essentially rewrites the poem into a script about the relationships among men, particularly fathers and sons, and the meanings of masculinity.[10] Peter Tremayne, who is in another life the Celtic scholar Peter Berresford Ellis, similarly writes a series of early medieval murder mysteries whose detective is an Irish nun, Sister Fidelma. A brehon, trained in traditional Irish law, Sister Fidelma journeys all over Ireland, England, and much further afield as a kind of Celtic travelling detective who brings resolution and absolution to the murders she decodes, and knowledge of the early medieval world to the reader. A shockingly modern figure (save for her lack of vices), she is also a thoroughly medieval one in all the details of her life, her pilgrimages, and her encounters.[11]

This note began with a brief discussion of the difficulties of defining the term "medievalism." "Trope" is another word that both resists and requires definition. In this case, there is a particular appropriateness to the origin of "trope" as a specific musical and liturgical element in chants of the European Middle Ages, melismas and variations on the pre-existing originals of the Western Christian church. The current usages of the term are proliferating, perhaps productively, in philosophy with respect to figurative and metaphorical language and also as a theory in metaphysics, and in literary criticism as both a specific rhetorical figure of speech and more generally as a pattern, theme, or motif so common as to become a trope. Medievalism has its tropes, because it has its general themes and patterns, and its variations and embellishments on those patterns. Nonetheless, what this brief survey of two tropes of medievalism may demonstrate most clearly is the double or triple lens of the study of medievalism: always a medievalist trope is perceived first through the sceptical modern eye of the twenty-first-century scholar, second (though not invariably) through the romanticizing eye of nineteenth-century medievalist scholarship and study that is the foundation of the medievalizing impulse in the contemporary world; and third through the variable (reaching toward 'authentic') eye of the creator(s) of the text. The balance among the lenses will vary according to the text and trope under consideration. In fact, this triple-faceted lens and the complications it brings to the study of medievalism may well be why texts using medievalism are almost invariably described in terms of the process, and why medievalism itself is so often defined with gerunds and participles, as something in the process of coming into being, and not – as would ordinarily be the case in the study of a text – as a product. Texts using medievalism are never quite finished, never quite authentic, never quite tangible, never quite over.

NOTES

1. For example, see R. R. K. Hartmann, ed., *Lexicography: Principles and Practice* (London: Academic Press, 1983).

2. Definitions of medievalism are many. Some of the more useful are:

Leslie J. Workman, Paul E. Szarmach, William D. Paden, and Richard J. Utz, "Medievalism, New Medievalism, Medieval Studies: Contested Territory or Common Ground? A Special Session at the 1995 Convention of the Modern Language Association," *Medievalism: The Year's Work for 1995* 10 (1999 for 1995): 223–43; the review of that volume by Stephanie Trigg, *Prolepsis* 9 (September 2001), at <http://www.as.uni-hd.de/prolepsis/01_06_tri.html>; Clare A. Simmons, "Introduction," in Clare A. Simmons, ed., *Medievalism and the Quest for the "Real" Middle Ages* (London: Frank Cass, 2001), 1–28; John Ganim, "Once and Future Medievalism: A Belated Afterword," *antiTHESIS* at <http://www.english.unimelb.edu.au/antithesis/forum-3>; and specifically on medievalism and Anglo-Saxon England, T. A. Shippey, "The undeveloped image: Anglo-Saxon in popular consciousness from Turner to Tolkien," in Donald Scragg and Carole Weinberg, ed., *Literary Appropriations of the Anglo-Saxons from the Thirteenth to the Twentieth Century* (Cambridge: Cambridge University Press, 2000), 215–36.

3. Michael Alexander, *Medievalism: The Middle Ages in Modern England* (New Haven, CT: Yale University Press, 2007), xiv. Alexander brings a traditional approach to thinking about medievalism, focusing chronologically on literature – especially poetry and fiction – in Britain from the nineteenth century to the present day. Veronica Ortenberg surveys a wider field, working partly diachronically and partly by themes in *In Search of the Holy Grail* (London: Hambledon Continuum, 2006).

4. J. E. Cirlot, *A Dictionary of Symbols*, trans. J. Sage, 2nd ed. (New York: Philosophical Library, 1974), 85, s.v. dragon.

5. Joyce Tally Lionarons, *The Medieval Dragon: The Nature of the Beast in Germanic Literature* (Middlesex, Eng.: Hisarlik Press, 1998), 111.

6. The literature on dragons is extensive from the middle of the nineteenth century onwards. Jones engages in a quite measured approach: David E. Jones, *An Instinct for Dragons* (New York: Routledge, 2002), 117. The pseudoscientific approach begins with G. Elliot Smith, *The Evolution of the Dragon* (Manchester: Longmans, 1919), and continues with such works as Ralph Whitlock, *Here Be Dragons* (London: George Allen & Unwin, 1983), which includes a gazetteer of dragons in England, including fonts, carvings, and sightings in literature and history (including, of course, the Loch Ness monster); and Carl Sagan, *The Dragons of Eden: Speculations on the Evolution of Human Intelligence* (New York: Random House, 1977). Serious scholarly analyses of medieval texts with dragons, such as Lionarons' *The Medieval Dragon* and Christine Rauer's *Beowulf and the Dragon: Parallels and Analogues* (Cambridge, Eng.: D. S. Brewer, 2000), tend also to refer to the role of dragons in the popular imagination, which is the focus of Anne C. Petty, *Dragons of Fantasy: The Scaly Villains & Heroes of Tolkien, Rowling,*

McCaffrey, Pratchett & Other Fantasy Greats! (Cold Spring Harbor, NY: Cold Spring Press, 2004). More intriguing from the populist point of view are Ash "LeopardDancer" DeKirk, *Dragonlore* (Franklin, NJ: Career Press, 2006); D. J. Conway, *Dancing with Dragons* (Woodbury, MN: Llewellyn Publications, 1994); and perhaps Dugald A. Steer, ed., *Dragonology: The Complete Book of Dragons* (Cambridge, MA: Candlewick Press, 2003), a spoof that suggests the biggest concern of a dragonologist is conservation of a scarce resource. These books recall F. W. Holiday, *The Dragon and the Disc: An Investigation into the Totally Fantastic* (London: Sidgwick & Jackson, 1973), which argues for dragon-worship as the earliest human religion, as well as for worship of the sun and the serpent; and Paul Newman, *The Hill of the Dragon: An Enquiry into the Nature of Dragon Legends* (Bath: Kingsmead Press, 1979), which canvasses dragon legends historically and more specifically studies British dragon legends and theories.

    7. See note 6, above.

    8. See note 6, above.

    9. Melvyn Bragg, *Credo: An Epic Tale of the Dark Ages* (London: Sceptre, 1996).

    10. *Beowulf and Grendel*, screenplay by Andrew Rai Berzins, dir. Sturla Gunnarsson, perf. Gerard Butler, Stellan Skarsgärd, Ingvar Eggert Sigurdsson, Sarah Polley (Burbank, CA: Warner Brothers, 2006).

    11. The first in the series, which has nearly twenty volumes at the moment, is *Absolution by Murder* (New York: St Martin's, 1994).

Medievalism and the Middle Ages

Elizabeth Emery

The term "medievalism" is sufficiently broad to describe the practices of a great number of different trends related to the Middle Ages in scholarship and popular culture, but also maddeningly vague for those who seek in it a clear definition. As both Tom Shippey and Nils Holger Petersen have pointed out in their contributions to this volume, it may be more accurate to speak of "medievalisms" because of the multiple forms through which interest in the Middle Ages tends to manifest itself. This is particularly true with regard to the divide separating historically based "high culture" studies of the medieval period and productions of "popular culture" inspired by it; the latter tend to focus less on the historical period known as the Middle Ages than on received ideas about it. J. R. R. Tolkien's publications as a specialist of medieval literature, for example, are quite different from his use of these sources as inspiration for his fictional *Lord of the Rings* series. Tolkien's knowledge of and engagement with Anglo-Saxon language, literature, and culture is not always replicated by his admirers, many of whom accept his work as "medieval," much as the "medieval" worlds represented in Second Life "islands" are more likely to have drawn their inspiration from Peter Jackson's cinematic adaptation of Tolkien's fiction than from either Tolkien's work or extant sources from the eighth century.

The editorial board of *Studies in Medievalism* should be commended for recognizing that the beginning of the twenty-first century – a period in which interpretations of the medieval world flourish through new visual and interactive media like video games and Second Life – represents a watershed moment for re-evaluating the definition of medievalism and for assessing the journal's mandate

with regard to it. I will contribute to the debate in the following pages
by underlining some of the problems inherent in the terms "medieval"
and "medievalism" before offering a few practical measures that may
allow us to speak more concisely about medievalism while respecting
the broad yet inclusive scope of the term as defined by Leslie
Workman.

Despite the frustration that inevitably arises when trying to find
common ground among the very different forms medievalism can take,
the problem is not with the term as Workman presented it: "the *study*
of the Middle Ages on the one hand, and the *use* of the Middle Ages in
everything from fantasy to social reform on the other, are the two sides
of the same coin."[1] Indeed, for him, medievalism was less a tidy field
consisting of a canonical group of names and works than a *method*, a
mode of engagement with the medieval. That medievalism is a method
can be inferred from both the *Oxford English Dictionary*'s and Workman's definitions: it consists of the relationship to the Middle Ages, the
ways in which people "devote" themselves to the period's ideals or the
ways in which they "study," "use," or "construct" them.[2] Medievalism
is thus an active and evolving process of engagement with things
medieval. As such, it can encompass different scholarly interpretations
of the Middle Ages over periods of time (Jules Michelet's, Joseph
Bédier's, and Ernst Curtius' different characterizations), different
artistic representations in varying media (Walter Scott, the Pre-
Raphaelites, Richard Wagner, and Ridley Scott), different political or
religious claims (Joan of Arc claimed by the Catholic Church, the
secular French Republic, the Action Française, and Le Front National),
"medieval" analysis of the Middle Ages (François Villon's fifteenth-
century ballad "en viel langage françois," written in Old French), and
even scholarly studies of the way individuals have been influenced by
other uses of the Middle Ages (analysis of Hugo's debt to Sir Walter
Scott in imagining the medieval world). Despite temporal and geographical differences, all these examples (chosen at random, but
favoring the French since this is my field) involve differing kinds of
engagement with the Middle Ages. It is surely to recognize this active
process that Workman entitled the journal he founded *Studies in Medievalism* and not *Studies of Medievalism*. The common denominator
among the multiple, interdisciplinary forms medievalism takes is
method: how and why various individuals and institutions have chosen
to engage with the Middle Ages.

The brilliance of Workman's definition lies less in identifying medievalism as a method (the *OED* also does this), than in acknowledging the extent to which the "Middle Ages" is itself an artificial construct, changing in accordance with the individual or the society imagining it. By recognizing that the concept of what we call "the Middle Ages" has been in flux since the phrase was coined in the fifteenth century, Workman cleverly recognized and circumvented the ambiguity at the heart of the *OED*'s definition, which makes the meaning of medievalism dependent on "medieval" and "Middle Ages," terms fraught with ambiguity. Scholars recognize that the term "Middle Ages" (from *medieum ævum*) was popularized by fifteenth-century Italian humanists in order to contrast their "Renaissance" with a "Dark Ages," thereby establishing a solid link between this "Renaissance" and the classical period it sought to emulate. The public, however, does not generally know the history of the term and knows little about the centuries ostensibly intended by the phrase "Middle Ages." Undergraduates, for example, when asked about the Middle Ages, rarely speak of the thousand years from the fall of the Roman Empire (476) to the fall of Constantinople (1453). Instead, they tend to identify stereotypes drawn from fairy tales: knights, princesses, magic.[3] Ultimately, the problem in defining medievalism lies with how we define "medieval."

The title of Régine Pernoud's 1977 classic *Pour en finir avec le moyen âge* makes this point clear: if scholars want the public to base its understanding of the period from 476 to 1453 on authentic sources instead of stereotypes, they should stop using the term "Middle Ages" ("en finir avec le moyen âge"). The book opens with an anecdote still pertinent today with regard to misunderstandings about the Middle Ages. While working for the French National Archives, she received a letter requesting the exact date of "the treaty ending the Middle Ages" and information about the city in which delegates met to draft it. The correspondent requested a quick response as he was to present a lecture on the topic in a few weeks' time.[4] Her point – and this has changed little since 1977 – is that the public knows nearly nothing about the Middle Ages. Indeed, as she notes, the roughly 1000 years of history tend to be reduced – largely by teachers and the mass media – to a handful of violent stereotypes. A woman putting together a television documentary, for example, asked Pernoud whether she might be able to send her some images "representing the Middle Ages."

When Pernoud was not sure what she meant, the woman continued: "Those giving a general idea of the Middle Ages: carnage, massacres, scenes of violence, famine, epidemics [...]."[5]

Indeed, for most Western European audiences the term "Middle Ages" refers less to specific historical reality than to a received set of historical and literary figures, events, places, practices, and monuments. When teaching courses about twelfth- to fifteenth-century French literature, I often begin the semester by asking students to identify five or six things that come to mind when they hear someone say "the Middle Ages." These invariably involve King Arthur, William the Conquerer, Charlemagne, Richard the Lionhearted, Robin Hood, Ivanhoe, Saladin, Quasimodo, Joan of Arc, the Crusades, The Hundred Years War, the Black Death, witchcraft, jousting, Gothic cathedrals, and castles, to name just a few. And this phenomenon is hardly new: nineteenth-century representations of the "medieval" similarly tended toward the picturesque, eliding temporal and social differences and blurring the line between fiction and reality: a Feast of Fools celebration held by students at the Sorbonne in 1898, for example, featured Charlemagne, Louis IX, and Louis XI rubbing shoulders with Quasimodo, beggars, and poet François Villon.[6] Today's Renaissance Fairs do the same, bringing together a kind of "greatest hits" of costumes and practices based on imagination or existing cultural artifacts on display in museums and in books, and, above all, from what has been portrayed in earlier representations of the Middle Ages. The Middle Ages as a popular concept is thus largely distinct from the historical reality of the centuries identified by the word "medieval".

As Pernoud notes, scholars are every bit as complicit in perpetuating myths about the "Middle Ages" as are the media because we accept the term in the name of our departments, our courses, and our scholarly dialogue. Richard Glejzer, in a piece for this journal, points out the dangers inherent in considering the Middle Ages as a single period, as "an object of knowledge" that can somehow be reconstituted through careful study and contextualization. No matter how hard scholars may try to reconstruct "medieval life" through the documents and artifacts remaining today, it is too vast a period and too vast a project to succeed. We continue to pursue the impossible nineteenth-century dream of "resurrecting" the Middle Ages.[7] To combat this kind of generalization and to better inform the public,

Pernoud asks scholars to rename the Middle Ages, to create other (though no less arbitrary) names (the "imperial age," the "feudal age") better reflective of historical trends from the fifth to the fifteenth centuries.[8]

Given the confusion that surrounds the term "medieval", how can we hope to define the term "medievalism," which depends so heavily upon it? It is entirely possible, for example, to be devoted to what one considers "medieval ideals and usages" (*Oxford English Dictionary* definition) without understanding that these are not actual ideals and usages from the historical period known as the Middle Ages. As a result, what one chooses to say about these 1000 years often reveals much more about the person evoking the "medieval" than about the historical period itself: "[medievalism] might well be defined as the Middle Ages in the contemplation of contemporary society," as Leslie Workman put it.[9] In the wake of Hayden White's work on the importance of subjectivity for history, we recognize that the conclusions drawn by figures such as Jules Michelet, Johan Huizinga, and Marc Bloch, who were all known as serious medieval scholars in their time, reveal as much about their own beliefs as they do about history. Workman's definition, which presents medievalism as the continued process of imagining the historical period called "the Middle Ages," recognizes the problem of the "medieval" in a way the *OED* does not. Above all, Workman's definition captures the impossibility of knowing a "real" Middle Ages. In this sense the vagueness of his definition is also its greatest strength: it recognizes the Middle Ages as an artificial construct while admitting that nearly all discussion of the period contributes another layer to the palimpsest we now call the Middle Ages. Moreover, because his definition of medievalism implies that each individual's or entity's vision of the medieval will be different, it obviates the need to speak of "medievalisms." Workmanian medievalism is itself a plural concept.

While the inclusiveness of Workman's definition is admirable, it often makes it difficult – as Tom Shippey has noted – to characterize the field as a whole, to find overarching patterns within the diverse works that claim to discuss "medievalism." I would argue that instead of looking for outward signs of similarity among the different forms that medievalism can take, it would be more effective to look at the *methods* used by individuals and institutions to construct the Middle Ages. The forms themselves are important, but even more so are the motives behind them. Why does a twenty-first-century game designer choose to represent a French Gothic cathedral like Notre-Dame de Paris in a game such as *Onimusha 3: Demon Siege*? Is it a realistic depiction of the cathedral? How does the cathedral relate to other elements of the game? Questions like these draw out the rationale behind the engagement with the medieval and provide a link among the many different forms medievalism can take.

Nevertheless, as new modes of engagement with the Middle Ages arise all over the world and in different media, we still need a way to speak of these forms of medievalism with greater precision. Umberto Eco's 1986 "Dreaming of the Middle Ages" (in *Travels in Hyperreality*) made a step in the right direction by insisting that any discussion of medievalism (what he calls "dreams" of the Middle Ages) should first spell out which Middle Ages is being evoked. But the ten types he proposes – among them "the Middle Ages as the site of an ironical revisitation," "the Middle Ages as a barbaric age," "the Middle Ages of national identities," "the Middle Ages of Decadentism," "the Middle Ages of Romanticism," "the Middle Ages of philological reconstruction" – tend to focus either on how the Middle Ages are envisaged or on the aesthetic movement responsible for interpreting the medieval period.[10] As such, his types do not account well for the great variation within these "dreams." While there may be a "Middle Ages of Romanticism," for example, Romantic-era writers and artists chose to evoke the Middle Ages for markedly different reasons (Chateaubriand to laud Catholicism or Hugo for local color and to preserve medieval architecture) and represented it in markedly different ways (Walter Scott's historical novels, for example, little resemble Matthew Lewis's "Gothic" novels). While Eco is absolutely correct about our need to specify which version of the Middle Ages is being discussed, his categories rely too heavily on the outward forms "dreams" of the Middle Ages take. As we have seen, medievalism is above all a method, a way of engaging with what we call the Middle Ages. As such, it might be more effectively classified by modes of interaction with the medieval period.

In this sense, one might speak of "scientific" or "scholarly" medievalism to refer to the ways in which specialists (of literature, art history, music, philosophy, archeology, theology) attempt to engage seriously with the cultural productions of the period known as the Middle Ages or of "dogmatic medievalism" to evoke the ways in which

religious, political, or nationalist groups have claimed various historical figures (Clovis, Joan of Arc, Robert the Bruce) for their own needs.
The term "creative medievalism" might allow one to encompass a
variety of cultural productions (in poetry, painting, literature, music,
film, comic books) that may or may not engage directly with historical
reality, but have been inspired by it to create new aesthetic products.
A subset of this kind of "creative" medievalism might be called "spec-
tacular medievalism": movies, plays, operas, and other multi-media
productions intended to entertain an audience. And within "spectac-
ular medievalism" would be located what Shippey terms "movie medievalism" and "music medievalism." A further subset of "creative
medievalism" might be entitled "living medievalism," to evoke activities like parades, fairs, or other events (like those sponsored by
AVISTA or the Society for Creative Anachronism), geared toward
involving the spectator in hands-on experience of activities from
various time periods. These kinds of activities attempt to bring aspects
of the Middle Ages back to life by implicating their participants in
ritualistic activities that help them understand the past. The flexibility
of the term "medievalism" also lends itself to popular authors, schools,
or geographical regions ("Tolkien medievalism," "American medievalism").

Creating such sub-categories corresponds to practices we employ
for another vague term used to define an amorphous genre: the novel.
Despite the infuriatingly imprecise definition of the word "novel"
(*OED*: "a fictitious prose narrative or tale of considerable length [...]
representing character and action with some degree of realism"), the
term functions successfully as an indicator of genre while allowing one
to adapt it to new descriptive subcategories as they emerge: the episto-
lary novel, the historical novel, the detective novel, the graphic novel,
the romance novel, the magical realism novel. "Medievalism" can do
the same.

Indeed, such sub-categories are effective in distinguishing those
who attempt to engage with the historical period known as the Middle
Ages from those who create a vision filtered through previous examples
of medievalism (Walt Disney operating through Grimm's and
Perrault's fairy tales, for example). In this case, it might be helpful to
apply Eco's term "neomedievalism" (coined in "Dreaming of the
Middle Ages"). The term "neomedievalism" is, in fact, redundant with
regard to Workman's sense of medievalism, which posits medievalism

as a constant evolution of the process of imagining the Middle Ages, yet "neomedievalism" has already gained cultural currency as a way of describing visions of the Middle Ages driven more by fantasy than by historical reality.

The examples I have given here are certainly not prescriptive; they are intended merely as a way to begin classifying different representations of the "Middle Ages" by mode of engagement with the period. In many cases, instances of medievalism seem to defy classification by overlapping with one another (Viollet-le-Duc's reconstructions of French cathedrals are at once "scientific," "creative," and "dogmatic," for example). I have thus proposed these possibilities as a very preliminary example of how, if we need to classify (and I am not sure we do need to replicate the structure of a positivist-inspired dictionary of medievalism), representations of the Middle Ages might usefully be organized by how and why the creator chose to interact with the period.

The multi-layered nature of medievalism, in which various representations of the "Middle Ages" constantly build upon prior representations of this constructed period, does not lend itself well to definition. It does, however, lend itself extraordinarily well to the kind of cross-referencing now common on the Internet. While it would, indeed, be a Herculean task for a single person to classify all medievalism past and present, there are a number of organizations that are currently using the Internet to good profit in doing so, at least for specific disciplines. The "Camelot Project" at the University of Rochester, for example, contains images, texts, bibliographies, and scholarly sources cross-linked by Arthurian character, place, and symbol,[11] while the association Modernités médiévales, run by a group of energetic French scholars, has been actively compiling (and invites contributions to) cross-referenced lists about all aspects of medievalism (<http://www.modernitesmedievales.org/>). Given the increasingly large number of online archival sources from the period we call "medieval," as well as the growing number of technologies (like Wikis) that make it simple for groups to share and post information, it is only a matter of time before such ventures succeed in capturing the richness and complexity inherent in medievalism as a mode of engagement with the "medieval" period. Compiled through the efforts of specialists in many disciplines, an active repository of links provides the most coherent picture of medievalism as a constantly evolving method, a form of engagement in constructing and reconstructing both the historical period known as the Middle Ages and the received ideas that have also come to be known as the Middle Ages.

Medievalism understood (in Leslie Workman's terms) as an active process makes the examples I used in my introduction much less shocking. In their attempt to capture aspects of the artificially constructed period known as the "Middle Ages," both "high" and "low" cultures perpetuate images that correspond to the dreams, beliefs, or needs of the individual producing them. Ultimately, then, medievalism is a constantly evolving and self-referential process of defining an always fictional Middle Ages.

NOTES

1. Leslie Workman, "The Future of Medievalism," in James Gallant, ed., *Medievalism: The Year's Work for 1995* (Holland, MI: Studies in Medievalism, 1999): 7–18 (12).

2. "The system of belief and practice characteristic of the Middle Ages […] the adoption of or devotion to mediaeval ideals or usages; *occas.* An instance of this."

3. My sense is that this is beginning to change, particularly with a generation used to sating its curiosity on the Internet where so many reproductions of images and texts from the fifth to the fifteenth centuries are now available.

4. Régine Pernoud, *Pour en finir avec le moyen âge* (Paris: Editions du Seuil, 1977), 5.

5. Pernoud, *Pour en finir*, 7.

6. See Elizabeth Emery and Laura Morowitz, *Consuming the Past: The Medieval Revival in Late Nineteenth-Century France* (Aldershot: Ashgate Press, 2003), 177–78.

7. Richard Glejzer, "The New Medievalism and the (Im)Possibility of the Middle Ages," *Studies in Medievalism* 10 (1998): 104–19.

8. Pernoud, *Pour en finir*, 136.

9. "Preface," to Kathleen Verduin, ed., *Medievalism in England II*, *Studies in Medievalism* 7 (Cambridge: D. S. Brewer, 1996): 1–2 (2).

10. Umberto Eco, "Dreaming of the Middle Ages," in *Travels in Hyperreality*, trans. William Weaver (San Diego, CA: Harcourt, 1983), 61–72 (68–71).

11. <http://www.lib.rochster.edu/camelot/cphome.stm?CFID=154794 08&CFTOKEN=44138786&jsessionid=5a3040b9d7bb37781322>.

Medievalism from Here

Karl Fugelso

On another occasion I have argued that many supposed departures from medievalism, particularly those often classified as "neo-medievalism" or "pseudomedievalism," do not, in fact, escape conventional definitions of our field.[1] Though they may be conveyed by comparatively new media, such as computers, or may incorporate overt fantasy, such as dragons and trolls, they almost always descend at least in part from the historical Middle Ages. That is to say, they almost always fall within what Leslie Workman has described as "the post-medieval idea and study of the Middle Ages and the influence, both scholarly and popular, of this study on Western society after 1500."

Yet hardly a month goes by that *Studies in Medievalism*, which was founded by Leslie and which features his definition on its title page, does not have its boundaries tested.[2] The most common parameter with which potential contributors play is the year 1500. Some authors observe the letter but not the spirit of that threshold, as they discuss post-fifteenth-century works from regions for which 1500 clearly does not mark the end of the Middle Ages, such as parts of Poland and of the Balkans.[3] Other authors observe the spirit but not the letter of Leslie's definition, as they concentrate on echoes of the Middle Ages in works that are widely perceived as post-medieval yet pre-date the sixteenth century, such as late-fourteenth- and fifteenth-century Italian poetry. And still other authors dance back and forth across the borders of Leslie's definition, as they address works that come from approximately 1500 or are part of an oeuvre that partly pre-dates that year, such as Albrecht Dürer's engravings. Indeed, in discussing both pre- and post-1500 works, many potential contributors call into question not only the flexibility of Leslie's definition but also the degree to which we can permit a paper to expressly depart from it, to openly concentrate on non-medievalism in a journal devoted to medievalism.

Of course, similar issues arise in relationship to the geographical borders of Leslie's definition, and often within the same papers that challenge its chronological parameters. For example, many authors who address manifestations of a prolonged Middle Ages concentrate on modern countries that border the West but are not always defined as Western, such as Turkey and Russia. Other authors discuss medieval influences on modern countries that are geographically far from the West but exhibit so much Western influence that they have sometimes been seen as part of the West, such as Japan and Argentina. And some authors address modern responses to a so-called medieval period in contexts that were not only geographically but also culturally distant from the West, such as pre-modern China.

Yet perhaps the most challenging submissions to identify as studies in medievalism are those that do not make a clear case for the influence of any middle ages on post-medieval culture.[4] As post-modernism has taught us, causality, at least to the degree that it revolves around intentionality, is impossible to prove with absolute certainty. Even if we have a plethora of parallels between a medieval and post-medieval work, and even if we have a statement in which the creator of the post-medieval work declares his or her intent to copy the earlier work, coincidence can never be completely ruled out as a factor in those parallels. However, some submissions to *SiM* do not even try to present any other explanation for such similarities. Apparently in hopes that readers will supply their own motives and causal connections, the authors merely compile a long list of possible references to the Middle Ages and then conclude with a summary of them. In fact, some authors do not even bother with such a list, much less a summary of it, as they opt instead for merely alluding to the Middle Ages in passing, for, say, mentioning Roger Bacon while deconstructing Lacanian psychoanalysis.

Of course, such superficial approaches to medievalism often come with other problems, particularly a failure to account for the possibility of non-medieval influences on ostensible examples of medievalism. Indeed, even some papers that are thoroughly devoted to medievalism occasionally overlook the fact that their post-medieval subjects may have been influenced by earlier post-medieval or pre-medieval works. Continuous narrative, for example, may be found in not only medieval and modern art but also that of Antiquity. In much the same manner that an anonymous fifteenth-century illuminator of British Library MS Yates Thompson 36 and the nineteenth-century painter Joseph Anton Koch include several figures of Dante within a single illustration of the *Divine Comedy*, so the anonymous second-century sculptors of Trajan's column depict the emperor and his army multiple times in a single frieze. And though the sign of Aries in Koch's illustration of *Inferno* I can be found in many medieval miniatures, including one for a *Commedia* manuscript, it can, of course, also be found in many images that post-date the Middle Ages and pre-date Koch's work.[5] Thus, Koch may have derived his supposed medievalism in these cases from entirely non-medieval sources and/or from long-term practices that were not exclusive to the Middle Ages.

In other cases, acts of supposed medievalism may have sprung solely from one or more anthropological common denominators. While some of our potential contributors do not even try to rule out coincidence, others fail to fully account for the possibility that apparent references to the Middle Ages may be nothing more than similar responses by like-minded people to similar circumstances. Though iconographic parallels may admittedly be so extensive that they are extremely unlikely to be the product of mere chance, they can never completely escape that possibility, and, like similarities in function or purpose, they are often so broad as to easily allow that their creators independently arrived at similar solutions to similar problems. For example, in comparing a guarded woman of great beauty to a rose, nineteenth- century American poets need not have derived that metaphor from the thirteenth-century text of the *Roman de la rose* or the pre-nineteenth-century afterlife of that text, for the qualities of a rose obviously invite such analogies. And not every story told during road-trip movies, much less the journey motif itself, necessarily derives from *The Canterbury Tales*. Thus, even scholars who wish for their readers to supply particular motives and causal connections for ostensible parallels to the Middle Ages, may wish to define their examples as, in fact, echoes of the Middle Ages.

Of course, that may be particularly difficult for attempts to trace medieval influence through more than one layer of post-medieval culture. Though some relayed aspects of the Middle Ages may remain so intact or distinctive that they leave little doubt about their roots, many others are so generic from their very origin, or become so attenuated and/or fragmented as they are passed on, that they are extremely difficult to detect in their later incarnations, much less to track in every stage of their development. For instance, the green man in medieval celebrations of nature may be an ancestor of the Jolly Green Giant and of the other, disturbingly numerous green men who populate modern culture, but establishing the full extent of his legacy has so far eluded scholars, and, given the amazing breadth of that legacy, it is likely to continue doing so.

Moreover, with each relay come additional opportunities for medieval influences to be not only diluted but also displaced by pre- or post-medieval influences. For example, many post-medieval tales of descent into the underworld have been traced via an intermediary to the *Divine Comedy*, when in fact the primary source for that intermediary may have been Orphic literature or Dante's own primary source, the *Aeneid*. And each relay introduces additional opportunities for a medieval influence to be displaced by another medieval influence, which, while not necessarily altering the quotient of medievalism in a work, may, of course, greatly affect the character of its reference to the past. For instance, the *Divine Comedy* has sometimes been characterized as a descendant of a particular, slightly earlier, vision of the afterlife, such as *Tundale's Vision*, when in fact it may have descended from one or more of the many other medieval visionary texts that pre-date it. Indeed, scholars who wish to discuss medievalism that is not a direct response to the Middle Ages may wish to make sure that their instance of medievalism, is, in fact, as indirect as they purport. Sometimes potential contributors to *SIM* do not take any steps to defend against the possibility that one or more relays assigned to an instance of medievalism were in fact skipped, that the medievalism was, in fact, more direct than the writer suggests. For example, some of the efforts to trace post-medieval tales of descent into the underworld via one or more descendants of the *Commedia* ignore the fact that the *Commedia* itself may have been the direct source of the tales on which the scholars are concentrating.

Of course, even if a submitter defends against such a possibility and in at least one part of his or her paper lays out a careful case for the history of an indirect reference to the Middle Ages, the introduction of intermediaries greatly multiplies the opportunities for confusion in characterizing the medievalism in question. Many an aspiring contributor to *SiM* has failed to stick to the order or completeness with which they have defined the genealogy for an act of medievalism. For instance, after cleanly and concisely tracing the roots of Gothic Revival architecture at a leading American university, one scholar proceeded to tie that lineage up in knots, as he confused points at which social and political concerns may have entered this chain of influence and as he shaped his evidence to support his over-arching thesis about the motives for that influence.

Yet, as great as may be the confusion in those instances, it hardly compares to the chaos of some papers that expressly allow for the possibility of multiple medieval and/or medievalist influences on a work. Especially when all of those sources may in fact constitute a single thread of influence, potential *SiM* contributors often get lost in the logic, or at least language, of their explanation. For example, in tracing the roots of an author-portrait in a modern facsimile of *The Canterbury Tales*, one scholar was ultimately unable to relate precisely what roles were played by the many medieval and Renaissance proto-types he presented as possible sources. And no scenario seems to present more of a challenge to our aspiring contributors than attempts to argue that interpretations of interpretations of the Middle Ages were also influenced directly by the Middle Ages. For instance, in arguing that medieval scholastic exegesis lies at the root of nineteenth-century responses to Howard Pyle's *Men of Iron*, one scholar ran into difficulties distinguishing that influence from at least ostensibly co-incidental parallels between, on the one hand, medieval responses to medieval texts, and, on the other hand, modern responses to medievalizing aspects of Pyle's novel.

But as confused as those complex explanations may be, they usually avoid the other pitfalls I have discussed. They generally concentrate on examples of medievalism from cultures that clearly have a rapport with the Middle Ages yet are not just extensions of it. They offer alternatives to the possibility that the similarities they are considering sprang solely from chance, but they do not entirely rule out the latter. And they at least strive to define how those apparent influences may have survived the Middle Ages. That is to say, they serve as a model in many ways for the sort of work that *Studies in Medievalism* has traditionally featured.

Yet that is not to say that *SiM* should be limited to papers that fit within those parameters. Though we should perhaps insist on clarity of explanation (especially as Lacan and other postmodern scholars have already explored the benefits of deliberate opacity), properly framed departures from the other parameters discussed above could foreground important issues for medievalism and related fields. Indeed, though I must admit that I brought up examples of such departures primarily to deter potential contributors from repeating them, I find myself hoping that this essay will inspire a backlash, a flurry of creative and cogent attacks on the traditional borders of our field, for though medievalism may seem at first glance to be a narrow, rather rigid discipline, it is in fact nothing if not broad and flexible, and we here at *SiM* aim to nourish those qualities.

NOTES

1. The 22nd Annual International Conference on Medievalism, London, Ontario, 5 October 2007.
2. For much more on the founding of *Studies in Medievalism*, see Kathleen Verduin's contribution to this volume.
3. Though it has been argued that the Middle Ages have not ended, I think their presence is definitely stronger in some areas than in others.
4. I use "post-medieval" here to refer to whatever an interpreter might denote as coming after what he or she has defined as the "Middle Ages".
5. The *Commedia* miniature with the image of Aries decorates the opening page of the *Inferno* for Biblioteca Civica Gambalunga MS 4.I.II.25, fol. 4, in Rimini.

A Steam-Whistle Modernist?: Representations of King Alfred in Dickens's *A Child's History of England* and *The Battle of Life*

Emily Walker Heady

The Victorians' attraction to the Middle Ages is a well-documented phenomenon. Charles Dellheim, for instance, has noted the paradox that as the Victorians became more technologically advanced, their fascination with the "preindustrial past and in particular its medieval inheritance" increased.[1] In addition to numerous Gothic railway termini, Londoners at mid-century would have been able to watch the construction of All Saints Church on Margaret Street (1849), view the Pre-Raphaelite exhibit at the Royal Academy (1851), and tour Pugin's Medieval Court at the Great Exhibition (1851). Strangely, however, Charles Dickens, one of Victorian England's most paradigmatic authors, seems largely to have resisted this typical impulse to idealize, use, and abuse the Middle Ages. Yet if in his major novels Dickens seems not to have any particular relation to the Middle Ages, some of his minor works suggest more specific engagements with the past, and particularly with the question of how the Victorians should relate to and narrate it. Not only does he explicitly demonstrate a version of historiography in *A Child's History of England* (1851), but he imports his favorite figure from English history, King Alfred, in the fourth of his five Christmas books, *The Battle of Life* (1846). Beyond this, he criticizes the ways in which some of his contemporaries, the Pre-Raphaelites, handled history in their own work. A reader would be hard-pressed, however, to find a coherent philosophy of history in

Dickens's works, for his statements about the medieval past remain irreducibly, yet interestingly, irreconcilable. Still, if Dickens cannot be counted among the great Victorian theorizers of history, his contradictory formulations of the problem that the medieval posed for the Victorians are important, for they reveal the doubled, hazy, and often conflicting attitudes with which the Victorians approached their national past. Among the Victorians, Dickens was not known for his historical acumen. John Ruskin, who argued that Gothic architecture represented human artistry at its highest, charged that he was "a pure modernist – a leader of the steam whistle party par excellence."[2] And indeed, trains make many more striking appearances in Dickens's fiction than does medieval architecture, which figures prominently only in Dickens's last (and unfinished) novel, *The Mystery of Edwin Drood*. Patrick Brantlinger largely accepts Ruskin's assessment of Dickens and traces the latter's legendary modernity to the good impression that the textile mills in Lowell, Massachusetts, with their advanced factory systems, made on him when he visited the United States in 1842.[3] If he was indeed such a modern, Dickens was in good company, for, according to Thomas Arnold:

> we must remember also not so to transport ourselves into the four-teenth century as to forget that we belong really to the nineteenth; that here, and not there, lie our duties; that the harvest, gathered in the fields of the past, is to be brought home for the use of the present.[4]

But, as George Ford argues, Dickens was not simply a fan of modernity and hater of history.[5] Indeed, both of these contradictory impulses are evident throughout Dickens's oeuvre. In *Bleak House*, for instance, Dickens has harsh words for both the backward-looking aristocratic throwback Sir Leicester Dedlock and for the progress-driven new-money industrialist Watt Rouncewell. Similarly, in *Great Expectations*, Dickens sees Magwitch's future-oriented efforts to secure Pip's financial happiness as an inverted but equally mistaken version of Miss Havisham's creepy nostalgia for her halcyon days of romantic bliss.

If Dickens does not discuss the medieval past – or the past at all – as explicitly as do some of his contemporaries, his doubled attitude toward history, which suggests that it should be approached with

simultaneous sympathy and wariness, was nevertheless typically
Victorian. Indeed, Victorian approaches to history ranged from elegy
to condemnation, and sometimes both at the same time. Despite the
failure of events such as the faux medieval tournament at the Earl of
Eglinton's castle in 1839, there was a vast proliferation from that time
on of local historical and archaeological societies dedicated either to
uncovering or to rebuilding English – and particularly medieval –
history. One of the most notable of these, the Camden Society,
comprised Cambridge undergraduates and worked to restore Angli-
canism to its former glory by increasing its formality, use of art, and
other medieval practices. Members of this group wanted to transform
medieval churches to make them fitting sacred symbols again. The
renovations they undertook were often vandalisms, however, and
involved moves such as "restoring" churches to cruciform shapes that
they never possessed, installing altars where none had been present,
and "retouching" art that did not previously exist.[6] That group and
others like it were, however, balanced to some degree by groups such
as SPAB (the Society for the Preservation of Ancient Buildings),
which was nicknamed "Anti-scrape" because of its stance against the
removal of plaster and which included among its members such
eminent Victorians as William Morris, John Ruskin, and Leslie
Stephen, who would later father Virginia Woolf.[7] If, as A. Dwight
Culler suggests, the idea of "medievalism" was less a set group of
ideologies, artistic values, or historiographical postulates, than a way
for the Victorians to register their complaints against the present,[8] its
possibilities as a coherent historiographical approach are, at best,
severely limited.

   Dickens's approach to a giant from medieval history, King Alfred,
in *A Child's History of England* and *The Battle of Life* and his explicit
commentary on Victorian medievalism in "Old Lamps for New
Ones" (1850) enact and play out the implications of some common
Victorian ways of responding to the artifacts and figures of history,
especially medieval history. Dickens responds specifically to the ways
in which his contemporaries use these artifacts and figures as models
or pedagogical tools, either by contrasting them with the weaknesses
of the present or treating them as monuments to an aesthetically
superior past age. At the same time, Dickens also mines the implications of a contradictory (yet also typically Victorian) attitude his
contemporaries often demonstrated toward the past: insisting on its

incomprehensibility, or, by extension, ignoring it altogether. If the diverse and often conflicting approaches to the Middle Ages that Dickens displays in these texts suggest that he had no coherent philosophy of history of his own, no single rhetoric about the Middle Ages, and no carefully delineated stance toward the figures of England's national past, they nonetheless suggest that he understood the implications of his contemporaries' medievalism very well. For Dickens, the past is interesting not for its own sake but because it demands a response; Alfred is less compelling as a figure in his own right than as a sharp, focused lens through which the present tense can – and should – be viewed.

Dickens's use of King Alfred in *A Child's History of England* demonstrates one common use to which his Victorian contemporaries – and various characters in his own novels – put historical figures: the medieval king serves as a pedagogical tool by which Dickens models good citizenship for his young readers. For Dickens, Alfred is praiseworthy for a number of reasons: he demonstrates judicious behavior in battle; with valiance and a "mighty heart,"[9] he subdues those who challenge him, especially pirates; he shows mercy to those he conquers and brings about their conversion to Christianity (18); and he establishes unity and order in a chaotic land, even establishing peace between the long-warring Saxons and Danes, whose children play together in the "sunny fields," fall in love, marry, and eventually talk of the greatness of Alfred at their familial firesides (18). In short, Alfred "possessed all the Saxon virtues" (21) in a way that was relevant for readers in Dickens's day. In fact, drawing a line between the virtues of Dickens's Saxon king Alfred and those of a hearty Victorian self-improver who is interested in self-acculturation and its benefits to society proves nearly impossible. Just as Samuel Smiles, the author of the 1859 bestseller *Self-Help*, uses famous figures from English history to urge his working-class audiences to cultivate character, virtue, a good work ethic, and an appreciation for knowledge, so also does Dickens impress the same lessons and values on his young readers with a history that looks up to Alfred as the model Englishman.[10]

Soon, however, Dickens's discussion of the ways in which Alfred embodies "all the best points of the English-Saxon character" – law, industry, respect for life and property, steadiness, perseverance, bravery, and grace – dissolves into a critique of Victorian England's artistic insensibility. Dickens begins this critique by suggesting that industry and artistry, work and pleasure, need not be seen as polar opposites. Indeed, Alfred enjoys the fruits of a formidable work ethic, for his disciplined time-management allows him to found schools, hear court cases, and, in the interests of measuring time more effectively, design the first lantern that allowed candles to keep time outdoors as well as in (19–20) – a list of accomplishments that any hard-working Victorian surely would have found impressive. At the same time that Alfred undertakes social and material improvements, so also does he establish the value of culture in an un-cultured age. For instance, Dickens attributes Alfred's defeat of the "pestilent Danes" to his musicianship rather than his military genius, as Dickens has Alfred gather vital information on the enemy while playing music in the tent of the Danish leader, Guthrum (18). But most importantly for Dickens, Alfred devotes himself to literary pursuits from a very young age: when the king was twelve years old, Dickens informs us, he taught himself to read and began a lifelong acquisition of knowledge:

> He loved to talk with clever men, and with travelers from foreign countries, and to write down what they told him, for his people to read. He had studied Latin after learning to read English, and now another of his labours was, to translate Latin books into the English-Saxon tongue, that his people might be interested, and improved by their contents. (19)

The way in which Alfred politically and culturally consolidates Saxon England, Dickens argues, means that his people are free to enjoy the finer things in life: food, drink, wall hangings, ornate furniture, elegant table service, jewelry, manners, music, and after-dinner storytelling (20–21). This close alliance during Alfred's time between, on the one hand, idealistic and aesthetic goals, such as beauty and literacy, and, on the other hand, concrete improvements such as lanterns, should, Dickens insists, serve as a lesson for the Victorian public, which, according to him, too often has the accoutrements of culture without the aesthetic richness that ought to infuse such commodities.

The way in which Dickens approaches his source materials for his depiction of Alfred in *A Child's History* also bears the marks of this two-fold engagement with the past, as he focuses simultaneously on its objective, measurable accomplishments and its aesthetics.

Comparatively objective sources about the Middle Ages would have been easy for Dickens to come by. For example, he almost certainly knew "The Anglo-Saxon Chronicle," which existed in Middle and Modern English translations well before the time Dickens began preparations for his *Child's History*, and which would have given him a strong record of the major events of Alfred's reign. He was surely also familiar with such widely known sources as David Hume's *History of England* and *Magnall's Historical Questions*. And the depiction of Arthur that Dickens gives us in *A Child's History* clearly owes much to J. A. Giles's 1847 translation of Asser's biography of Alfred, which Dickens paraphrases multiple times and from which he directly draws several episodes and pieces of dialogue.[11] Dickens would have found it more challenging to capture the aesthetic side of King Alfred, but he was not without sources even so. It seems likely, for instance, that he had either seen or knew of the Alfred Jewel, a gold, enamel, and crystal artifact that bears an image of Christ or an allegorical representation of Sight, along with the words "*AELFRED MEC HEHT GEWYRCAN*" ("Alfred ordered me to be made").[12] This objet d'art, discovered in 1693 and residing at the Ashmolean Museum at Oxford,[13] depicts the figure's features in a manner remarkably similar to those Dickens uses in *A Child's History of England* to describe Alfred himself: "long fair hair, parted on the forehead[,] […] ample beard, […] fresh complexion, and clear eyes" (21). We do not know if Dickens intentionally collapsed Christ and Alfred with his physical description in *A Child's History* or whether he was simply confused about what the Alfred Jewel represents. Yet asking this question is in some ways to miss the point, for Dickens is concerned much less with the accuracy of his aesthetics than with their appropriateness, much less with the objective and measurable content of the past than with the rhetorical ends that history can be made to serve.

This rhetorical maneuver of looking for keys to the present in the recesses of the past, especially Alfred's reign, is typically Victorian. As Charles Dellheim argues, not only did the Victorians "happily interpret […] [Alfred] in their own images and appropriate him for their own causes," but they also often made an alliance between medievalism and modernity in order to imagine a society that was both technologically advanced and spiritually lively.[14] Indeed, as G. K. Chesterton argues, *A Child's History* may be less about Alfred than about the man who penned the volume: "It may not be important as a contribution to history, but it is important as a contribution to biography; as a contribution to the character and the career of the man who wrote it, a typical man of his time."[15] This sort of historiography is best exemplified by Thomas Carlyle's treatment of the strong leader Abbott Sampson in *Past and Present* (1842), in which figures from the past serve to critique the present.[16] Just as Carlyle's Sampson is able to bring order to a disordered community of monks whose worst characteristics resemble those Carlyle most abhorred in his own society, so also is Alfred able to improve his people in just the ways Dickens would see Victorian England bettered: better schools, better courts, more beauty, and thus more general happiness. Moreover, Dickens here seems to mimic Carlyle's tendency to search for something aesthetic or spiritual in the past, "a source of permanent value capable of sustaining human community on earth and their longings for transcendence beyond it,"[17] in order to inject meaning into Victorian everyday life. Dickens's Alfred, like Abbott Sampson, seems to be just the sort of leader – both politically and aesthetically – that England needs.

But here the similarity stops. Although Dickens and Carlyle react against the same sorts of abuses in Victorian society, Carlyle uses the Middle Ages to trace the Victorians' spiritually impoverished materialism, what he calls "mammonism," to a confluence of particularly nineteenth-century historical developments: the Corn Laws, the aftermath of the Industrial Revolution, the rise of the "captains of industry," the development of advertising culture, and so forth. Dickens, by contrast, has a much hazier relation both to his own time and to the past. As Patrick Brantlinger argues, Dickens's philosophy of history, though hardly systematic, reveals a persistently doubled relationship to history, where the past is on the one hand an object of repulsion – "a nightmare from which we are always trying to awake" – and on the other an object of attraction, a treasure trove of wisdom and improvement to which we owe the comforts of the present.[18] *The Battle of Life* demonstrates this complexity and adds to it, as Dickens's varied and often confusing attitude toward the past mirrors similar confusion in his own culture.

The central action of *The Battle of Life* revolves around the characters' relationship to an idyllic past that seems to be lost forever, and the plot foregrounds the issues that arise from the simultaneous attractiveness and inaccessibility of the past. Yet, for Dickens, the view that various characters take toward the past is inextricable from their views in general, especially about the most emotively and morally complicated elements of living in the present. Dickens's discussion of everyday life, both in the past and the present, thus continually stretches toward the timeless realm of allegory, while his discussion of history collapses into a discussion of the individual's emotive life. Dickens reads the past through the sentimental lens provided by a tangled love triangle: the young hero Alfred loves the allegorically named Marion, but Marion's sister Grace, who also has an allegorical name, loves Alfred. In the second book, Marion, recognizing that her sister's affections turn toward her own fiancé, feigns an elopement with a mysterious traveler, thus leaving Alfred free to forget her and Grace free to claim his affections. In the third and final book, Grace and Alfred live happily ever after, and, after the space of some years, Marion returns home, older but no less allegorically self-sacrificial.

This plot, which does not present Dickens at his most subtle, revolves around a historical figure – Alfred – yet it does so largely to suggest that both the debates about history that plagued Dickens's contemporaries and the romantic entanglements that complicated Dickens's own everyday life are, in the end, timeless, ahistorical, and universal. As we shall see, the process of mourning and marrying that Marion's disappearance inaugurates both suggests certain lessons about how to relate to the collective, national past and serves as a field on which the conflicts infecting Dickens's personal life from the mid-1840s through mid-century could be worked out as well. Dickens, it seems, has no problem conflating medieval history with his own romantic and artistic difficulties; further, he has no problem reading the particularities of collective and personal history in a largely allegorical register. This highly unusual narrative approach has left readers and literary critics largely unable to approach *The Battle of Life* in any coherent way. With the exception of William B. Todd's article about the authenticity of the plates used for the book's title page and an occasional mention of the work or comparison of it to Dickens's other writings, recent critical interest in *The Battle of Life* has been confined to two extremely short articles by Frank Gibson and Katherine Carolan in 1962 and 1973 respectively.[19] And from the first printing of the *Battle of Life*, reviewers' responses have been almost entirely negative, from Edward FitzGerald's 1846 assessment of the piece as a "wretched affair"[20] to Steven Marcus's 1965 mourning of its hopeless, dismal, and depressing mood.[21] Nevertheless, despite the bad reviews, *The Battle of Life* sold well, and seventeen dramatic adaptations based on it were produced.[22] Dickens too was displeased with the Christmas book, but not because he thought it had failed. Rather, he thought its ideas were too good to be wasted on anything other than a full-length novel: "I was thoroughly wretched at having to use the idea for so short a story. I did not see its full capacity until it was too late [...]."[23] As we shall see, the "full capacity" of *The Battle of Life* has less to do with its intricate plotting or compelling characterization than with its historical flexibility – its ability to play simultaneously in the past, the present, and the eternal.

Dickens's nods to medieval history are most visible. Although his use of Alfred in *The Battle of Life* does not bear the specific marks of historical research into the life of Alfred that *A Child's History* does, the figure of the medieval king is unmistakable in the book's aptly named protagonist, Alfred Heathfield. The fictional Alfred Heathfield is an "active[, ...] handsome young man" and proves as attractive to those he is close to in *The Battle* as King Alfred does in the battles he wages.[24] From the first, Alfred Heathfield is associated with music, as is the historical King Alfred before him, for the book opens with a revelation that Alfred "sent the music" – a group of traveling minstrels – to his love interest Marion on her birthday (289). Like King Alfred, who, Dickens informs us in *A Child's History*, traveled twice to Rome, Alfred Heathfield goes abroad, where he acquires knowledge. He continually devotes himself to education, even spending a good portion of the book away from the central action so he can help others with the medical knowledge he acquires. And most importantly, like his predecessor, Alfred Heathfield demonstrates the best of the Saxon virtues, including a "true heart" (290). Given this, it seems that Alfred Heathfield represents an early version of the fully fledged king who emerged four years later in *A Child's History*; he is, we might infer, a figure who can demonstrate a proper relationship to history. But while in *A Child's History* Dickens sees King Alfred as a positive figure who can offer a solution to Victorian errors in vision, in *The Battle of Life*, by contrast, Alfred Heathfield is part of the problem, for his view of history is as skewed as everyone else's.

At least initially, though, Dickens does seem to want to use *The Battle of Life* to teach a complex (and by now familiar) doubled attitude toward the past: we must, Dickens says, embrace

historiography as an act of simultaneous remembrance and forgetfulness. Yet as Dickens's prose demonstrates what this sort of
forgetful remembrance might look like in practice, *The Battle* seems
less like an object-lesson and more like an exposé, for it plays out
the contradictions inherent in Victorian historiography. For
instance, Dickens says, "Heaven keep us from a knowledge of the
sights the moon beheld upon that field," just before he lists off
what precisely Heaven should keep us from knowing (284) – a
truly disconcerting authorial maneuver. The book's resident
Christ-figure, Marion, shares a similarly split consciousness. When
Marion leaves, ostensibly because she hopes that Alfred will be able
to forget her in favor of Grace, she also leaves a note in which she
begs her family *not* to forget her, an act that leaves her family
deeply confused. And although the good-hearted servant Clemency
carries a thimble that reads "for-get and for-give," she also has in
her pocket a collection of odd bits and pieces of how she has passed
her time in Dr. Jeddler's service: handkerchiefs, good-luck charms,
needles, thread, balls of fuzz, curl-papers, a padlock, and – King
Alfred's innovative marker of the passage of time – the end of a
wax candle (303). The past imagined in this register, like the
objects in Clemency's pockets, comes to seem less like a coherent
text that can be interpreted and used to good ends than a jumbled
collection of odds and ends cut loose from the contexts that give
them meaning in the first place.

Dickens introduces another Victorian debate about history –
whether it exists primarily as a collection of artifacts or as a text that
teaches right living – in the book's overriding metaphor, the battle-
field. With their readings of the historical objects taken from the
battlefield, Jeddler and Alfred Heathfield enact two common ways in
which Victorians read the artifacts that so often turned up in English
soil. While Jeddler and Alfred find bits of battle armor and bone fragments, Dickens's contemporaries often found vestiges of England's
Roman past. In addition to the coins, plates, goblets, and other articles that laborers sometimes discovered, so also were there relics of
battles fought on English ground – a real-life *Battle of Life*. As Dickens
describes it in *A Child's History*:

> In some old battle-fields, British spear-heads and Roman armour
> have been found, mingled together in decay, as they fell in the

thick pressure of the fight. Traces of Roman camps overgrown with grass, and of mounds that are the burial-places of heaps of Britons, are to be seen in almost all parts of the country. (10–11)

The Jeddler family home is built on the site of just such a battle-ground. Although, as Dickens says, "It matters little when" this battle occurred, and though Daniel Maclise's illustrations for the first edition include a strangely anachronistic rifle in the hand of a fallen drummer boy, they otherwise suggest a medieval battle, complete with appropriate armor, spears, battle standards, and richly bedecked horses. Moreover, Dickens tells us that the battle was fought in "stalwart England" (283), a phrase that calls to mind England's noble and honest Saxon past. If Dickens's understanding of the medieval past seems here vague, littered with artifacts of the present, that is a symptom, he might argue, of Victorian historiography, which remembers and forgets at the same time, and which, apparently, cannot keep England's buried Roman past in the ground.

Neither can characters in *The Battle of Life* keep from unearthing the past they thought was buried. Dickens tells us that the years following this great battle routinely see it brought back to memory by farmers who turn up pieces of armor, or even by patches of unusually green turf growing over the bones of fallen horses, indeed, the repressed past makes so many cameo appearances in those years that it is hardly repressed at all. Yet as years pass, the artifacts begin to appear with less frequency, and as a result, people find their memory of the battle growing dim. As Dickens explains, the passage of years has "obliterated [...] even these remains of the old conflict; and wore away such legendary traces of it as the neighbouring people carried in their minds, until they dwindled into old wives' tales, dimly remembered round the winter fire, and waning every year" (286). Despite the virtual invisibility of history on a daily basis, though, Jeddler, like some of Dickens's contemporaries, keeps willfully dredging it up at the most inappropriate of times. As Jeddler says:

"On this ground where we now sit, where I saw my two girls dance this morning, where the fruit has just been gathered for our eating from these trees, the roots of which are struck in Men, not earth, – so many lives were lost, that within my recollection, generations afterwards, a churchyard full of bones, and dust of bones, and chips of cloven skulls, has been dug up from underneath our feet here." (297)

Surely Dickens knows he is contradicting himself: the bones are either there or not there; the battle is either an old wives' tale or a physical reality. But Jeddler's understanding of the past represents only one way of doing historiography. Because Jeddler sees history as a collection of material objects, he sees it not as an instructive textbook but as a muddled and random text that cannot teach anything in particular:

> "Yet not a hundred people in that battle, knew for what they fought, or why; not a hundred of the inconsiderate rejoicers in the victory, why they rejoiced. Not a half a hundred people were the better, for the gain or loss. Not half-a-dozen men agree to this hour on the cause or merits; and nobody, in short, ever knew anything distinct about it, but the mourners of the slain." (297)

By contrast, Alfred embodies a second approach to history: he seeks lessons in the past at the expense of its varied and often indeterminate concrete details. For Alfred, the fact that a churchyard full of bones has been unearthed matters little, if at all, and he cheerfully, and perhaps rather dimly, urges Jeddler "to try sometimes to forget this battle-field" because it distracts from "that broader battle-field of Life, on which the sun looks every day" (299). Alfred believes that refocusing the battle as a metaphor for life, not a relic of past foolishness, makes possible a new sort of meaning – everyday heroism:

> "I believe [...] there are quiet victories and struggles, great sacrifices of self, and noble acts of heroism in it – even in many of its apparent lightnesses and contradictions – not the less difficult to achieve, because they have no earthly chronicle or audience; done every day in nooks and corners, and in little households, and in men's and women's hearts." (299–300)

Dickens admires Alfred's idealism so much that he paints him in terms that render him remarkably physically similar to his medieval predecessor. Despite the loveliness of Alfred's idealistic speech, though, his argument fails to convince Jeddler for the simple reason that it cannot be proven. Alfred believes that all sorts of good deeds that are never chronicled or narrated are happening all around, which may be true, but could just as easily be a lie, for his belief, unlike Jeddler's disenchantment, relies on no concrete evidence, no artifacts, and no acts of remembrance. Dickens, then, places us in the center of a Victorian historiographical problem: given that our entries in the past always combine forgetting and remembering, how then should we approach history when we encounter it? If we attend to the past, should we try to see pedagogical patterns in it, or should we simply admit our helplessness before the vast data we encounter? In short, should we read the past through its scattered material artifacts, as Jeddler does, or through aesthetically beautiful but largely imagined reconstructions, as Alfred does? Dickens's obvious answer is "neither," for both Jeddler and Alfred understand the past incompletely.

Dickens at first seems to offer this critique in order to set up an obvious solution to the problems that the past poses: if neither Jeddler nor Alfred sees things completely, should we not simply try to combine the ways they see into a more complete vision of the past that bridges matter and meaning, artifacts and artistry? Indeed, this solution would seem to be supported by *A Child's History*, for, as we have seen, Dickens argues via the figure of Alfred that we should attend at once to both the material and aesthetic components of everyday life. One could martial other examples from Dickens's oeuvre as well to suggest that he wants us to mimic Alfred Heathfield and Jeddler at once. In *A Christmas Carol* (1843), for instance, Scrooge infuses his materially bound everyday life with aesthetic richness and spiritual depth when he learns to "live in the Past, the Present, and the Future!"[25] Given figures like Scrooge and King Alfred, it seems – at least initially – that for Dickens, refusing to occupy any one historical realm is tantamount to balancing material and aesthetic lives and practicing responsible historiography.

But, to be fair, the historical problems that Dickens poses in *The Battle of Life* are simply too intricate to be so easily resolved. Indeed, as Dickens suggests, many of the historiographical problems that face his contemporaries derive from the fact that they simply do not know how to live, like Scrooge and Alfred, in multiple temporal and epistemological spheres at once. It is not that they do not want to attend simultaneously to the past and to the present, to artifacts and artistry, but that they do not know what these mean in relation to each other. As Peter Ackroyd notes, the very phrase "the battle of life" enacts just this problem, for, as it refers to the Darwinian and Malthu-sian struggle for existence, as well as to the political turmoil Gladstone described as "perpetual conflict,"[26] it carries with it a plethora of asso-ciations that blur historical boundaries; the battle of life is, we must remember, a battle. Indeed, *The Battle of Life* is only one of many complex attempts Dickens makes to enact the difficulties the Victo-rians had as they approached history. In the years between 1846 and 1851 especially, Dickens's works revolve almost obsessively around these questions. For instance, Dickens's final Christmas book, *The Haunted Man* (1848), complicates *A Christmas Carol*'s approach to the question of memory, as the protagonist Redlaw embraces an opportunity to eliminate the pain of his past by having his memory erased. Redlaw, in the end, learns the hard way that there is no one right way to relate to the past: in remembering, he is in pain yet kind to others, while in forgetting, he is numb to pain yet harsh to those he loves. In *Dombey and Son* (1846–48), Dickens offers a similarly complex treatment of historical memory, and he heals the title char-acter by forcing him to remember – and then to correct – the sins of his past. Finally, *Bleak House*, which Dickens began in 1851, suggests an extremely intricate understanding of family history, as Esther Summerson learns about her parentage only after a case of smallpox erases her strong physical resemblance to her mother. In all these texts, artifacts and meaning, materiality and aesthetics, do not always line up, and none of them offers a coherent way to understand the signifi-cance of the past in the present.

Dickens discusses this problem explicitly in his 1850 *Household Words* article "Old Lamps for New Ones." Here, Dickens takes to task those most prominent Victorian medievalists, the Pre-Raphaelite Brotherhood, for the ways in which their "great retrogressive prin-ciple" has led them astray. For Dickens, the Pre-Raphaelites are ridicu-lous primarily because the idea of being pre-anything is itself absurd: we might as well found a pre-Galileo Brotherhood to protest the movement of the earth around the Sun, a Pre-Harvey Brotherhood "against the circulation of blood," or a pre-Newtonian Brotherhood to object to that iron-fisted modern construct known as gravity.[27] Yet Dickens does not simply react against the ways in which the "Pre-Raphael Brotherhood," that "dread Tribunal,"[28] aims to correct Victorian historiographical errors. Rather, he uses the PRB to demon-strate that a proper approach to history – if such a thing is even

possible – involves much more than uniting materiality with
aesthetics. The PRB, Dickens says, imagines history as an "admirably
painted" collection of details, such as "the shavings [...] strewn on the
carpenter's floor," all of which come together in a spiritually impoverished homage to "ugliness of feature, limb, or attitude."[29] One can be
aesthetically perfect and materially responsible and still, Dickens
suggests, miss the point.

    Yet what the point is, what moral Dickens wants us to take away
from the works that fall into this period, remains strangely murky.
Although Dickens issues harsh critiques and admonitions of
medievalists ranging from Jeddler to Alfred Heathfield to the PRB to
Sir Leicester Dedlock, he seems to have no specific ideas about how
one ought to approach or understand the Middle Ages. Moreover, his
discussions of the Middle Ages are, at best, vague, as they lack in the
historical specificity that characterizes other Victorian medievalist
texts. What he does suggest, however, is that these figures understand
the Middle Ages wrongly because they do not, in the end, understand
themselves. And this, in the end, is Dickens's most forceful point:
Victorian medievalism is less important for the historiographical
errors and tendencies it demonstrates than for the way in which it can
serve as a key to the psychology of the age. Similarly, Dickens's own
statements about history prove less useful as keys to the way he understands his nation's past than as indices of how he understands his own
life. For Dickens, history is autobiography, and reflecting on the struggles of the Middle Ages is a way to meditate on his own personal
issues.

    It makes sense, then, that Dickens's personal life imbeds itself to a
great degree in *The Battle of Life*. For instance, the central romance
plot of the book, in which Marion relinquishes her claim on Alfred in
order to allow Grace to marry him, carefully reverses Dickens's
marriage to Catherine despite his strong attraction to her sister Mary
Hogarth. If only Catherine had stepped aside, Dickens seems to
suggest, he could have been spared an unhappy marriage and could
have been with Mary instead; he could have traded the wrong sister
for the right one. And, on an equally personal but less tragic level, *The
Battle of Life* similarly invokes and then revises the frustrating writing
process that gave rise to the book. Dickens composed the piece when
he was away from London in the Swiss countryside just outside of
Lausanne. His creative energies were, at that time, at a very low ebb,

and he had to finish the book in a rush when he fell behind the writing schedule he had set for himself. In fact, Dickens was deeply worried he would not get *The Battle* to press in time for Christmas at all, and he wrote to his friend and biographer John Forster just a few weeks before his deadline, "I fear there may be NO CHRISTMAS BOOK!"[30]

Dickens blames his writer's block on the fact that he was in Switzerland and not in England in another letter to Forster: "a day in London sets me up again and starts me. But the toil and labour of writing, day after day, without that magic lantern, is IMMENSE!!"[31] And indeed, the Swiss landscape seems to have been intrusively present – even omnipresent – to Dickens during the composition of *The Battle of Life*. He walked miles per day in the countryside around Lausanne while he was conceiving of the idea for the book,[32] and he dedicated the *Battle of Life* to three English friends – William Haldimand, who directed the Bank of England and engaged in phil-anthropic labors, the former liberal MP Richard Watson, and the latter's wife, Lavinia[33] – who accompanied him on a trip to the Great St. Bernard convent during the drafting process, a trip that was notable to Dickens largely for the desolate scenery: "Nothing of life or living interest in the picture, but the grey dull walls [...]. No vegeta-tion of any sort of kind. Nothing growing, nothing stirring."[34] This landscape serves as a symbol that allows Dickens to issue a tri-fold critique against the spiritual deadness of Switzerland's monastic popu-lation, the deadening historiography of the PRB, and his own artistic impotence. Consolidating these three critiques in one central symbol, Dickens suggests they all stem from the same errors in vision and, indeed, that there is no real difference between them. To be spiritually impoverished is to be historically deficient, and to be historically defi-cient is to lack creativity. Spirituality dissolves into history, and history into biography.

In *The Battle of Life*, similarly, historical, biographical, and spiri-tual questions coalesce in yet another lengthy meditation on the battlefield, which serves not just as a repository of history, but a synecdoche of the English countryside. And here again Alfred's name comes into play, for he is not just Alfred but Alfred *Heathfield* – an embodiment of the English landscape. Dickens shows that the way characters read the environment, like the way they approach history, attests to their spiritual and personal state. But reading the battlefield as a site that contains both artifacts and vegetation, that features both scars and new growth, suggests the possibility for personal spiritual and emotional renewal in the midst of conflict and violence. In *The Battle of Life*, that is, the artifacts of history are integrated within the natural environment and its cyclical patterns of death and rebirth. If in 1877 Gerard Manley Hopkins would meditate on the way in which the earth, despite being "seared with trade; bleared, smeared with toil," continually shows that "nature is never spent,"[35] so also does Dickens in 1846 assert that history, like nature, is replete with self-renewal and rebirth. Hardly a dry, cold repository for artifacts, the battle ground is instead a field where history can produce fruit in the present: "there were deep green patches in the growing corn at first, that people looked at awfully. Year after year they re-appeared; and it was known that underneath those fertile spots, heaps of men and horses lay buried, indiscriminately, enriching the ground" (285). An almost direct anticipation of Dickens's description of the appearance of Roman artifacts and strange green patches in nineteenth-century England, this passage reminds us that history – in Christmas Books and in real life – stubbornly and persistently insists that it is anything but dead.[36]

Moreover, Dickens reminds us that we cannot mark history without also marking rebirth. Strangely but appropriately, all the major events in *The Battle of Life*, including the battle itself, occur on the birthday that Marion and Alfred share; long after Marion has vanished, in fact, Grace and Alfred acknowledge the fact that "changes and events within" mark time in tandem with her birthday, and Grace, in fact, expects her return on that same day (356). Marion's disappearance, the key event in the Jeddler family's history, promises to reverse itself as she surfaces like an artifact from the past. Yet Marion's promised reappearance does not simply rewrite the past, blot it out, or make it any less important. Rather, as Alfred acknowledges, it reminds them that they have "tender relations stretching far behind [them], that never can be exactly renewed" but others as well dawning day by day (297). History goes hand in hand with rebirth, and the past renews itself continually in the movements of human affection.

Fittingly, then, both Alfred and Jeddler learn a right relation to history and to their own personal stories when a "rebirth" happens and Marion returns. Marion's disappearance accomplishes this work of historical correction because in leaving she reminds them of the simultaneous presence and absence of history in culture – the way it depends on us to remember it, and the way it presses down on even those who would, if they could, forget it. For Alfred, losing Marion means that he cannot ignore what has been; he cannot rely on his belief in everyday heroism alone at the exclusion of the past, reality, and personal memory. He mourns Marion by learning to love Grace. Similarly, for Jeddler, grief enriches his reading of history, for as he comes to identify with those "mourners of the slain" who knew what the original battle was about, so also does he find that history reverberates almost mystically in the hearts and minds of those alive in the present and that it thus comprises far more than senseless artifacts. As Jeddler says, "It's a world full of hearts [...] and a world we need be careful how we libel, Heaven forgive us, for it is a world of sacred mysteries, and its Creator only knows what lies beneath the surface of His lightest image" (362–63).

For both Alfred and Jeddler, a process of loss and mourning allows them to make a space for a new sort of love – one they had not envisioned before. For Alfred, mourning Marion means that he must learn to give his belief in human nature a basis in reality by marrying, raising a family, and attempting to record acts of everyday heroism on a daily basis. And for Jeddler, losing Marion reminds him that the world is indeed meaningful, that it signifies insofar as we infuse its traces and artifacts with personal emotive significance. Similarly for Marion, people in the world who are "trying to assist and cheer it and to do some good" (361) point to divine kinship relations, the tie between artifact and interpretation, past and present. For Dickens, then, the proper way to approach the past is as a key to human kindness: we study history in order to learn to mourn; we learn to mourn in order to cultivate deeper affection for our fellow men. In so doing, we make objective reality subjectively significant, and we assert the place of each individual's experience in the rich fabric of the heavenly order. And thereby, like King Alfred before us, we learn to devote ourselves to serving our fellow men, to enriching their existence both materially and spiritually.

NOTES

1. Charles Dellheim, *The Face of the Past: The Preservation of the Medieval Inheritance in Victorian England* (New York and London: Cambridge University Press, 1982), viii.

2. Charles Kostelnik, "Dickens's Quarrel with the Gothic: Ruskin, Durdles, and *Edwin Drood*," *Dickens Studies Newsletter* 8 (1977): 104–08 (104).

3. Patrick Brantlinger, "Dickens and the Factories," *Nineteenth-Century Fiction* 26 (1971): 270–85 (276).

4. Rosemary Jann, *The Art and Science of Victorian History* (Columbus: The Ohio State University Press, 1985), 6.

5. George H. Ford, "Dickens and the Voices of Time," *Nineteenth-Century Fiction* 24 (1970): 428–48 (437).

6. Dellheim, *The Face*, 80–81.

7. Dellheim, *The Face*, 85–86.

8. A. Dwight Culler, *The Victorian Mirror of History* (New Haven, CT, and London: Yale University Press, 1985), 159.

9. Charles Dickens, *A Child's History of England* (New York: P. F. Collier, n.d.), 19. All further references will be given parenthetically in my main text.

10. Samuel Smiles, *Self-Help* (1859; repr. London: Sphere, 1968).

11. Bishop Asser of Sherborne. *The Life of King Alfred from A.D. 849 to A.D. 887*, trans. J. A. Giles, The Online Medieval and Classical Library (2006), <http://omacl.org/KingAlfred/> (accessed 14 November 2006).

12. Ken Roberts, "The Alfred Jewel" (1997), <http://www.mirror.org/ken.roberts/alfred.jewel.html> (accessed 14 November 2006).

13. David A. Hinton, *A Catalogue of the Anglo-Saxon Ornamental Metalwork 700–1100 in the Department of Antiquities, Ashmolean Museum* (London: Oxford University Press, 1974), 29–48.

14. Dellheim, *The Face*, 4, 71.

15. G. K. Chesterton, *Appreciations and Criticisms of the Works of Charles Dickens*, <http://www.lang.nagoya-u.ac.jp/~matsuoka/CD-Chesterton-A&C-2.html#XVI> (accessed 6 May 2006).

16. Thomas Carlyle, *Past and Present* (New York: New York University Press, 1965).

17. Jann, *The Art*, 33.

18. Patrick Brantlinger, "Did Dickens Have a Philosophy of History?: The Case of *Barnaby Rudge*," *Dickens Studies Annual* 30 (2001): 59–74 (70–71).

19. William B. Todd, "Dickens's *The Battle of Life*: Round Six," *The

Book Collector 15 (1966): 48–54; Frank A. Gibson, "Nature's Possible: A Reconsideration of *The Battle of Life*," *Dickensian* 58 (1962): 43–46; Katherine Carolan, "*The Battle of Life: A Love Story*," *Dickensian* 69 (1973): 105–10.

20. Carolan, "*The Battle*," 105.

21. Steven Marcus, *Dickens: From Pickwick to Dombey* (New York: Basic Books, 1965), 289–92.

22. Peter Ackroyd, *Dickens* (London: Sinclair-Stevenson Limited, 1990; repr. New York: HarperCollins, 1990), 514.

23. Ackroyd, *Dickens*, 515.

24. Charles Dickens, *The Battle of Life*, in Sally Ledger, ed., *The Christmas Books* (London: Everyman, 1999), 294. All further references will be given parenthetically in my main text.

25. Charles Dickens, *A Christmas Carol*, in Ledger, ed., *The Christmas Books*, 79.

26. Ackroyd, *Dickens*, 514–15.

27. Charles Dickens, "Old Lamps for New Ones," *Household Words* 12 (15 June 1850), <http://www.engl.duq.edu/servus/PR_Critic/HW15jun50.html> (accessed 8 May 2006).

28. Dickens, "Old Lamps," <http://www.engl.duq.edu/servus/PR_Critic/HW15jun50.html> (accessed 8 May 2006).

29. Dickens, "Old Lamps," <http://www.engl.duq.edu/servus/PR_Critic/HW15jun50.html> (accessed 8 May 2006).

30. Ackroyd, *Dickens*, 512.

31. Ackroyd, *Dickens*, 511.

32. Ackroyd, *Dickens*, 503.

33. Ackroyd, *Dickens*, 498.

34. Ackroyd, *Dickens*, 512.

35. Gerard Manley Hopkins, "God's Grandeur," in Stephen Greenblatt, ed., *The Norton Anthology of English Literature: The Major Authors* (New York: Norton, 2006), 2160.

36. While Dickens was writing *The Battle of Life*, he was also summarizing and rewriting parts of the New Testament, particularly the Gospels, for his own children, a work that he would later publish as *The Life of Our Lord*. For Dickens, making the Gospel narrative come alive means attending to the ability of the "New Testament spirit" to produce new growth and new life in those it seizes. Indeed, he says that all his Christmas Books contain "an express text preached on, and that text is always taken from the lips of Christ." See Ackroyd, *Dickens*, 504.

Writing Medieval Women (and Men): Sigrid Undset's *Kristin Lavransdatter*

Mark B. Spencer

The historical novel is a conservative genre. Although Sir Walter Scott in many respects paved the way for the great nineteenth-century masterpieces of contemporary realism, as Georg Lukács claimed,[1] he also firmly established romance as the dominant mode for historical fiction. Nowhere is this stark division more evident than in the work of Gustave Flaubert, for while Emma Bovary's dreams of romance wither amid the mud and manure of rural Normandy, the Carthaginian princess Salammbô soars to the heights of romantic fantasy, rescuing the veil of the goddess Tanit, inspiring the impossible love of a Moorish rebel chieftain, and dying of a broken heart as her Moor is torn to pieces by a frenzied crowd. A few notable exceptions can be found, above all William Makepeace Thackeray's *Henry Esmond* (1852) and Tolstoy's *War and Peace* (1863–69), but, as Ernest Leisy and Peter Green were among the first to recognize, it was not until the twentieth century that historical novelists began making a serious effort to think their way into the mentalities of the past and create characters and plots that were as plausible and authentic as the costumes, settings, and other antiquarian lore of their fictions.[2] Prominent among the pioneers of this new model of full-fledged realism in the historical novel, a tradition that would ultimately boast such luminaries as Robert Graves, Marguerite Yourcenar, and Mary Renault among many others, stands Sigrid Undset and her medieval trilogy *Kristin Lavransdatter* (1920–22).[3]

Surprisingly enough, it is unclear to what extent Undset was conscious of being an innovator. She had been researching her novel for almost twenty years, both in the extensive collection of her father, a distinguished archeologist of the Scandinavian Iron Age, who died when Undset was eleven, and in the local public and academic libraries.[4] Reading *Njal's Saga* at the age of ten had left her thunderstruck, and she went on to devour the other Icelandic sagas in the modern translations of N. M. Petersen, while imbibing the methods of modern medieval scholarship from her father. Already as a teenager she dreamed of recreating the world she had encountered in the sagas, not in the manner of Scott, but "realistically," so that "everything that seems so romantic from here – murder, violent episodes, etc., becomes ordinary – comes to life."[5] Her first effort, however, "received one of literature's more memorable rejections" in 1905, when the editor advised her to try her hand at something more modern, since she had no talent for historical novels.[6] Undset doggedly took this advice, as she was determined to become a successful author, living by her pen and freeing herself from the drudgery of the office work by which she supported her mother and sisters. A string of very successful novels and stories soon followed in the vein of modern Scandinavian realism, as established by Henrik Ibsen and Auguste Strindberg for drama, that largely drew upon her own experience to portray the travails, sorrows, and moral dilemmas of the young women who flocked to the cities seeking work as clerks and secretaries in Norway's rapidly modernizing economy. Undset returned to the Middle Ages with *Gunnar's Daughter* in 1909, closely modeled on the old Icelandic manner and style, but not until after a trip to Italy, marriage, and a rapidly burgeoning family, did she hit upon the serendipitous formula of bringing the skills and techniques she had honed in her realist novels of modern life to bear in her medieval fiction.

Kristin Lavransdatter has long enjoyed phenomenal popular appeal, both in Undset's native Norway and abroad in translation to some eighty languages. The 1929 edition of Charles Archer and J. S. Scott's original English version is now in its twenty-ninth printing, and the blurb on the back cover from the Book-of-the-Month Club calls it "the best book our judges have ever selected" and "better received by our subscribers than any other book."[7] In 1928 Undset won the Nobel Prize in Literature, largely for *Kristin* and her subsequent medieval tetralogy *The Master of Hestviken*,[8] and in terms of "sales, number of translations, significant honors, and reader loyalty," she was "probably the most successful woman writer in the world."[9] A fresh English translation was undertaken by Tiina Nunnally in the late

1990s for Penguin Classics, recently published in a deluxe combined edition,[10] while Liv Ullman directed a film version that generated a huge sensation in Norway on its release in 1995 and has been viewed by "as much as two-thirds of the population."[11] The Norwegian media eagerly covered the progress of the filming, and the reconstructed medieval farmstead that served as Kristin's childhood home at Jørundgard (spelled "Jørundgaard" in the novel) is now an open-air cultural center complete with website and gift shop. The full panoply of tours, school classes, and accommodations for special occasions such as weddings and birthdays are readily available, and every summer there is an annual *Kristen Lavransdatter Kulturfestivalen* in the nearby town of Sel, where Undset and her family frequently spent the summer. Obviously, "Kristin-mania" is alive and well in the twenty-first century.[12]

Undset has always received a respectable share of academic attention, more so at home than outside of Scandinavia.[13] Recent appreciative studies in English include that of Claudia Berguson, who adopts Mikhail Bakhtin's dialogic approach to explore the tensions among the competing polyphonic voices of saga, epic, sacred legend, ballad, and gossip in *Kristin Lavransdatter*.[14] Christine Hamm uses a theoretically enhanced conception of melodrama to illuminate Undset's vision of the body and the problematic communication between the sexes as a medieval projection of the "gender trouble" debate in the early twentieth century.[15] However, much of the criticism over the last few decades has turned rather negative. According to Liv Bliksrud, the novel is too popular, too Catholic, and ironically too demanding for contemporary Norwegian critics, who lack the adequate grounding in medieval and religious culture necessary to properly understand it.[16] But Otto Reinert claims it is Undset's unfashionably realist approach that forms the principal issue:

> Her novels are product not process literature: the reader does not participate in the novel's progressive discoveries or experience them as being conscious of the difficulties of their own coming into being. They do not invite deconstruction into multiple meanings held in suspension. Their narrative shifts among authorial omniscience, characters' inner speech, and objective reporting do not mirror the shattered certainties and the bottomless self-reflexiveness of postmodernism. The truth value of their literary closure is doubtful. Their realism skirts anachronism: characters

feel, think, and behave more like Undset's contemporaries than like people of the thirteenth and fourteenth centuries.[17]

There is more in this vein, but the main point is clear. Undset was not a "proto-postmodernist," although how anyone could expect her to be seems rather bemusing. Reinert is almost apologetic about "the unexciting labor to claim merit for the conventional and call great a work that comes late in a long line of works great in the same way," and he emphasizes her powerful command of the epic mode as manifested in the best nineteenth-century realist novels, replete with "plausible characters and events, recurrent themes and motifs, charged images, poignant ironies, and moral givens."[18] However, as discussed above, historical novels in the nineteenth century most certainly were not "great in the same way," above all in regard to plausible characters and events. Given the recent resurgence of interest in *Kristin Lavransdatter* and the downturn in its academic critical estimation, it seems worthwhile to look again at how well the novel stands up as a popular representation of the Middle Ages some eighty years after its first publication.

One problem voiced by early critics and still heard occasionally today can be dispensed with in short order, and that is the notion that *Kristin Lavransdatter* is not really a historical novel, because it is set in one of the most poorly documented periods of medieval Scandinavia and barely concerns itself with identifiably historical characters and events.[19] Such a judgment reflects a far too narrow definition of historical fiction. Undset's novel is indeed almost entirely invented, although a handful of the background figures are historical, and there is no evidence of any conspiracy to detach Norway from the dual monarchy with Sweden under Magnus VII by establishing Magnus' half-brother Haakon Knutssøn as the Norwegian king, which Kristin's husband unfortunately becomes involved in. Undset was apparently rather uneasy about making up this aborted plot, but subsequent historians have affirmed that it was precisely the sort of political effort that might have been made at the time.[20] Kristin's story may be timeless in many ways, and more than a little tinged with modern psychology, but it is firmly rooted in a specific historical milieu, namely the Norwegian High Middle Ages, some three hundred years after the Viking conversion but long before the emergence of a new religious and cultural sensibility in the Reformation and Renaissance.

To be precise, the book opens in 1306 with Kristin as a small child and ends when she succumbs to the Black Death in 1349.

Although over a thousand pages long, the story is actually quite simple and has been described as "a daddy's girl who refuses daddy's choice of a husband and marries for love, with often harrowing long-range consequences."[21] The only surviving child of Lavrans Bjørgulfssøn and his wife Ragnfrid when the novel opens, Kristin spends her early years spoiled and pampered at Jørundgaard, a prosperous and comfortable manor, but by no means a wealthy one. Both parents are quiet, reserved, God-fearing folk, their marriage somewhat darkened by the deaths of three sons in infancy, and secret sins that they have long nursed in their hearts: Ragnfrid giving herself to another man before marrying Lavrans, and he marrying Ragnfrid although he could not love her. Two more girls ultimately follow Kristin at some remove, although one becomes crippled in an accident and also dies before reaching adulthood. Kristin is engaged by her father to Simon Andressøn, whose patrimonial lands lie adjacent to Jørundgaard. Kristin harbors no special regard or ill-will towards Simon and at first seems willing enough to obey the wishes of her father, until, while spending a year at a convent in Oslo, she meets Erlend Nikulaussøn, a knight with a scandalous reputation who is attached to the king's court. At eighteen Erlend had run off with an older married woman, Eline Ormsdatter, ultimately having two children by her and being forced to relinquish some of his lands in order to make amends with her relatives and the king. Kristin had heard of Erlend before, as he was the nephew of a family friend, Lady Aashild, and although they merely plighted their undying love at the first meeting, their relationship soon escalates into a clandestine affair, and Kristin becomes determined to break her troth with Simon and marry Erlend. This was no easy business, as Lavrans will have none of it at first, but eventually he is worn down, and the first book of the trilogy ends with their wedding, the bride already about three months pregnant.

Not surprisingly, this marriage born in sin and deception proves a stormy one. Erlend's mistress arrives at Husaby, his ancestral estate, and, after a desperate attempt to poison her former lover and his new bride, is driven to suicide by Erlend. The birth of Kristin's first child proves exceptionally difficult, and, convinced that God must be punishing her for her sins, she makes a pilgrimage to the grave of St.

Olav. Husaby had fallen into considerable disrepair and neglect under Erlend's careless tenure, and upon her return Kristin sets out to remake it in the thrifty and industrious image of Jørundgaard. Several more children follow, in addition to Eline's son and daughter, but Erlend grows restless and becomes involved in political affairs, first taking up command of a distant frontier outpost against the heathen Lapps, and then entering a conspiracy to separate the crown of Norway from Sweden. The plot is exposed, and Erlend is arrested and tortured, but he refuses to reveal the identity of his fellow conspirators. The intervention of Simon Andressøn saves Erlend's life and wins his release, but all his lands are forfeited, so he and Kristin must retire to Jørundgaard, which passed to her upon the death of her parents.

The final book details Kristin's life from her return home to her death. She smarts under the disgrace that has fallen upon her family, and relations with her former neighbors are strained. Erlend adapts to his new, idle life rather more easily, roaming the forests and teaching his sons the arts of the hunt and war. Kristin resents Erlend's lack of interest in husbandry or providing a secure future for their sons on the land, and after she accuses him in a quarrel of not being the man her father was, their married life together finally collapses. Erlend retires to a small derelict farm in the mountains, the last stray bit of his patrimony remaining in his possession. When Simon Andressøn dies, he begs Kristin to patch things up with her husband, and she visits Erlend up in his mountain lair. Erlend entreats Kristin to stay with him, but her concern for their sons renders this impossible, although she does become pregnant with one last child. When rumors begin circulating that the father is the foreman on her estate, Erlend comes down from his retreat to defend her honor and is slain in a misunderstanding with several villagers. The local priest had been one of Kristin's slanderers, and Erlend refuses to accept Christian last rites from him before he dies.

As Carl Bayerschmidt has remarked, the novel could have ended here.[22] Religious themes have been prominent up to this point but not necessarily central to the story. The final portion of the novel, however, relates Kristin's return to God, from whom she has been estranged by her stubborn self-will. One of her sons has married and settled his wife at Jørundgaard, assuming its stewardship, while the others have sought their various fortunes in the wider world. Kristin decides to make another pilgrimage and then join the convent of Rein. Along the way she looks back over her life and comes to feel the full extent of God's presence, mercy, and grace for the first time. When the Black Death reaches Rein, she dedicates herself to caring for the sick and saves the young son of a prostitute from being sacrificed in a pagan ritual as a last desperate measure against the pestilence. The boy is released to her on the condition that she bury the dead mother, and in transporting her body Kristin catches the disease herself. Before she dies she offers her bridal ring to God, and, removing it from her finger, interprets the impression it has left – a tiny "M" for the Virgin Mary – as a sign that all her life she has been marked as "a servant of God."

The tale is a powerful and moving one, despite a few critical sneers that have been recently raised about the "middlebrow" appeal of its modern psychologizing.[23] An early critic, Hanna Larsen, claimed that there is only one excessively melodramatic incident, and that is Erlend's death.[24] But in an age when few men ventured abroad without a weapon, the slightest altercation could turn deadly in an instant. In some ways the first meeting of Erlend and Kristin is rather more strained, as he rescues her from an attempted rape after she had become lost with a fellow convent guest during a trip to town. Kristin's childhood friend, Arne Gyrdsøn, had been killed defending her good name after another thwarted rape attempt, and two such incidents within a single year is perhaps a bit much. Given Erlend's rather feckless character, one also wonders whether he would command sufficient influence to overturn the government, and the details of the conspiracy are left rather hazy. Still, compared with such works as Scott's *Quentin Durward* (1823) or Charles Reade's *The Cloister and the Hearth* (1861), once the most widely admired historical novel of the Middle Ages and Renaissance, the advance toward plausibility is far greater than the "irreducible minimum" claimed by Peter Green for modern historical fiction.[25]

One hallmark of realism in the novel at its best is the complexity and three-dimensionality of the leading characters, and evidence for Undset's achievement in this vein can be found in the sharp disagreements that have arisen among critical interpreters in responding to *Kristin Lavransdatter*. The two lead characters will suffice as examples, especially as both serve as strongly archetypal medieval figures in a number of ways. Erlend is both the romantic lover and the warrior chieftain in the old Viking mode, albeit sadly out of place as the latter in the more domesticated fourteenth century, and some critics view him in a highly positive light. Frank, noble, and generous in spirit, courageous in battle, a born leader inspiring his men and sharing their hardships, a restless adventurer more at home on the open sea or wandering the forests and mountains than sitting by a cozy hearth, he also manages to sweep Kristin off her feet, being equally slim, handsome, charming, courteous in the chivalric manner, and somewhat dark and mysterious with an exciting whiff of scandal. Even Lavrans, though loath to bestow his daughter on such a man, later comes to like Erlend "more than he would," enjoying his ingenuous and boyish qualities. Erlend's unimpeachable loyalty is shown by his refusal to reveal the name of his fellow conspirators even under torture, and unlike Kristin he does not nurse old grudges, but gladly forgives and forgets. On his deathbed, Erlend bids his sons to remember their mother's love for them, but Gaute, the future master of Jørundgaard, declares "that you, Father, seemed to us all our days as the most courageous of men and the noblest of chieftains. We were proud to be called your sons – no less so when fortune forsook you than in your days of prosperity" (977).[26] By this interpretation Kristin is seen as the one primarily responsible for the failure of their marriage, as she attempted to remake him in the mold of her father, just as she brought order, thrift, and cleanliness to his manor at Husaby but ultimately succeeded only in driving him away.[27]

Other critics view Erlend as an essentially irresponsible figure, a boy who never manages to grow up and become a proper husband and father. Lavrans puts it nicely when he says early on that Erlend "doesn't look as if he were much good for anything but seducing women" (205). Erlend's sins are indeed numerous. Eline Ormsdatter, considerably older than himself, may well have seduced him, rather than vice versa, but he seeks only to wash his hands of her once she becomes troublesome, all but forcing her to commit suicide when she arrives with poison at Husaby. He pledges to treat Kristin honorably at their first meeting but cannot resist seducing her at the second, drawing her into a secret love affair that would have proved disastrous had Kristin conceived earlier. His family estates were once extensive, but his knack for getting into trouble had reduced them considerably even before his marriage, and his aspiration to play high politics took the rest. Like all warriors, he is basically lazy, preferring to idle away the long stretches between the few short bursts of violent action. Kristin may be wrong-headed in attempting to change him, but he makes little effort to meet her halfway. He actually enjoys living in his filthy mountain lair, for as he tells Kristin, here "I don't have to think about anything but whatever happens to cross my mind and can come and go as I like. And you know that I've always been the kind of person who can fall asleep if there's nothing to keep watch over" (205). Up on the mountain Erlend is still a free man and "no one glares at my footprints or talks behind my back" (920, 925). Given his reduced circumstances, he is probably more prescient than she in realizing that his sons will have to make their own way in the world. On his deathbed he confesses that he has not done well by them, but, as noted above, they do not agree.[28]

The character taking center stage, of course, is the eponymous heroine, who has been described as "one of the most fully realized female characters in all of literature."[29] Through Kristin's eyes the modern reader is introduced to not only the manifold aspects of the traditional feminine roles of maiden, wife, and mother in the Middle Ages, but also an even more alien realm, the vast medieval Catholic drama of human sin and redemption. Although most readers probably empathize with Kristin's joys and travails, a number of critics portray her in a highly unsympathetic light, insisting upon her multiple "betrayals" of her father, Simon, Erlend, herself, and God, as well as more than a few petty acts of "anger, cruelty, and revenge."[30] At one point Erlend tells her "you can be cruel to those you love too dearly" (532), and prime examples can be found when she reveals to her father the most sordid details of her clandestine meetings with Erlend just as he was coming to like his son-in-law, or when she ultimately drives Erlend from Jørundgaard with her self-righteous taunts about his worldly failures. Her mother was heavy and somber of spirit, as much by temperament as her secret sin, and Kristin as well seems occasionally possessed by a perverse "black residue" that wells up from within.[31] When she resorts to sorcery in order to save the life of Simon's son, digging up the turf of a poor man's grave and sacrificing a gold ring, she acts partly from a desperate love for the young boy, but she may also be rather spitefully seeking to humble Simon for his unstinting fidelity, and to bring him down a notch from his complacent superiority, by binding him with her in a sinful and disgraceful deed.[32]

There can be no question that Kristin is tenaciously willful, determined to have her own way and highly resourceful in its pursuit, but
becoming bitter and resentful when things do not turn out as she
would have them. As Erlend again tells her, "it's a sin to brood over
and dwell on the sins we have confessed to the priest and repented
before God" (562). Later he adds, "I know you're more pious than I
can ever be. And yet, Kristin, I have difficulty accepting that this is the
proper interpretation of God's words: that you should go about
storing everything away and never forgetting" (858). Not that her
intentions are malicious, for in the first instance she merely wishes to
wed the man of her choice, and once married she seeks only the best
for her family as she conceives it. Ultimately, she is perhaps a victim of
both her overwhelming passion for Erlend and her "savage maternal
devotion."[33]

Seen from a purely secular perspective, Kristin's story is tragic, a
typically inexplicable product of the complex interaction of character,
fate, and circumstance. Brunsdale describes the last book of the trilogy
as built "out of a succession of sad good-byes, an elegy not so much
for what was or what had to be, but like all the deepest human
sorrows, for what might have been."[34] From a more religious point of
view, however, Kristin's willfulness becomes emblematic of all human
self-will in opposition to the will of God, and her ultimate reconciliation with God makes her life a triumph of the medieval Catholic
faith. Brother Edvin, a traveling monk who often stayed at
Jørundgaard when Kristin was a child, once told her, "There is no
one, Kristin, who does not love and fear God. But it's because our
hearts are divided between love for God and fear of the Devil, and
love for this world and this flesh, that we are miserable in life and
death".[35] Kristin's "love for this world and this flesh" primarily takes
the form of her husband and children, whom she loves "too dear,"
shutting out her love for God. Throughout most of the novel, Kristin
is torn between "the love of God she knows she ought to feel and the
prideful love of the flesh she cannot resist."[35] She feels her sins sharply
and takes to heart the spiritual instruction she receives from Brother
Edvin and Gunnulf Nikulaussøn, Erlend's deeply learned ecclesiastical
brother. She faithfully undertakes with deep contrition the penances
and pilgrimages they prescribe, experiencing some minor spiritual
epiphanies along the way, especially during her trek to the shrine of St.
Olav. But whereas Erlend enjoys full absolution from his participation

in the formal rituals of the church, Kristin "can never say of herself that she is saved," for the tug of her earthbound and selfish desires is too great, always pulling her back into obstinate self-will and the vexing cares of her daily life.[36] She remains fully *capax dei*, but she cannot cross the threshold into full resignation to his will. A quotation from Augustine's *Confessions* appended as the motto to one scholar's study of Undset's work exemplifies well this struggle in Kristin's soul: *Fecisti nos ad te et inquietum est cor nostrum donec requiescat in te* (You have made us for yourself, and our hearts know no peace until they rest in you).[37]

Only after the death of Erlend and the arrival of her sons at young manhood is Kristin freed from her bondage to the world and able to finally understand that:

> the interpreters of God's words were right. Life on this earth was irredeemably tainted by strife; in this world, wherever people mingled, producing new descendants, allowing themselves to be drawn together by physical love and loving their own flesh, sorrows of the heart and broken expectations were bound to occur as surely as the frost appears in autumn (1056).

She also begins to understand "that her love of the world has also been a form of and desire for God – that the devil in the flesh is not alien to, but part of the divine plan."[38] As she wanders over the Dovre mountains on her way to St. Olav's, she marvels at the immensity of God's creation lying below, and the infinitesimal part an individual's sorrows and travails must play in God's larger plan. Once she accepts the divine will in place of her own, she enters a life not of joy and delight, but rather of thankfulness, humility, and strength, which will help bear her through the further trials of the Black Death. As she lies dying, her last conscious thoughts are that in some mysterious way, which she cannot fathom but surely knows to be true, "God had held her firmly in a pact which had been made for her, without her knowing it, from a love that had been poured over her" (1122). In spite of her headstrong self-will and "melancholy, earthbound heart" she had always been a servant of God:

> a stubborn, defiant maid, most often an eye-servant in her prayers and unfaithful in her heart, indolent and neglectful, impatient toward admonishments, inconstant in her deeds. And yet He had

held her firmly in His service, and under the glittering gold ring a mark had been secretly impressed upon her, showing that she was His servant, owned by the Lord and King who would now come, borne on the consecrated hands of the priest, to give her release and salvation. (1122)

As Bliksrud argues, this religious theme has probably contributed to *Kristin Lavransdatter*'s currently "unfashionable" status, but it is a refreshing change to see medieval religious faith portrayed so sympathetically. Undset was working her way towards a formal conversion to Catholicism in 1924, a highly unfashionable thing to do in turn-of-the-century, liberal-Protestant Scandinavia, and this partly explains the ring of authenticity in her description of Kristin's difficult spiritual progress. At the time of her formal conversion, Undset wrote, "Only supernatural intervention can save us from ourselves."[39] Critics have also noted several other features in Undset's life similar to that of her medieval heroine, including an idealized father, marriage to a feckless and irresponsible artist that ended in annulment, and the heavy burden that befell her of rearing alone not only their three children but also three more from a previous marriage of her husband, two of whom were mentally handicapped. Amazingly, it appears that *Kristin Lavransdatter* was written at night on cigarettes and coffee after the children had been put to bed.[40] The many photographs of her certainly reveal a rather "heavy, earthbound spirit," which is hardly surprising given the weight of her many cares and responsibilities. When Undset's younger son, Hans, asked his mother whether one of her sisters might be the model for Kristin, she supposedly replied, "I am Kristin."[41]

These autobiographical aspects undoubtedly contributed to the seemingly modern psychology of her characters frequently noted by critics and even mentioned in the Nobel Prize presentation speech.[42] But Undset also believed on principle that people in the past were fundamentally the same as in the present, with as complex and highly developed emotions as people today, especially in regard to spiritual needs and romantic passions.[43] The last two sentences of her Norwegian version of the King Arthur legend declare, "For mores and manners are always changing as time passes, and people's beliefs change and the way they think about many things. But people's hearts do not change: they remain the same through all the days, forever."[44]

However, dramatic changes in both religious beliefs and romantic relationships during the last century have certainly made the psychology of her characters far less "modern" than it was even a generation ago. Thus, the idiom into which she has translated medieval experience for the contemporary reader may already be a little dated, although this also furnishes a slight distancing effect, which coats the characters with an additional patina of otherness. Like Thackeray's predilection for the eighteenth century, there seems an almost mystical connection between Undset and medieval Norway, which perhaps bears more than a few traces of nostalgic romanticism.[45] Whether Undset's characters will seem as quaintly unreal in another fifty years as those in *Quentin Durward* or *The Cloister and the Hearth* remains to be seen. One would be very hard put today, however, to find any historical novel with more convincing representatives of medieval humanity than *Kristin Lavransdatter*.

A certain amount of modernization is inevitable in all historical fiction. Lukács addressed this problem in his seminal study, basing his discussion on Goethe and Hegel. The "necessary anachronism" found in the novels of Scott, according to Lukács:

> consists, therefore, simply in allowing his characters to express feelings and thoughts about real, historical relationships in a much clearer way than the actual men and women of the time could have done. But the content of these feelings and thoughts, their relation to their real object is always historically and socially correct. The extent to which this expression of thought and feeling outstrips the consciousness of the age is no more than is absolutely necessary for elucidating the given historical relationship.[46]

Obviously, Kristin could never have formulated her experiences and the development of her inner life with quite the same comprehensive assurance as the narrative voice of Undset's novel (the word "Freudian" often pops up in these discussions), but that does not mean that the content of those "feelings and thoughts" is not historically accurate. As mentioned above, Peter Green praises the way twentieth-century authors such as Graves and Yourcenar steeped themselves in all the available evidence and were able almost shamanistically to think their way into the essentially alien and remote mentalities of individuals in the past, but he is also the first to admit that this was partly driven by the cultural relativism of the modern era. Nineteenth-century historical novelists were unable to penetrate and represent mentalities essentially alien to their own because of their "unthinking, unquestioning, unconscious yet absolute belief" in the superiority of their "inherited ethics and institutions."[47] In the twentieth century the pendulum had swung in the opposite direction, and "our only prejudice is against having prejudices: we tolerate everyone except the intolerant,"[48] so that it may be merely a matter of replacing "one set of prejudices and *idées reçues* with another."[49]

In recent decades postmodernist critics have become skeptical of this alleged ability to step outside ourselves and grasp the essence of the historical "Other." Frederick Jameson has argued that no matter how deeply immersed in the sources we might be:

> our apparent "comprehension" of these alien texts must be haunted by the nagging suspicion that we have all the while remained locked in our present [...] and that we have never really left home at all, that our feeling of *Verstehen* is little better than a mere psychological projection, that we have somehow failed to touch the strangeness and the resistance of a reality genuinely different from our own. Yet if, as a result of such hyperbolic doubt, we decide to reverse this initial stance, and to affirm, instead and from the outset, the radical Difference of the alien object from ourselves, then at once the doors of comprehension begin to swing closed and we find ourselves separated by the whole density of own culture from objects or cultures thus initially defined as Other from ourselves and thus as irremediably inaccessible.[50]

If it seems unlikely that a Marxist interpretation of history, no matter how sensitive, will succeed in surmounting this impasse as Jameson believes, it cannot be said that anyone else has figured out a way to break the "hermeneutic circle" of alterity and identity either.[51] Unless all historical fiction is to be cast in the postmodern ironic mode of Umberto Eco's *The Name of the Rose*, the historical novelist must be accorded a certain indulgence in this regard. Henry James famously dismissed historical novels as mere humbug a century ago for precisely the same reason. Perhaps it is an inherent flaw in the genre, which partly explains why so few historical novels have achieved enduring canonical status in academic literature departments. At any rate, Undset's work has to be judged on the ground she stakes out for herself, which is traditional realism as practiced by the novelists of contemporary life in the nineteenth century, and any demand for "deconstruction," "self-reflexiveness," and "process" rather than "product" literature is itself a critical anachronism.

The same holds true for the treatment of gender relations and identity in *Kristin Lavransdatter*. Recent scholarship has tended to be sharply critical of the way Undset insists on:

> remaining a part of discursive systems in which "woman" and "man" *must* function in accordance with an ethics of self and an aesthetics of writing that do not allow for any radical transgression of the very gender-bound notions of so-called human nature, and in this case, in particular that of "woman's nature."[52]

But such a decision is surely the author's prerogative, especially in a historical novel, for as much as we might be drawn to medieval women who challenged received notions of patriarchy and gender, they were most likely to have been the exception rather than the rule. Undset was intensely aware of the deeply problematic status of young women in early twentieth-century Norway, and it forms a major theme of her modern novels. She seems to have been something of a pessimist on the possibility of harmonious concord between the sexes, or what she would call the "marriage problem," perhaps in part as a result of her own unhappy experience.[53] From this standpoint, Kristin's romantic dream drawing her to Erlend is doomed not just by her own stubborn and willful character, but by a fundamental disconnect in what women and men are seeking from each other. However much *Aucassin and Nicolette*, *The Chatelaine of Vergy*, or the tales of Marie de France might posit the near total sufficiency of romantic love for human self-realization, Chaucer, in the closing stanzas of *Troilus and Criseyde*, reminds us that such can only come from putting our trust in the love of God and not the "feigning loves" of this world, which is the lesson that Kristin ultimately learns.[54]

For Undset was steeped very deeply indeed in the historical sources for her chosen time period, above all in the great Scandinavian and Icelandic saga tradition. As mentioned above, she wrote in her later autobiographical reminiscences how reading *Njal's Saga* for the first time at the age of ten was the turning point of her entire life.[55] During the last period of her father's long illness, she read selections from the sagas to him, and he helped by explaining strange grammatical constructions or obscure old folkways. *Gunnar's Daughter* was written in direct imitation of the Icelandic sagas, and she published several translations of these in 1923. Set in the eleventh century, before Christianity had exerted much influence on Norse society, and when the thirst for revenge remained a primary motivating factor in life, *Gunnar's Daughter* is full of brutal violence as the pagan priestess Vigdis spends half a lifetime wreaking vengeance upon a man who had raped her when he failed to win her consent in marriage, spawning a host of collateral tragedies in her wake. Sherrill Harbison, in her introduction to the recent Penguin reissue, calls it "a gripping psychological novel, a terse, swiftly moving tale of naive trust, betrayal, violation, and vengeance."[56] Bayerschmidt is more typical when he judges it less successful than *Kristin Lavransdatter* because Undset's penchant for minute descriptive detail and acute psychological analysis does not mesh well with the bald, terse, and objective style of the saga writers, who leave the audience to visualize the scenes and draw the moral conclusions. Undset had not yet adequately integrated and interpreted the saga material into her own more modern manner.[57]

As many critics have noted, it is precisely Undset's power of description and the small but telling insights she offers into the most mundane operations of everyday life that generate the vivid and palpable historical realism of *Kristin Lavransdatter*. Unlike the antiquarian novels of the nineteenth century, these descriptions do not take the form of set-pieces tacked on or slipped into the narrative, but rather are minutely interwoven with the story as it unfolds in a seamless web. To be sure, Undset benefited enormously from nearly a century of additional historical and archaeological research in these matters, including the work of her father, but the skill with which she deploys this knowledge of the deep past is largely unprecedented.

The central focus, naturally, is the domestic sphere of hearth and home, whether at Jørundgaard or Husaby. Kristin's arrival at the latter as a newly wedded bride affords the occasion for a particularly striking picture of a medieval Norwegian nobleman's agricultural estate, albeit one that was somewhat old and decrepit after having suffered from neglectful management and household economy. There were two courtyards, a smaller one surrounded by the various structures used as living quarters, storehouses, cookhouse, weaving house, and brewhouse, and beyond that a larger one flanked by the farm buildings, including the stables, cowsheds, sheep-pens, and barns. All were made from large fir-wood logs with a thatched roof, except for the main hall, which at Husaby was of stone and looked "more like the interior of a church or a king's hall than the hall of a manor" (300). Down the center of the hall ran the hearth, with enough space for several fires in colder weather, although the lack of chimneys or other proper ventilation beyond a vent in the roof meant that the room inevitably filled with smoke. The high seat was placed against the east end with a table and bench in front of it, while wide benches ran along the walls to the right and left. Additional tables were set up for meals, and here everyone gathered in the mornings and evenings, although at Husaby the servants retired to their sleeping quarters after the evening meal, unlike at Jørundgaard where all remained together until bedtime, mending their clothes or tools, drinking from the ale keg, taking turns singing or playing the harp, and recounting tales of high romance and knightly adventures, or "bawdy, ribald stories from the sagas" (343).

On Kristin's first night in her new home, the hall was decked out in lordly splendor to receive both her and the many guests, with candles burning everywhere, the high seat covered in velvet, tables groaning with precious vessels and platters, and weapons and shields hanging on the walls between the draped tapestries. Tucked into the corners next to the high seat were two boxed beds, and though the one prepared for Kristin and Erlend was spread with "silk-covered pillows, a linen sheet, and the finest blankets and furs," she could not help noticing that "underneath lay filthy, rotting straw" with "lice in the bedclothes and in the magnificent black bear pelt that lay on top" (302). In the days that followed she discovered caked dirt and soot behind the costly tapestries, nearly empty storerooms and stalls, a loft half-filled with flax from several years' harvests left untouched, and a huge pile of "ancient, unwashed, and stinking wool, some in sacks and some lying loose all around, full of tiny brown worm eggs" from moths and maggots (302). The animals were mostly old and poorly cared for, the cattle "feeble, gaunt, scabrous, and chafed," although the horses were magnificent and well-groomed. Kristin quickly set to work, restoring cleanliness, good order, and proper husbandry at the estate, as had been practiced at Jørundgaard, where similar domestic arrangements were conducted on a smaller scale, but solid comfort still prevailed.

A good bit of the novel is taken up by the marriage negotiations of the various characters, including obviously Kristin herself, illuminating the essentially kinship-based and customary nature of such social contracts in medieval Norway. Although as Erlend's brother Gunnulf observes, "the Church has created laws regarding marriage," in the final analysis it was primarily a matter for the families to work out among themselves, and "we priests must not marry man and maiden against the will of their kinsmen" (387). The Church insisted on the consent of the betrothed, but it could be difficult for young girls especially to stand against the will of their fathers. In Kristin's case, she was already engaged for some time to Simon Andressøn before she met Erlend, and it was a delicate business for this long-standing and sensible agreement between neighbors to be dissolved without ill-will, which indeed never fully evaporated even after Simon married Kristin's younger sister, Ramborg. Luckily for Kristin, Lavrans was well-known for being highly indulgent toward his womenfolk.

Considerably more dramatic was the elopement of Kristin's son, Gaute, and his future wife, Jofrid. Her father, Helge Duk, was a rich and powerful man, and Gaute's abduction, however willing on Jofrid's part, was an offense unredeemable by the mere payment of fines and could result in unconditional banishment, if the aggrieved party demanded it (1026). Jofrid was already pregnant, and her marriage with Gaute was solemnized upon his arrival back home by nothing more than his oath: "Now you have seen the woman who will be my wife here at Jørundgaard. This woman and no other – I swear this before God, our Lord, and on my Christian faith" (1029). Not until after Jofrid had given birth to a son did Helge Duk finally appear at the head of a great procession of family, friends, retainers, and the local sheriff to demand his rights. Gaute had similarly collected a large crowd of his own kinsmen with their armed men, along with his friends from the neighboring countryside. Fortunately, negotiations rather than fighting ensued, and after a good bit of haggling, terms were agreed upon. Gaute offered "sixteen marks in gold for Jofrid's honor and taking her by force," which was far beyond his means to pay, but it was canceled out by Jofrid's dowry from her father. Ultimately, Jofrid brought little more to the marriage than the personal effects she had carried with her when she eloped, but now that she would be lawfully married and her son fully legitimate, their inheritance rights were restored, and in return Gaute "gave her documents for almost all that he owned as betrothal and wedding gifts." The next day Jofrid made her first appearance in the church after giving birth, "honored as if she were a married woman." The "beautiful and grand" ceremony itself was held a month later, and people judged that everything had been brought to "the most honorable of ends" (1048–50).

Although domestic affairs predominate in the novel, there are abundant views of the wider world as well. Erlend's conspiracy introduces an element of high politics, which the reader learns only indirectly as Kristin hears it from the men of her family. During most of her lifetime, the king of Norway was Magnus VII (1319–43), who inherited the thrones of both Norway and Sweden while still a boy. Independent councils were set up to rule the two newly joined kingdoms under the regency of his widowed mother, Lady Ingeborg. She soon became involved in a number of political intrigues with her Danish lover, Sir Knut Porse, whom she later married, and she was ultimately removed from power first in Sweden and then Norway. Young Magnus, meanwhile, was growing up in Sweden, and the feeling began to grow that Norwegian interests were being subordinated to Swedish ones. As a kinsman of Erlend puts it, "For far too long we up here in the north have had to settle for smelling the soup cooking while we spoon up cold cabbage" (422). Even worse, it was rumored that the king had been led into the most "unmentionable" of sins by his Swedish tutor, presumably homosexual relations (534). In 1330 Magnus turned sixteen and was declared of age to rule. He stayed on in Sweden and continued to neglect Norwegian affairs, while not neglecting to demand money and supplies to further his ambitious plans for detaching the province Skaane (Scania) in what is now southern Sweden from Danish rule. Erlend's entirely fictional conspiracy was part of an effort to detach the kingdom of Norway from the dual monarchy, placing Ingeborg's son, Haakon, from her marriage with Knut Porse, on the throne. If successful, the result would probably have been broadly welcomed among the Norwegian nobility, but after the plot is exposed through Erlend's negligence, he is left to suffer the consequences alone. Although tortured, he refuses to reveal his fellow conspirators, and the intercession of his powerful friends and kinsmen manages only to preserve his life. Almost all his former lands and offices, including the estate at Husaby, are stripped from him, and he is forced to retire to Kristin's ancestral manor at Jørundgaard.

Looming even larger throughout the novel, however, is the wider world of medieval religion. After the birth of her first child, conceived in sin before her formal marriage to Erlend, Kristin makes a pilgrimage to Christ Church cathedral in Nidaros as an act of penance, walking the full twenty miles in bare feet from Husaby and carrying her child in her arms all the way. When she arrived, she was overwhelmed by the cathedral's architectural magnificence, the blooming profusion of sculpted figures, spires, and towers: "a reflection of the splendor of God's kingdom." Three times she walked around the church praying and nearly "sank to the ground beneath her sin." The interior was even more dazzling, with its soaring pillars "furrowed like ancient trees," the animals and people that "frolicked in the stone foliage," the dizzying height of the arches and vaults, and the deep hues cast by the stained glass windows. A service was underway as she entered, and Kristin fell to her knees: "The song cut through her like a blinding light. Now she saw how deep in the dust she lay" (401). Looking up beyond the altar, she beheld the gleaming shrine of Saint Olav, the king who had converted the kingdom to Christianity, and imagined how on Resurrection Day, "the lid would spring open and he would rise up," striding forth through the church with axe in hand. Then all "the dead yellow skeletons" would also rise from beneath "the stone floor, from the earth outside, from all the cemeteries of Norway" to be clothed in flesh anew, crowding about the saint and begging for his intercession with God, Kristin herself among them (402, 406).

At opposite ends of her life Kristin spends a brief period at two very different nunneries. The convent of Nonneseter in Oslo, where she went to stay before her proposed marriage to Simon Andressøn, was an amply appointed refuge of pious comfort, and a large number of well-born maidens lived for a year or two there "to learn to obey and to serve" before they would be "charged with giving orders and commands" (102). Kristin was overwhelmed on her arrival by the gray stone buildings, paved courtyards, and large glass windows, and she was equally impressed by the midday meal in the great hall, where all the sisters and maidens showed "such elegant comportment" (103). The very best food and drink were laid out in abundance, but "everyone took only modest portions, using only the tips of their fingers to help themselves from the platters," and "they ate so carefully that not a sound could be heard" (103). Nor were the sisters entirely cut off from interaction with the bustling town around them, for the abbess and several of the eldest sisters occasionally attended civic events, such as the first day of the farmers' guild celebrations, and the reader catches a glimpse of medieval town life when Kristin and another resident maiden go shopping for some shoes. All this forms a striking contrast to the convent of Rein outside of Nidaros, where Kristin lived her last days. The sisters there were "truly dead to the world" (1084), and none had set foot outside the cloister walls in years. Solemn austerity ruled, and meals were taken in silence, as one of the sisters read from a devotional text. The nuns themselves worked in the flax fields and prepared the linen cloth for which the convent was famous. The poor came for charity every day, "the ill, the crippled, and the leprous" among them (1091), and all were diligently attended to, pouring out their sorrows and troubles in the nuns' patient ears.

Nor is the full spectrum of male religious experience neglected. The simple but devout traveling monk Brother Edvin provided Kristin's earliest introduction to the mysteries of the faith during his occasional visits at Jørundgaard. Although Kristin's pious parents were always generous in offering hospitality to religious itinerants, Edvin insisted on sleeping in the cowshed because of the lice in his clothing, which he cherished more than any scourge for chastising his "proud hide" (70). Later Kristin developed a close relationship with Sira Eiliv, the parish priest of Husaby, for "with him she could talk as much as she liked about her children; the priest was willing to discuss with her all the small bits of news that bored Erlend and drove him from the room" (437). Sira Eiliv was also fond of good food and drink, and Kristin often prepared special dishes for him, while he gave her gardening advice and read to the family from the lives of the saints and martyrs. Erlend's Paris-educated brother, Gunnulf, rises to considerable ecclesiastical prominence in the service of the archbishop of Nidaros but remains tortured by doubts regarding his spiritual worthiness. He describes at length to Kristin the pilgrimage to Rome he undertook in his youth and his visits to the catacombs and the "caves and oratories" of the first Christians, with their attendant relics cherished by the resident monks (447). Eventually, he relinquishes his privileged position and dons the robes of a friar to take the gospel to the half-wild and still heathen peoples of the north, partly as a way of testing his religious vocation (452, 495).

Although the Christian faith had sunk deep roots in Norway in the three centuries since its introduction, vestiges of former pagan beliefs and practices still endured. In the opening pages of the novel, Kristin wanders off while on an expedition to the mountains with her father and spies an elf-maiden by a stream. During a year of bad weather and crop failure, some of the local men around Jørundgaard take to sacrificing boars and cats before "great white stones that were shaped like the secret parts of human beings," forcing the parish priest to smash the stones flat (251). Erlend's kinswoman, Lady Aashild, who lived in the mountain croft at Haugen during Kristin's youth, was regarded by the people around Jørundgaard as a sorceress, and she taught Kristin some of her alleged black arts. When Simon Andressøn's only son is deathly ill, Kristin secretly resorts to one in order to save his life, stealing a bit of turf from the grave of a poor man who had been a stranger in the parish and leaving in return her grandmother's betrothal ring, a piece of gold that had been passed down three generations. At the boy's bedside she covers his face and chest with a linen cloth and places the strip of sod on top. When he shows signs of life again the next morning, she casts the linen and sod into the fire. Worst of all, though, is the effort of the men from Nidaros to appease the wrath of Hel, the plague giantess, by burying alive an outcast beggar boy named "Tore" as a human sacrifice when the Black Death reaches their vicinity. Kristin and a group of nuns from the convent of Rein go out and successfully intervene, but this leads Kristin to bury the boy's mother as well, who has been lying dead for over two weeks. During the horrifying recovery of the putrid and decayed body, she becomes infected herself and soon dies.

Finally, a few words must be said about Undset's depiction of the natural world and its deep interpenetration with everyday life. Few historical novels can match this sensual apprehension of the medieval landscape, from the smallest and most delicate flowers to the sweeping vistas of mountain and sky. Through her words the reader sees, feels, hears, and smells this landscape in a way that is hopelessly irretrievable in our modern climate-controlled and sanitized environments. The inner being of her characters often seems to well up from the clouds, rain, mud, and snow, or the smiling verdant fields and bright sunshine, whether on the broad rolling plateau of Jørundgaard, or in the narrow valley of Husaby, perched between the fjord below and the mountains above.[58] The following passage depicting a particularly cold winter is typical:

For those who were waiting for the redemption of spring, it seemed as if it would never come. The days grew long and bright, and the valley lay in a haze of thawing snow while the sun shone. But frost was still in the air, and the heat had no power. At night it froze hard; great cracking sounds came from the ice, a rumbling issued from the mountains, and the wolves howled and the foxes yipped all the way down in the village, as if it were midwinter. People scraped off the bark for livestock, but they were perishing by the dozens in their stalls. No one knew when it would end. (236)

Several recent critics have complained of Undset's lack of "style," especially her "readable but pedestrian" prose and slow narrative pace, which makes "reading her an experience somewhere between mild appreciation and mild boredom."[59] Obviously, it is difficult for the non-Norwegian reader to judge her prose through translation. According to Otto Reinert, the characters speak "essentially modern Norwegian," but the debt Undset's language owes to the vocabulary and syntax and cadences of Old Norse is never intrusive, and "the archaizing modulations work. They sound authentic, not strange."[60] For many years the only available English version had been that of Archer and Scott, and they employ a number of noun–verb syntactical inversions and archaisms such as "methinks," "forsooth," and "it boots not" to impart a heightened medieval flavor in a manner typical of Victorian historical fiction.[61] The new translation by Tiina Nunnally evokes a plainer style, closer to Undset's original. Nunnally tells us she was intent on "removing the soot and grime" that had "muddied and obscured" Undset's "lucid prose, hiding her true voice [...]. My goal was to match her clear and straightforward style and to make her characters sound as natural in English as they do in Norwegian." She readily admits that "Undset is not a great stylist [...] although she can be quite lyrical in her descriptions of the beautiful mountain landscape in Norway."[62] The following two comparative passages from the first volume, *The Wreath*, will serve as a good example:

> Ay, now I see the word that has gone about concerning this little maid of yours was no wise too great – a lily-rose she is, and looks as should the child of a knightly man. Mild eyes hath she too.
>
> (Archer and Scott, 9)

> Now I see that the rumors did not exaggerate about your little

maiden. She's a lily, and she looks like the child of a knight.
Gentle eyes she has as well. (Nunnally, 11)

In his introduction to the new combined deluxe edition, Brad
Leithauser confesses that despite his enthusiastic admiration for
Nunnally's translation, which "unquestionably brings us closer to the
heart of the book," he still retains "a lingering fondness" for the earlier
rendition.[63] However, it seems likely that more than a few English
readers over the years have probably begun the book in the older
translation and quit in frustration over its "pseudo-antique language,"
as a friend of Thom Satterlee reports.[64] Nunnally's fresh new version
certainly eliminates that hurdle, as it could hardly be more accessible.

As far as narrative pace is concerned, that is mostly a matter of
taste and fashion. Some critics, such as Alrick Gustafson, claim that
the leisurely narrative movement is actually one of the novel's great
strengths, endowing it with "a quiet, deliberate solemnity." At times
this "stateliness" bursts into a "blazing intensity" in individual
episodes, but then recedes back into its unhurried way, "as unhurried
as the ceaseless processes of nature and eternity and God." Given the
novel's elevated and rather somber moral theme, "any other narrative
tempo would be inconceivable."[65] According to Walter Allen, both
Kristin Lavransdatter and *The Master of Hestviken* (1925–27), Undset's
later four-part novel set in the eleventh century, are "written gradually,
laboriously, and with a patience which soaks into the spirits of their
readers. They neither excite nor entertain: they win our attention inch
by inch; appealing, not to our sense of the sublime, but to our knowledge of the normal."[66] It must be admitted, however, that a thousand-
page novel is a tall order for most readers today, in a world where,
surrounded by every conceivable labor-saving device, we all have less
time than ever.

If *Kristin Lavransdatter* is not read quite as much as it used to be
outside of Scandinavia, perhaps Nunnally's translation will stimulate
fresh interest, endowing the tale with a long life well into the
twenty-first century. Since the heyday of Scott and Dumas, only a
handful of historical novels have managed to break out of their seemingly inherent literary marginality. In terms of a larger overall evaluation, the comparison that came most readily to the early critics was
with Tolstoy's *War and Peace*, above all for the totality of Undset's
vision in the sense used by Lukács.[67] Of course, Tolstoy was writing of

events a mere generation or two before his own time, while Undset was recreating a world many centuries in the past. Even if one might wish to demur a bit from such a lofty comparison, there can be no doubt that *Kristin Lavransdatter* is unquestionably a pioneer of modern historical realism, and surely "one of the greatest historical novels of all time," perhaps even "first among novels dealing with the Middle Ages."[68]

NOTES

1. Georg Lukács, *The Historical Novel*, trans. Hannah and Stanley Mitchell (Lincoln: University of Nebraska Press, 1962).

2. Ernest E. Leisy, *The American Historical Novel* (Norman: University of Oklahoma Press, 1949), 18–19; and Peter Green, "Aspects of the Historical Novel," *Transactions of the Royal Society of Literature* 3rd series 31 (1962): 35–60. Green's paper was originally read to the Society in 1958.

3. The original Norwegian titles are *Kransen* (1920), *Husfrue* (1921), and *Korset* (1922). They were translated into English by Charles Archer and John S. Scott as *The Bridal Wreath* (1923), *The Mistress of Husaby* (1925), and *The Cross* (1927). They first appeared together as a three-volume *Kristin Lavransdatter* set in 1927 (the Lillehammer edition), and a new combined Nobel Prize edition was issued in 1929, all from Alfred A. Knopf of New York.

4. A. H. Winsnes, *Sigrid Undset: A Study in Christian Realism*, trans. R. G. Foote (New York: Sheed and Ward, 1953), 100–01; and Mitzi Brunsdale, *Sigrid Undset: Chronicler of Norway* (New York: St. Martin's Press, 1988), 66.

5. Letter to Dea Hedburg, a pen-pal confidant of Undset from 1898, quoted by Sherrill Harbison in her introduction to *Gunnar's Daughter*, trans. Arthur G. Chater (New York: Penguin Books, 1998), x.

6. Harbison, introduction to *Gunnar's Daughter*, xi–xii. The manuscript was an early draft of what later became *The Master of Hestviken*.

7. The novel was chosen as the Book-of-the-Month Club main selection in February 1929. Interestingly, the chairman of the selection board, Henry Seidel Canby, a distinguished professor from Yale, was not enthusiastic about it, as noted in Charles Lee, *The Hidden Public: The Story of the Book-of-the-Month Club* (Garden City, NJ: Doubleday & Company, 1958), 163.

8. The tetralogy was originally published in two halves of two books apiece, *Olav Audunssøn i Hestviken* (1925) and *Olav Audunssøn og hans born*

(1927). These were translated into English by Arthur G. Chater and published by Alfred A. Knopf as *The Axe* (1928), *The Snake Pit* (1929), *In the Wilderness* (1929), and *The Son Avenger* (1930). The combined edition, entitled *The Master of Hestviken*, appeared from Knopf in 1932.

9. Brad Leithauser, "Introduction," *Kristin Lavransdatter*, trans. Tiina Nunnally (New York: Penguin, 2005), xii. Originally published as "Love in a Cold Climate," *New York Review of Books* 52.15 (6 October 2005): 43–45.

10. Nunnally's translations appeared as *The Wreath* (1997), *The Wife* (1999), and *The Cross* (2000). The third volume won the PEN/Book-of-the-Month Club Translation Award in 2001. The combined edition was published in 2005, as cited in the note above. Nunnally has translated numerous other works of Nordic literature by such authors as Hans Christian Anderson, Knut Hamsun, and Jens Peter Jacobsen.

11. Ellen Rees, "Dreaming of the Medieval in *Kristin Lavransdatter* and *Trollsyn*," *Scandinavian Studies* 75 (2003): 399–416 (400). Rees principally addresses the film, which covers only the first book of the trilogy, ending with Kristin's marriage to Erlend Nikulaussøn.

12. Rees, "Dreaming of the Medieval," 412. The Jørundgard website address is <http://www. jorundgard.no/>, and the annual festival can be found at <http://www.kristindagene.no/>.

13. For works in English see Marie Maman, *Sigrid Undset in America: An Annotated Bibliography and Research Guide* (Lanham, MD: Scarecrow Press, 2000).

14. Claudia Berguson, "Questions of Narrative Authority and Authenticity in Sigrid Undset's *Kristin Lavransdatter*," *Edda* 4 (2005): 344–56.

15. Christine Hamm, "The Maiden and the Knight: Gender, Body and Melodrama in Sigrid Undset's *Kristin Lavransdatter*," *Scandinavica* 45 (2006): 5–27.

16. Liv Bliksrud, "Norsk utakt: Sigrid Undset i litteraturvitenskapen," *Norsk Litteraturvitenskapelig Tidsskrift* 8.1 (2005): 72–81, as noted in Hamm, "The Maiden and the Knight," 5.

17. Otto Reinert, "Unfashionable *Kristin Lavransdatter*," *Scandinavian Studies* 71 (1999): 67–80 (67–68).

18. Reinert, "Unfashionable *Kristin Lavransdatter*," 69.

19. Carl Bayerschmidt, *Sigrid Undset* (New York: Twayne Publishers, 1970), 111; Victor Vinde, *Sigrid Undset, a Nordic Moralist* (Seattle: University of Washington Press, 1930), 25–26; and Harry Slochower, *Three Ways of Modern Man* (New York: International Publishers, 1937), 44–45.

20. Bayerschmidt, *Sigrid Undset*, 109–11.

21. Leithauser, "Introduction," ix.

22. Bayerschmidt, *Sigrid Undset*, 102.

23. Reinert, "Unfashionable *Kristin Lavransdatter*," 73.

24. Hannah A. Larsen, "Sigrid Undset," *American-Scandinavian Review* (June and July, 1929): 406–14 (410).

25. Green, "Aspects of the Historical Novel," 50.

26. Sigrid Undset, *Kristin Lavransdatter*, trans. Tiina Nunnally (New York: Penguin, 2005). All quotations from the novel in this paper are taken from the latest combined edition, and henceforth will be indicated by page numbers in parentheses.

27. Sister Margaret Dunn, *Paradigms and Paradoxes in the Life and Letters of Sigrid Undset* (Lanham, MD: University Press of America, 1994), 15; Andrew Lytle, *Kristin: A Reading* (Columbia: University of Missouri Press, 1992), 48–54, 60, 68; and Brunsdale, *Sigrid Undset*, 77–78.

28. For the critics taking this predominantly negative line, see Winsnes, *Sigrid Undset*, 117–18, 121, and Walter Gore Allen, "The Catholic: Sigrid Undset," in his *Renaissance in the North* (London: Sheed and Ward, 1946), 41. For a mixed assessment see Reinert, "Unfashionable *Kristin Lavransdatter*," 70–72, and Larsen, "Sigrid Undset," 408.

29. Mary Reichardt, *Exploring Catholic Literature* (Lanham, MD: Rowan & Littlefield, 2003), 100.

30. Brunsdale, *Sigrid Undset*, 68–69; and Maura Boland, "Rediscovering Sigrid Undset," *Commonweal* 107/20 (7 November 1980): 620–23.

31. Dunn, *Paradigms and Paradoxes*, 11.

32. Dunn, *Paradigms and Paradoxes*, 14; and Reinert, "Unfashionable *Kristin Lavransdatter*," 72.

33. Brunsdale, *Sigrid Undset*, 70.

34. Brunsdale, *Sigrid Undset*, 73.

35. Mitzi Brunsdale, "A Lifetime of Penance for an Hour of Happiness: The Life and Fiction of Sigrid Undset," in Deal Wyath Hudson, ed., *Sigrid Undset on Saints and Sinners* (San Francisco, CA: Ignatius Press, 1993), 135.

36. Winsnes, *Sigrid Undset*, 122.

37. Eugenia Kielland, *Ord och Bild* (Oslo: Aschehoug, 1926), cited in Winsnes, *Sigrid Undset*, 113; and Bayerschmidt, *Sigrid Undset*, 91. The quotation is from Book I of the *Confessions*.

38. Reinert, "Unfashionable *Kristin Lavransdatter*," 77.

39. Colman McCarthy, "Sigrid Undset," *Critic* 32 (1974): 59–64 (60); and Bayerschmidt, *Sigrid Undset*, 38–39.

40. Brunsdale, *Sigrid Undset*, 64, and "A Lifetime of Penance," 122–23, 128, 133.

41. Dunn, *Paradigms and Paradoxes*, xii.

42. Available at <http://nobelprize.org/nobel_prizes/literature/laureates/1928/press.html>.

43. Larsen, "Sigrid Undset," 13–14.

44. Sigrid Undset, *Fortellinger om Kong Arthur og ridderne av det runde bord* (1915). The passage is cited and translated in Reinert, "Unfashionable *Kristin Lavransdatter*," 69.

45. Boland, "Rediscovering Sigrid Undset," 621–22.

46. Lukács, *The Historical Novel*, 63.

47. Green, "Aspects of the Historical Novel," 42.

48. Green, "Aspects of the Historical Novel," 48.

49. Green, "Aspects of the Historical Novel," 50.

50. Frederick Jameson, "Marxism and Historicism," *New Literary History* 11 (1979): 41–73 (43–44).

51. Davis D. Day, "Monty Python and the Medieval Other," in Kevin J. Harty, ed., *Cinema Arthuriana: Essays on Arthurian Film* (New York: Garland Publishing, 1991), 83–92 (84–85). See also Lee Patterson, "On the Margin: Postmodernism, Ironic History, and Medieval Studies," *Speculum* 65 (1990): 87–108; and David Aers, "A Whisper in the Ear of Early Modernists; or, Reflections on Literary Critics Writing the 'History of the Subject,'" in David Aers, ed., *Culture and History, 1350–1600: Essays on English Communities, Identities and Writers* (Detroit, MI: Wayne State University Press, 1992), 177–202.

52. Pål Bjørby, "Recent Trends in Sigrid Undset Criticism," *Scandinavian Studies* 58 (1986): 308–12 (308).

53. Hamm, "The Maiden and the Knight," 10.

54. For the most readily accessible text with this quote, see the Penguin edition (Harmondsworth: Penguin, 1971), 308. This edition is rendered into modern English by Nevill Coghill, and the precise translation is in the singular "feigning love," while the original is "feynede loves." For the latter, see the abridged edition of *Troilus and Criseyde* edited by D. S. Brewer and L. E. Brewer (London: Routledge and Kegan Paul, 1969), 100.

55. Brunsdale, *Sigrid Undset*, 11; and Bayerschmidt, *Sigrid Undset*, 62–63.

56. Harbison, introduction to *Gunnar's Daughter*, vii–viii.

57. Bayerschmidt, *Sigrid Undset*, 62–67; and Brunsdale, *Sigrid Undset*, 124–25.

58. Alrick Gustafson, "Christian Ethics in a Pagan World: Sigrid Undset," *Six Scandinavian Novelists* (Princeton, NJ: Princeton University Press, 1940), 319–23.

59. Reinert, "Unfashionable *Kristin Lavransdatter*," 67.

60. Reinert, "Unfashionable *Kristin Lavransdatter*," 68–69.

61. Thom Satterlee, "*Kristin Lavransdatter I: The Wreath* by Sigrid Undset," *Translation Review* 57 (1999): 39–41.

62. Tiina Nunnally, "Removing the Grime from Scandinavian Classics: Translation as Art Restoration," *World Literature Today* 80.5 (2006): 38–42.

63. Leithauser, "Introduction," xv.
64. Satterlee, "*Kristin Lavransdatter I*," 41.
65. Gustafson, "Christian Ethics in a Pagan World," 324.
66. Allen, "The Catholic: Sigrid Undset," 38.
67. Lytle, *Kristin: A Reading*, vii–viii, xi; Boland, "Rediscovering Sigrid Undset," 622; and Vinde, *Sigrid Undset*, 35.
68. Gustafson, "Christian Ethics in a Pagan World," 311.

J. K. Rowling's Medieval Bestiary[1]

Gail Orgelfinger

The world of J. K. Rowling's seven Harry Potter novels is inhabited by not only witches, wizards, and Muggles, who are ordinary folk generally oblivious to and protected from magic, but also a vast assortment of real and imaginary creatures.[2] Young wizards bring owls, cats, and the odd rat to Hogwarts School of Wizardry and Witchcraft, where Harry enrolls at the age of eleven. In The Care of Magical Creatures classes, Keeper Rubeus Hagrid's misplaced love of the exotic leads him to domesticate a hippogriff and engage in dangerous breeding experiments. In Professor McGonagall's Transfiguration classes, students begin by changing porcupines into pincushions or tortoises into teapots. A very few wizards have the ability to become *Animagi*, and can transform at will into a particular animal.[3] And Professor McGonagall herself initially appears in the books as a tabby cat (*SS*, 2).

Of course, some of these references to real and imaginary creatures derive from folklore about magic, but Rowling's general conformance with Christian doctrine in characterizing the struggle between good and evil[4] also invokes the medieval literary tradition of the bestiary, which is perhaps best defined as "a compilation of pseudo-science in which […] fantastic descriptions of real and imaginary animals, birds, and even stones were used to illustrate points of Christian dogma and morals."[5] The specific model for the medieval bestiaries was the fourth-century Greek *Physiologus*, which derived its descriptions from the writings of earlier Greek and Latin authors such as Aristotle and Pliny the Elder. The bestiaries are often illustrated and typically contain around fifty chapters, each beginning with a biblical quotation, continuing with a *précis* of a creature's purported natural history, and ending with an allegorical interpretation of the beast, chiefly according to the exegetical or interpretative tradition of the Church Fathers' commentaries on the first six books of the Old Testament, especially Genesis and Exodus.[6]

In 2001, Rowling overtly signaled both her interest in and knowledge of this rich tradition of animal symbolism by publishing the Hogwarts schoolbook *Fantastic Beasts and Where to Find Them* (under the pseudonym Newt Scamander).[7] Though this text does not include overt moralization, and features a number of creatures that are Rowling's own invention, it does include a number of the same creatures as do the medieval bestiaries. By doing so, it concomitantly underscores the symbolic potential of the bestiaries to serve as an index for the many animals that either chart Harry's human potential to combat evil, or foreshadow the Christ-like sacrifice that enables him to conquer evil by the end of the series, or both.[8] By understanding the symbolism of the bestiaries, we can perhaps better appreciate how Harry's interaction with animals or their avatars reveals his innate mettle or highlights his unpreparedness, endows him with crucial powers for fighting his reptilian nemesis Lord Voldemort, and gives him important allies against the so-called Dark Lord and other foes.

The chief exemplar of such an alliance is perhaps the Weasley family. In most bestiaries the weasel can defeat the basilisk, which is a form of serpent that has a paralyzing gaze and is sometimes depicted with the head of a rooster.[9] Voldemort unleashes a basilisk in the second book of the series, *Harry Potter and the Chamber of Secrets*, and Ginny Weasley is one of its victims. In fact, none of the Weasleys singlehandedly or collectively defeats that basilisk. But the Weasleys do lend Harry direct moral support for that defeat, and, except for a brief desertion by Harry's best friend Ron Weasley in the last book, they do stand by him throughout the rest of the series. That is to say, they contribute to a textual pairing between Rowling's work and the bestiaries that not only plays a significant part in her general characterization of good and evil but also promotes, even as it complicates, her identification of Harry with Christ.[10]

Especially in retrospect, knowledge of the bestiary tradition deepens, while it answers, such questions as "Is There Christian Meaning Hidden in the Bestselling [Potter] Books?" which is the subtitle of John Granger's *Looking for God in Harry Potter*.[11] Although

Granger and other authors who purport "to help [...] determine if [the Potter series] is an edifying message for Christians"[12] do not specifically cite bestiaries, they do note, as Granger puts it, that animals can embody "the various qualities, actions, and promises of Christ."[13] And in claiming that the Potter books "foster a Christian perspective" by "baptizing the imagination,"[14] Granger borrows a concept and a phrase from C. S. Lewis – the renowned scholar of the Middle Ages whose Chronicles of Narnia famously deploy animals as Christian allegories. But Rowling's Christian references differ in form, tone, and degree from those of Lewis, as the Potter series invokes bestiaries more overtly and complexly than do the Narnia books. For example, while Lewis's lion Aslan adheres to the mainstream medieval tradition in which the "king of beasts" represents solely the virtues of the "King of Kings," Rowling draws more comprehensively from the bestiaries. Not only does she associate a leonine Harry with Christ-like attributes, but she also associates the young wizard with certain negative attributes of the lion's principal foe, the serpent.

Those reptilian associations with Harry begin before he even knows such a place as Hogwarts exists, when we learn that he can understand and talk to snakes. During a trip to a zoo in honor of his cousin Dudley Dursley's birthday, Harry expresses sympathy for a sluggish boa constrictor in its cage. As a result of his as-yet-unrevealed magical powers, Harry's unspoken address to the snake causes it to change places with Dudley, and the boa thanks Harry as it makes its escape. This unusual linguistic ability, which Harry does not notice at the time, marks the young wizard as a Parselmouth and represents a gift his peers fearfully associate with Voldemort. As Harry matures, he not only speaks and understands Parseltongue but also seems – at first in his nightmares and later in an alternate but simultaneous reality – to inhabit the deadly serpent Nagini, Voldemort's constant companion. It is troubling that the boy whose parents were murdered by Voldemort should manifest this affinity with evil. But early on we learn that Harry and Voldemort are further linked by another important bestiary creature.

Before embarking on the train for his first year at Hogwarts, Harry visits Diagon Alley to purchase school supplies, including his copy of *Fantastic Beasts*, and his wand, which is more than a matter of simply choosing the latest model off the shelf. Mr. Ollivander, the proprietor of the shop, tells Harry, "It's really the wand that chooses the wizard" (*SS*, 82). These words, although we may not know it then, are prophetic of the final downfall of the Dark Lord (another name for Voldemort), yet not for the reasons hinted at throughout the first six books. Famously, only Harry's wand and Voldemort's include a phoenix feather. As Ollivander explains, "It so happens that the phoenix whose tail feather is in your wand, gave another feather – just one other. [...] its brother gave you that scar" (*SS*, 85). (Harry has a distinctive lightning-bolt-shaped scar on his forehead from the wound he suffered when Voldemort attempted to kill him as an infant.)

The phoenix to which Ollivander refers is Fawkes, the companion of Hogwarts' headmaster Albus Dumbledore. Its most striking attribute is its ability to regenerate itself; as described in *Fantastic Beasts*, the phoenix is:

> a magnificent, swan-sized, scarlet bird with a long golden tail, beak, and talons [...] [that] lives to an immense age as it can regenerate, bursting into flames when its body begins to fail and rising again from the ashes. [...] [Its] song is magical; it is reputed to increase the courage of the pure of heart and to strike fear into the hearts of the impure. Phoenix tears have powerful healing properties." (32)

To the standard bestiary accounts of the phoenix, which emphasize its symbolic representation of Christ's resurrection, Rowling has added the power of its song (an element of the classical tradition on which the bestiaries were based)[15] and the healing property of its tears. Fawkes' ability to help Harry in *Sorcerer's Stone* and other books in the series lies largely in its inspirational song because, at this stage, the twelve-year-old Harry is clever and courageous but cannot rely on those characteristics alone to combat the power of Voldemort. For example, in *Harry Potter and the Chamber of Secrets*, before Tom Marvolo Riddle (the schoolboy who grows up to be Lord Voldemort) summons the basilisk and after he claims he will become "the greatest sorcerer in all the world" (314), Harry defies Tom by reminding him that Dumbledore was and remains a greater wizard, whereupon a strain of "unearthly" music enters the chamber and makes Harry's "heart feel as though it was swelling to twice its normal size" (*CS*, 315). Fawkes enhances Harry's native courage because of the boy's unwavering loyalty to Dumbledore. As a further reward for his loyalty,

Fawkes brings the Sorting Hat, out of which Harry will shortly draw the sword of Godric Gryffindor (the founder of Harry's House at Hogwarts) so that he can duel the basilisk. Of course, Fawkes' help with the basilisk is not limited to an inspiring song, or even the provision of a weapon. The phoenix also pierces the basilisk's eyes so that Harry can fight it without being petrified. (Petrification from the basilisk's gaze is an effect that had already afflicted several Hogwarts denizens.[16]) Subsequently, Fawkes' "thick, pearly tears" heal Harry of the poison of the basilisk's fang.[17] But neither of these helpful deeds, nor, for that matter, Fawkes' song, would have even come into play if Harry had not already possessed the potential for evincing a great deal of courage, just waiting to be roused in defense of the Headmaster of Hogwarts.

That courage, which is one attribute that even Voldemort acknowledges in Harry,[18] evokes another bestiary foe of the snake – the lion. During Harry's first night at Hogwarts, he is assigned by the magically articulate Sorting Hat to the House of Gryffindor, whose symbol is not a golden griffin, as its name suggests, but a lion. The Sorting Hat's song emphasizes that "Their daring, nerve, and chivalry/ Set Gryffindors apart" (SS, 118), a theme it reiterates at the beginning of Harry's fourth year (GF, 177). Medieval bestiaries agree that the lion is the king of beasts, known for its courage, strength, and firmness, and they maintain it is so vigilant that it sleeps with its eyes open. Yet they also claim: "A lion, although he is the king of beasts, gets harassed by the tiny sting of a scorpion, and snake poison kills him," which echoes St. Ambrose's interpretation in the *Hexameron*, a commentary on the first six books of the Old Testament.[19] And in so doing, the medieval bestiaries betoken the fact that without Fawkes' aid, Harry, poisoned by the basilisk, is unprotected. The courage of the lion alone cannot counteract this vulnerability. Moreover, the lion fears the cock, which the basilisk resembles and from which, according to at least one source, the cock was born.[20] The young Harry certainly demonstrates Gryffindor nerve in the battle with the basilisk at the climax of *Chamber of Secrets*, but without Fawkes' aid, Harry's defiance alone could not have defeated the basilisk or Tom Riddle.

The lion's courage, however, is not its only attribute, and a physical resemblance to this king of beasts does not necessarily convey bravery. The latter equivocation holds true for the character of the new Minister of Magic, introduced at the beginning of *Harry Potter* and the Half-Blood Prince: "Rufus Scrimgeour looked rather like an old lion," with his "mane of tawny hair" and "keen yellowish eyes" (16). Scrimgeour is not a secret Death Eater (a follower of Voldemort), but despite his physical resemblance to the courageous lion, he is thoroughly frightened by the Dark Lord's return. Not only does he try to suborn Harry when they first meet, but later Arthur, the patriarch of the Weasley family, tells Harry of Scrimgeour's reluctance even to acknowledge Voldemort's growing power (*DH*, 91). Nonetheless, Scrimgeour dies as the Ministry falls, leonine courage coming to the fore as he refuses to reveal even under torture that he knows where Harry is hiding (*DH*, 159, 206).[21]

Despite Harry's intrinsic courage, his behavior, as he grows into adolescence, exhibits a quality antithetical to the lion. In the bestiary, the lion is said to be slow to anger. Yet in book five, *Harry Potter and the Order of the Phoenix*, Harry is constantly, dangerously angry, a state brought on by a combination of teenage angst, frustration at internecine strife in the Ministry of Magic (the bureaucracy that functions as the governing body of the wizard world and threatens to close down Hogwarts), and the increasing influence of Voldemort in his thoughts and dreams. At age fifteen, Harry must also reconcile his youthful idealization of his father with new knowledge that James Potter was far from perfect and was, in fact, something of a bully.[22] While Harry struggles with this disillusionment, he chafes at restrictions placed on him by his substitute father-figures: his godfather Sirius Black, Dumbledore, and Arthur Weasley.

Notwithstanding his occasional rebellion against the advice of his mentors, the young Harry does recognize his own weakness and lack of readiness to fight the Dark Lord. Moreover, his deepest fear concerns something else. In the third book, *Harry Potter and the Prisoner of Azkaban*, the thirteen-year-old must learn a difficult and potent new spell to fend off the dementors, the soul-sucking guards of the wizard prison mentioned in the title. He first encounters one on the Hogwarts Express train on his way to his third year at school. Nothing can be seen of the dementor except its hand, "glistening, grayish, slimy-looking, and scabbed" (*PA*, 83),[23] but it freezes Harry's very soul. (Opportunely, the train carriage is shared by Professor Remus Lupin, who is able to repel the dementor and revive Harry by feeding him chocolate.) Later that semester, during a lesson with Lupin on the Riddikulus charm, the third-year students are faced with a shape-changing boggart that first assumes the form of the student's greatest fear but, with the successful completion of the charm, is transformed into a figure of ridicule – thus the name of the charm. At first Harry anticipates "a Voldemort returned to full strength," but this abstract fear is soon displaced by a memory of the dementor (*PA*, 136). Dementors represent a different kind of threat to humans than does Voldemort, and they are not his allies. They seek to destroy souls, not to control the wizard world.

Fortunately for Harry, the class ends before it is his turn to face that fear, for only a more powerful charm than the Riddikulus could help him withstand the soul-sucking dementors. That charm is the Patronus, a spell that, in Professor Lupin's words, works as "a kind of anti-dementor – a guardian" and "a kind of positive force" (*PA*, 237). Despite practice, not until a nearly fatal encounter with dementors does Harry's Patronus take shape: something "bright as a unicorn" (*PA*, 385), "a blinding, dazzling silver animal" that shone "brightly as the moon above" and "looked like a horse" but whose "hooves made no mark on the soft ground as it stared at Harry with its large, silver eyes" and which was neither a horse nor a unicorn (*PA*, 411). Indeed, as Harry himself realizes, his Patronus has come to him in the form of Prongs, his father's cervine *Animagus*, or animal shape.[24] And in accord with the medieval bestiaries, the ability of Harry to withstand the dementors at this juncture associates his nascent Patronus spell with the ability to defeat some very powerful evil by magical means.

The white stag or hart, and, to a lesser extent, the white hind or doe, was as ubiquitous a Christian symbol in the Middle Ages as were the lion and phoenix, established as such very early in the patristic tradition, and appearing often in saints' lives, in romances, and in bestiaries.[25] The last of these tell us: "These creatures are enemies to serpents. When they feel themselves to be weighed down by illness, they suck snakes from their holes with a snort of the nostrils and, the danger of their venom having been survived, the stags are restored to health by a meal of them."[26] According to the modern scholar Marcelle Thiébaux, one allegorical reading of the stag relates its thirst to the desire for baptism and to that sacrament's defeat of "snakish sin."[27] Another reading, however, identifies the stag with "Christ harrowing hell and overcoming the serpent, Satan," according to Thiébaux.[28]

While the stag may renew itself by ingesting the serpent, some bestiaries claim it also destroys the serpent: "When the stag knows where the snake is, it fills its mouth with water and spurts it into the hole, drawing the snake out by its breath. The stag then tramples it to death underfoot."[29] Rowling adapts both of these motifs. First, in the fight between Voldemort and Dumbledore at the end of *Order of the Phoenix*, the Dark Lord transforms a rope of flame from Dumbledore's wand into a serpent that turns back on the headmaster (*OP*, 814). As the snake strikes at Dumbledore, Fawkes saves him by "swallow[ing] the jet of green light whole," so that Dumbledore can destroy the snake (*OP*, 815). Here Rowling transforms the snake-sucking power of the stag into the phoenix's power to inhale the dangerous spell. Second, at the beginning of *Order of the Phoenix*, dementors invade the Muggle world and attack Harry's cousin Dudley. When Harry speaks the Patronus spell, and the now familiar stag leaps forward, it attacks the dementor with its antlers "in the place where the heart should have been" (*OP*, 18). When he commands the stag to prevent a second dementor from sucking Dudley's soul, "the silver antlers caught it; the thing was thrown up into the air, and like its fellow, it soared away" (*OP*, 19). A very early manuscript of the *Physiologus*, whose images are available in the online bestiary cited above, also illustrates a stag attacking a snake with its antlers, not trampling it.[30]

In keeping with a reading of the first several books in terms of Christian doctrine, but not the bestiary tradition, Granger concludes: "That Harry's father appears in the form of a Christ symbol (the stag), and that Harry's deliverance (as son) comes at his realization that he is his father (in appearance and will), are poetic expressions of the essential union of Father and Son for our salvation."[31] In different terms, outlining a Jungian analysis of the series, Gail A. Grynbaum notes:

> The stag has archaic symbolic links to the Tree of Life due to the resemblance of its antlers to the cyclic life of branches. It is also seen as the forerunner of daylight or guide to the light of the Sun; it is a harbinger of supreme consciousness. Like the shaman that aligns with special animals, Harry connects with his father's [animagus] animal spirit and it gives him new strength to fight against the takeover and loss of his soul.[32]

In keeping with such mystical unions, whether Christian or not, Harry and his father are periodically reunited throughout the books.

As a first-year student, Harry can see his parents through the Mirror of Erised (backwards for "Desire"), which reflects the observer's dearest wish. At the end of that year, Hagrid gives him a magical photo-album containing animated snapshots of his parents. And during Harry's second duel with Voldemort, at the end of *Goblet of Fire*, James's image heartens his son as it emerges from the connection formed between the two wizards' wands.[33] Similarly, when Harry, having come to terms with the likelihood of his own death, approaches Voldemort, he is accompanied through the Forbidden Forest by the spirits of all but one of those who sacrificed their own lives and lent him their love, wisdom, and talents. In both instances, "their presence was his courage" (*DH*, 700). Soon thereafter, Harry is reunited in some form of afterlife with another of his father figures, the deceased headmaster Albus Dumbledore. Thus, the stag is simultaneously a manifestation of Harry's own power and of the complex web of protection forged by his parents and Dumbledore.

In part because of this protection, Harry rarely has to combat Voldemort completely alone; at crucial moments, Rowling "ingathers" the symbolic powers of the bestiary animals as a measure of his progress and potential for overcoming the increasing threat of Voldemort.[34] In preparation for his duel with the Dark Lord, the fourth book, *Harry Potter and the Goblet of Fire*, focuses on a series of tests that constitute the quadrennial Triwizard tournament among international wizarding schools. The tests ostensibly measure magical ability, such as Harry's use of his superior broom-flying skills to snatch an egg from its dragon protector, but they also require a highly developed sense of empathy. It is Harry's empathy for a fellow Hogwarts student that springs the trap that reveals the entire enterprise has been co-opted by an agent of Voldemort to force a confrontation. When Harry and the revivified Voldemort simultaneously fling deadly spells at each other, a golden dome of light forms around them, isolating their fight. As Harry struggles to maintain control, he hears again the phoenix song. But, this time, "he felt *as though the song were inside him instead of just around him*" (*GF*, 665; emphasis mine).[35] Note the difference from Harry's encounter with the basilisk: then, the phoenix song heartened him; now, he has integrated its potency.[36] (We are noticeably not told what the "unearthly and beautiful" song sounds like to Voldemort.) Now Harry wields his own wand, containing its phoenix feather and the power of advanced spells, not the sword of

Godric Gryffindor delivered to him earlier by Fawkes. With this wand Harry forces Voldemort's wand to expel the ghosts of its victims, one by one, until his mother emerges and heartens him to: "Hold on for your father" (*GF*, 667). And when his father James emerges, he tells Harry not how to vanquish his enemy but how to escape and fight another day. It takes all three snake foes to protect Harry at this stage, the middle book of the series, as Rowling integrates features and attributes shared by the snake-hating beasts of medieval lore with Harry. His leonine courage, the song of the phoenix, and the human avatar of the white stag combine to suggest that Voldemort is not necessarily invincible.

Indeed, in the tradition of commentary in the bestiary, the battle between Harry and Voldemort in *Goblet of Fire*, with each wizard wielding a wand containing phoenix feathers, evokes *Exodus* 7:8–12:

> And the LORD spake unto Moses and unto Aaron, saying, When Pharaoh shall speak unto you, saying, Show a miracle for you: then thou shalt say unto Aaron, Take thy rod, and cast *it* before Pharaoh, *and* it shall become a serpent. And Moses and Aaron went in unto Pharaoh, and they did so as the LORD had commanded: and Aaron cast down his rod before Pharaoh, and before his servants, and it became a serpent. Then Pharaoh also called the wise men and the sorcerers: now the magicians of Egypt, they also did in like manner with their enchantments. For they cast down every man his rod, and they became serpents: but Aaron's rod swallowed up their rods.[37]

This passage is striking not only because it explicitly talks about magicians, but also because the instrument of proof is a rod (or wand), and because the enchantment produces serpents. Its resemblance to the battle of wands between Harry and Voldemort foreshadows the repeat battle with quite different wands in *Deathly Hallows*.[38]

From this time on, Voldemort's effect on Harry takes on new force. The link between their wands during the inconclusive duel opens a dangerous mental connection and leads Harry to understand that the knowledge and power he seeks in order to defeat his foe at the same time make him vulnerable to evil in ways the younger Harry who battled the basilisk was not. The fifteen-year-old Harry now sometimes observes the world through Voldemort's (or the snake

Nagini's) eyes, and thus it seems that he himself is responsible for a near-fatal attack on Arthur Weasley.[39] Despite attempts by Professor Severus Snape to teach him Occlumency – the "branch of magic" that "seals the mind against magical intrusion and influence" (*OP*, 530) – Harry remains in danger. Paradoxically, Harry must ultimately give up both magical protections and the peace of the afterlife in order to have any hope of victory.[40]

From the beginning, it has been clear that Rowling is conversant with the most important elements of the bestiary tradition but not bound to it where it does not suit her artistic purposes. I do not mean to suggest that Rowling expects her readers to know the medieval significance of the weasel or to recognize the lion as an evangelical symbol, or to accept the phoenix as a symbol of Christ's Resurrection.[41] The variations she introduces often serve to ground the books' magic in the human world. Although she adds healing tears to the legend of the phoenix, that anodyne does not extend to the feather contained in Voldemort's wand, which harmed Harry and murdered his parents and many others. She identifies Harry, with all his leonine strengths, from the start as a Parselmouth, although the significance of that talent does not become immediately apparent and by *Order of the Phoenix* is positively ominous. Rowling's method accommodates symbolic multivalency, much as the Church Fathers' commentaries on the Bible, which underlie the moralizing in the bestiaries, do.

Harry's ultimate defeat of Voldemort is also firmly grounded in human virtues. He must accept and surrender to the probability of his own death. But before Harry reaches the maturity that enables him to sacrifice himself, he could never defeat his nemesis alone, not even with the help of the real and symbolic foes of the snake. Omnipresent in the story of "the boy who lived" – an epithet he is given because Voldemort could not kill him as an infant – is the figure of his mother, Lily Evans Potter, and the power of her maternal love and sacrifice. It was her humanity and its enduring effects on Harry that undermined Professor Quirrell, who was possessed by Voldemort in *Sorcerer's Stone*. It was her voice that surpassed even the song of the phoenix in heartening Harry to be strong. Yet even Lily's love for Harry is not the complete answer.

We actually learn very little about Lily in the first five books. We do not know what spells she may have mastered with a willow wand Mr. Ollivander describes as "Nice [...] for charm work" (*SS*, 82). We do not know if she was an *Animagus*. And we are given no hints as to the identity of her *Patronus*. But at the end of *Sorcerer's Stone*, Dumbledore reminds Harry of the power of human love (which, in the household of his mother's sister, was in short supply during his childhood), a protection so strong that Quirrell, the human host for an as yet disembodied Voldemort, could not even touch the boy without being burned. Dumbledore explains more at the end of *Order of the Phoenix*: that by dying to save Harry, Lily conferred on him a special protection that was sustained by the charm sealed when her sister, Petunia Dursley, agreed to give Harry a home. Voldemort's complete incomprehension of a mother's sacrifice is expressed by Tom Riddle at the end of *Harry Potter and the Chamber of Secrets* – the book Rowling herself once stated contains the key to the series.[42] There, Tom acknowledges that Lily's sacrifice was "a powerful counter-charm" but believes "it was merely a lucky chance that saved you from me" (*CS*, 317). Harry, too, only incompletely understands the complexity of love – until he witnesses Professor Severus Snape's disinterested sacrifice. The man he had taken to be his enemy, who had sneered at and belittled him both in and out of class, who was a Death Eater and a double agent, and who had killed Albus Dumbledore, loved Lily so deeply for so long that he lays down his own life to protect her son Harry. And his love manifested itself in his own Patronus, which, like hers, was a doe (*DH*, 740).

In the bestiary, female deer are noted for their maternal care. When they give birth, they hide the fawn, "and, having tucked them up in some deep shrubbery or undergrowth, they admonish them with a stamp of the foot to keep hidden."[43] However, Rowling complicates the question of maternal love by having Severus Snape, not Lily, cast his Patronus to lead Harry to the frozen pool where the sword of Gryffindor lies concealed.[44] Harry sees a doe, "silver-white [...] moon-bright and dazzling [...] leaving no hoofprints in the fine powdering of snow" (*DH*, 366). And her form seems familiar to Harry, as it should, evoking as it does the love he shares unknowingly with Severus Snape for Lily: "instinct, overwhelming instinct, told him that this was not Dark Magic," that "her presence had meant safety" (*DH*, 366–67, 373). But neither Harry nor we discover that this is not Lily's Patronus until Snape reacts, instinctively, to protect him (*DH*, 687).

Severus Snape's given name suggests his divided loyalties, with its plays on both "sever" and "severe." His surname means "to be hard upon [...] to rebuke or snub" (*OED*), which accords with not only his treatment as a schoolboy by James Potter and Sirius Black but also with his own treatment of Harry. He is the head of Slytherin, the Hogwarts House associated with snakes, with Voldemort, and with purity of blood (Snape is the "half-blood Prince" referred to in the title of the sixth book of the series, while Lily is Muggle-born). And he and Harry are destined to be antagonists from their first encounter in Potions class, when Snape's black eyes sweep the room, "cold and empty" (*SS*, 136), recognizing in Harry a strong physical resemblance to his own schoolboy nemesis, James Potter (except for Harry's green eyes, which are often described as exactly the same as Lily's). But as Snape dies and magically releases his memories of Lily's childhood kindness to him, he reveals his love to Harry, and "The green eyes [find] the black" (*DH*, 658). Harry finally understands that there was not one great sacrifice to enable him to live, but two, and though Tom Riddle dismisses human love as unimportant, it is revealed to be all-important. Rowling has succeeded in extending the Christological symbolism of the bestiary to encompass the human heart, in adapting the focus of the bestiary on the Christian struggle between good and evil, as she affirms that "Greater love hath no man than this, that a man lay down his life for his friends."[45]

NOTES

1. Preliminary versions of this article, based on the first five books in the series, were presented at the 29th Patristic, Medieval, and Renaissance Conference at Villanova University, 17 September 2004; the UMBC English Department Colloquium on 8 December 2004; and the UMBC Honors Forum on 31 October 2005. A written inquiry to Ms. Rowling about her interest in the bestiary has gone unanswered as of this writing (September 2007). I thank the readers and especially the editor of *Studies in Medievalism* for extremely helpful critiques and suggestions to improve earlier drafts.

2. The seven books are, in chronological order of appearance: *Harry Potter and the Sorcerer's Stone* (*SS*), *Harry Potter and the Chamber of Secrets* (*CS*), *Harry Potter and the Prisoner of Azkaban* (*PA*), *Harry Potter and the Goblet of Fire* (*GF*), *Harry Potter and the Order of the Phoenix* (*OP*), *Harry Potter and the Half-Blood Prince* (*HBP*), and *Harry Potter and the Deathly Hallows* (*DH*). Another view of the layered worlds in the books that also

harks back to a medieval construct is argued by Iver B. Neumann, "Naturalizing Geography: Harry Potter and the Realms of Muggles, Magic Folks, and Giants," in Daniel H. Nexon and Iver B. Neumann, ed., *Harry Potter and International Relations* (Lanham, MD: Rowman & Littlefield, 2006), 157–73.

3. Harry's best friend Ron Weasley has a pet rat that turns out to be the villainous Animagus Peter Pettigrew. Amusingly, his brother Fred Weasley refuses to accept "Rodent" as his code name for underground radio broadcasts in *Deathly Hallows* (443).

4. There are myriad ways of viewing this struggle, and it is not the purpose of this paper to argue metaphysics. Still, the Harry Potter books have engendered much discussion as to the nature of evil in the modern world. One interesting view that ties methodology to myth, somewhat analogous to my argument that allusion to the bestiary informs Rowling's narrative and thematic methodology, is that of Martin Hall, "The Fantasy of Realism, or Mythology as Methodology," in Nexon and Neumann, ed., *Harry Potter and International Relations*, 177–94.

5. Florence McCulloch, *Medieval Latin and French Bestiaries* (Chapel Hill: The University of North Carolina Press, 1960), 15.

6. McCulloch, *Medieval Latin and French Bestiaries*, 16. A more recent reconsideration of the second-family bestiary (which represents most of the medieval exemplars) is by Willene B. Clark, *A Medieval Book of Beasts: The Second-Family Bestiary: Commentary, Art, Text, and Translation* (Woodbridge: The Boydell Press, 2006). The most accessible translation is T. H. White, *The Bestiary: A Book of Beasts* (New York: G. P. Putnam's Books, 1960). Unless otherwise noted, all quotations from the bestiary refer to this version.

7. Newt Scamander [J. K. Rowling], *Fantastic Beasts and Where to Find Them* (New York: Scholastic, 2001). She mentions the book as a required Hogwarts text in *Sorcerer's Stone*, 67. Earlier considerations of fantastic creatures in the Harry Potter series have focused on their Classical mythological significance, and only to a much lesser extent on their medieval Christian symbolism. See Peggy J. Huey, "A Basilisk, a Phoenix, and a Philosopher's Stone: Harry Potter's Myths and Legends," in Cynthia Whitney Hallett, ed., *Scholarly Studies in Harry Potter: Applying Academic Methods to a Popular Text*, Studies in British Literature 99 (Lewiston, NY: The Edwin Mellen Press, 2005), 65–83; and Sarah E. Gibbons, "Death and Rebirth: Harry Potter & the Mythology of the Phoenix," in Hallett, *Scholarly Studies in Harry Potter*, 85–105.

8. Based on a reading of the first four books, Dan McVeigh uses the word "subterranean" to describe the nature of their Christian reference, but he does not consider the medieval symbolism of the bestiary, although he

does point out the influence of C. S. Lewis and others of the 1930s Oxford literary group "the Inklings": "Is Harry Potter Christian?" *Renascence* 54/3 (Spring 2002): 196–216 (210). Rowling's method seems quite medieval in a sense: in a study of *La Queste del Saint Graal* (The Quest of the Holy Grail), itself replete with animal symbolism, Albert Pamphlet refers to its author's symbolic method as a means to "traduire ses idées en langage concret: il lui suffisait de choisir dans l'infinité des apparances terrestres, ainsi qu'en un immense dictionnaire, celles qui etaient capables d'exprimer ses pensées" (translate his ideas into concrete language; he is content to choose from an infinity of earthly objects, just as from an immense dictionary, those which were able to express his thoughts): Albert Pamphlet, *Études sur la Queste del Saint Graal attribuée à Gautier Map* (Paris: É. Champion, 1921), 106. See also Lesley Kordecki, "Making Animals Mean: Species Hermeneutics in the *Physiologus* of Theobaldus," in Nona C. Flores, ed., *Animals in the Middle Ages: A Book of Essays* (New York: Garland, 1996), 87–101.

9. According to Pliny the Elder, "to a creature so marvelous as this [...] the venom of weasels is fatal." Quoted in David D. Gilmore, *Monsters: Evil Beings, Mythical Beasts, and All Manner of Imaginary Terrors* (Philadelphia: University of Pennsylvania Press, 2003), 39. For a medieval depiction of the basilisk with the head of a cock, see Kongelige Bibliothek National Library of Denmark Gl. kgl. S.1633 4o, fol. 51r at <www.bestiary.ca>. This site offers many images and quotations from the medieval bestiaries. It cannot be determined, unfortunately, where Rowling found her information about the bestiary, whether online, or in a widely read book such as White's, although her university studies included Latin and French. In *Order of the Phoenix*, we learn that Harry's godfather Sirius Black had a brother who was a Death Eater (that is, a Voldemort follower) who died after trying to desert from the Dark Lord's army. His name was Regulus, or ruler, which matches the Latin bestiaries' gloss of the basilisk as the king of serpents (this is why the basilisk is sometimes depicted as a cobra, whose hood resembles a crown).

10. The manifestation of Arthur Weasley's defensive spell, or Patronus, is itself a weasel, as we learn in *Deathly Hallows*, 121. Another level of Rowling's allusion to the bestiary has nothing to do with the major themes of the book but provides additional evidence for her multi-dimensional method: that is, cats form an amusing thread in the books. Harry's friend Hermione Granger's pet Crookshanks exemplifies the bestiary cat's predominant characteristic as a mouse- (or rat-) catcher. McGonagall's protective presence as Head of Gryffindor exemplifies the bestiary cat's watchfulness; cf. White, *The Bestiary*, 91. Hogwarts caretaker Argus Filch patrols the halls with the help of his cat, Mrs. Norris, ready to pounce on infractions of the rules. And the ghastly Ministry of Magic bureaucrat, inquisitor, and

sometime headmistress of Hogwarts, Dolores Umbrage, decorates her office with plaques of "beribboned kitten[s], gamboling and frisking with sickening cuteness" (*DH*, 251). She employs "a bright-silver, long-haired cat" to "protect the prosecutors from the despair that emanated from the dementors" in the Ministry hearing room (259). Its color and its effect on dementors suggest that this is Umbrage's Patronus.

11. John Granger, *Looking for God in Harry Potter* (Carol Stream, IL: Tyndale House, 2004). He is also the author of *The Hidden Key to Harry Potter* (Wayne, PA: Zossima Press, 2002) and *Unlocking Harry Potter: Five Keys for the Serious Reader* (Wayne, PA: Zossima Press, 2007). He hosts the website <http://hogwartsprofessor.com/>.

12. Granger, *Looking for God*, 171.

13. Granger, *Looking for God*, 171.

14. Granger, *Looking for God*, 100.

15. The power of the song is mentioned by Herodotus in *History* II.73, cited in N. F. Blake, ed., *The Phoenix* (Manchester: Manchester University Press, 1964), 9. Herodotus reports that the song is "performed when [the phoenix] is on the point of death," but Fawkes' song occurs in a different context. In the poem *De ave phoenice*, the third-century Christian apologist Lactantius writes, "as soon as the soft glow of the first light becomes visible, the bird begins to sing a sacred song and to summon the new day with a beautiful sound." Cited from R. Van Den Broek, *The Myth of the Phoenix According to Classical and Early Christian Traditions*, trans. I. Seeger (Leiden: E. J. Brill, 1972), 282–83. Fawkes regenerates in *Chamber of Secrets* and *Order of the Phoenix*, but on neither occasion does it sing.

16. In *Deathly Hallows*, Fred Weasley scotches the rumor that "You-Know-Who can kill with a single glance from his eyes. That's a *basilisk*, listeners," 443. And while Rowling's use of the bestiary is wholly serious, her love of wordplay can also encompass puns associated with the basilisk. See Bill McCarron, "Basilisk Puns in *Harry Potter and the Chamber of Secrets*," *Notes on Contemporary Literature* 36/1 (January 2006): 2.

17. This is attested by Hermione Granger in *Deathly Hallows*, 104.

18. *Deathly Hallows*, 659.

19. White, *Bestiary*, 11. Cf. St. Ambrose, *Exameron* Vi.6.37, cited from Carolus Schenkl, *Sancti Ambrosii Opera* (Vindobonae: F. Tempsky, 1896), I.i, 229: "leo quidem rex ferarum exiguo scorpionis aculeo exagitatur et venemo serpentis occiditure. eximia Leonis pulchritudo: comantis cervice toros excutit vel sublato pectore adtollit ora: sed quis non miretur tam verui scorpionis aculeo, ut incorporeum putes, ingentium corporum exire mortem?"

20. Joseph Nigg, *A Guide to the Imaginary Birds of the World* (Cambridge, MA: Apple-wood Books, 1984), 30. According to White, the

twelfth-century naturalist Alexander Neckham added this fact to the legend of the basilisk (*Bestiary*, 169n). For a medieval illustration of the lion's fear of the cock, see Kongelige Bibliotek, Gl. kgl. S. 3466 8°, fol. 10r, at <www.bestiary.ca>.

21. Rowling's treatment of courage also reflects the Aristotelian mean that Harry must learn: "a motivated and measured response to perceived danger by a person who is willing to face that potential harm for the sake of securing or promoting a greater good," as stated by Tom Morris in "The Courageous Harry Potter," in David Baggett and Shawn E. Klein, ed., *Harry Potter and Philosophy: If Aristotle Ran Hogwarts* (Chicago, IL: Open Court, 2004), 13.

22. Learning to distinguish mere human nefariousness from the sort of evil embraced by the Death Eaters and to cope with the disillusionment all children must face when they recognize their parents, too, are merely human, is a crucial element in Harry's maturation. See Donna C. Woodford, "Disillusionment in *Harry Potter and the Order of the Phoenix*," *Topic: The Washington & Jefferson College Review* 54: *Harry Potter* (Fall 2004): 63–72.

23. That the dementors reflect St. Augustine of Hippo's definition of evil as the *privation* or *diminution* of good rather than as a duality opposing good is argued by Jean Bethke Elshtain, "Harry Potter, St. Augustine, and the Confrontation with Evil," lecture at the Library of Congress, 12 November 2003; <www.loc.gov/locvideo/elshtain> (accessed 23 October 2005).

24. And this is apparently widely known, for when he casts it in *Deathly Hallows* (556), it is recognized as his. James Potter and three schoolmates (Lupin, Peter Pettigrew, and Black) created the Marauder's Map, which shows every room and corridor in the school and locates where any inhabitant is at a given time. They signed it with names corresponding to their *Animagi*: Prongs (Potter's stag), Moony (Lupin's werewolf), Wormtail (Pettigrew's rat), and Padfoot (Black's dog). Appropriately, Harry's friend and ally Hermione Granger's Patronus is an otter, which is a translation from the Greek "ichneumon," a foe of the dragon (a type of serpent) in some bestiaries.

25. It was also the heraldic emblem of both Richard II of England and Charles VI of France. In heraldry, especially in the iconography of the Wilton Diptych, the white hart suggests legitimate succession and was perhaps associated with a secret order. See Michael Bath, *The Image of the Stag: Iconographic Themes in Western Art* (Baden-Baden: Verlag Valentin Koerner, 1992), 188. See also Margaret Haist, "The Lion, Bloodline and Kingship," in Debra Hassig, ed., *The Mark of the Beast: The Medieval Bestiary in Art, Life, and Literature* (New York: Garland Publishing, Inc., 1999), 3–22. John Granger notes "The stag in Harry Potter, like the

unicorn, is a symbol for Christ," in *Looking for God*, 95. But the minor role of the unicorn in the series (its blood is a source of the disembodied Voldemort's strength) argues against this identification in the books, despite its medieval symbolism.

26. White, *Bestiary*, 37.

27. Marcelle Thiébaux, *The Stag of Love: The Chase in Medieval Literature* (Ithaca, NY: Cornell University Press, 1974), 40–42. The association of the stag with water is based on commentaries on Psalm 41, verse 2 (in the King James translation): "as the hart panteth after the water brooks, so panteth my soul after thee, O God." For example, St. Augustine writes: "Hear what else there is in the hart. It destroys serpents [...]. The serpents are thy vices, destroy the serpents of iniquity; then wilt thou long yet more for 'the Fountain of Truth.'" Cited from A. Cleveland Coxe, ed. & trans., *Expositions on the Psalms by Saint Augustin, Bishop of Hippo* ([1888]; repr. Grand Rapids, MI: Wm. B. Eerdmans publishing Co., 1983), 133a.

28. Thiébaux, *The Stag of Love*, 40–42.

29. McCulloch, *Medieval Latin and French Bestiaries*, 174, as illustrated in BL Royal MS 2 B. vii, fol. 116r.

30. MS Bern 318, fol. 17. For the image, see Christoph von Steiger and Otto Homburger, ed., *Physiologus bernensis Voll-Faksimile-Ausgabe des Codex Bongarsianus 318 der Burgerbibliothek Bern* (Basel, Alkuin-Verlag, 1964).

31. Granger, *Looking for God*, 145.

32. Gail A. Grynbaum, "The Secrets of Harry Potter," *San Francisco Jung Institute Library Journal: Reviews From a Jungian Perspective of Books, Films and Culture* 19/4 (2001): 17–48 (<http://www.cgjungpage.org/content/view/145/28/> [accessed 10 September 2004]).

33. In *Chamber of Secrets*, 316ff, Harry had briefly challenged Voldemort's schoolboy avatar Tom Riddle.

34. The poet and Inkling (a member of the circle that included C. S. Lewis and J. R. R. Tolkien) Charles Williams uses the term "ingathering" to describe how all the images in Dante's *Divine Comedy* converge in the Celestial Rose: *The Figure of Beatrice* (London: Faber & Faber, 1943). The term is apt, I think, for what Rowling does with the bestiary in this important scene. In a way, John Granger intuits this, for he observes that, unlike allegories, "symbols [...] can be stacked up," *Looking for God*, 100.

35. This feeling recurs when Fawkes sings "a stricken lament of terrible beauty" after Dumbledore's death (*HBP*, 61–62).

36. Yet, in the subsequent book, it is no longer the song of the phoenix that feels "as though it were inside him" but the evil consciousness of the Dark Lord himself.

37. *The Holy Bible* [King James Version] (New York: New American

Library, 1974). I am grateful to John R. Fortin, O.S.B., of The Institute for
Saint Anselm Studies, who suggested this analogue to me in an e-mail dated
21 September 2004.

38. In their final duel (*DH*, 742–43), neither Voldemort nor Harry
uses his original wand with the phoenix feather. Voldemort has stolen the
Elder Wand, an ancient instrument of great power, from Dumbledore's
tomb, and Harry wields Draco Malfoy's wand.

39. Harry dreams vividly about a serious attack on Arthur Weasley,
and when trying to convince Professor McGonagall that the danger to
Arthur is real, explains that he knows he was dreaming but that he suddenly
felt he was present during the attack and witnessed it (*OP*, 462–65).

40. Jerry L. Walls astonishingly anticipates this dénouement in his
essay "Heaven, Hell, and Harry Potter," in Baggett and Klein, ed., *Harry
Potter and Philosophy*, 67–76, remarking on Dumbledore's comment that "to
the well-organized mind, death is but the next great adventure." Walls
writes, "perhaps it is not up to us to prolong our lives at any cost. Perhaps
immortality is a gift, but a gift to be received only under certain conditions."
And he cites one of the Hogwarts resident ghosts, Nearly Headless Nick,
whose fear of death suspends him between the two states, but who recognizes his condition as a "feeble imitation of life," anticipating Harry's afterlife conversation with Dumbledore in *Deathly Hallows*. Dumbledore tells
Harry, "I think [...] that if you choose to return, there is a chance
[Voldemort] might be finished for good. I cannot promise it. But I know
this, Harry that you have less to fear from returning here than he does." And
Harry recognizes that "Leaving this place would not be nearly as hard as
walking into the forest had been, but it was warm and light and peaceful
here, and he knew that he was heading back to pain and the fear of more
loss" (*DH*, 722).

41. See, for example, Valerie Jones, "The Phoenix and Resurrection,"
in Hassig, ed., *The Mark of the Beast*, 99–115.

42. In a 13 November 2002 interview, Rowling said, "Key things
happen in book two. No one knows how important those things are ... yet.
There's a lot in there. And I know how difficult it was to get it all in there
without drawing too much attention to the clues." Cited from <http://
www.scholastic.com/harrypotter/books/author/interview3.htm>. As we subsequently learn, Tom Marvolo Riddle's childhood was as unhappy as Harry's
curtailed time with his parents was enduringly happy.

43. White, *Bestiary*, 37.

44. The sword contains a Horcrux, which must be destroyed before
Voldemort himself can be defeated. A Horcrux is an object into which the
Dark Lord has magically cached a fragment of his soul for immortal protec-
tion: *Half-Blood Prince*, 496ff.

45. John 15:13. Note that Harry learns this lesson as well, for of his and Ginny (Weasley)'s three children, only the middle child had "inherited Lily's eyes" (*DH*, 758), and his name is Albus Severus.

Seamus Heaney's Audio *Beowulf:* An Analysis of the Omissions[1]

Douglas Ryan VanBenthuysen

The significance of Seamus Heaney's translation of *Beowulf* struck me when I saw it on sale at the airport, alongside works by Tom Clancy and Sue Grafton. Three hundred years after the sole copy of this early medieval classic was literally on fire, it is now ubiquitous.

Yet Heaney's *Beowulf* has achieved more than a mere appearance on newsstand shelves, for it has also earned recognition as a credible translation for Beowulfian scholarship. The inclusion of Old English on the facing pages in the North American edition makes the translation an academic tool, and the choice of this translation for the latest Norton Critical Edition of the poem suggests it is the best available lens through which to engage scholarly criticism of the work. Indeed, the editor of the Norton edition, Daniel Donoghue, says that Heaney's mode of making poetry through his translation of *Beowulf* has been a way "to breathe life back into the body of the language."[2] And, in fact, reading Heaney's *Beowulf* makes clear the greatness of this translation, much as Chapman's translation of the *Odyssey* led John Keats to a new awareness of the poem's immediacy and relevance.[3]

That vivacity may explain why, despite the elimination of the Anglo-Saxon requirement at Oxford,[4] and despite other recent evidence of resistance to studying *Beowulf,* general interest in the poem appears to have grown in the last several years, as exemplified in the appearance of the graphic-novel adaptation by Gareth Hinds[5] and several films related to the story, including *Beowulf and Grendel*[6] and a big-budget production featuring Angelina Jolie as Grendel's mother.[7] Of course, the mere fact that Heaney's *Beowulf* has been made available in an audio version suggests that there is non-scholarly interest in his work, as does the response to that audio version. Originally recorded for the BBC and licensed for sale in the United States by HighBridge Audio,[8] it has outsold all other audio versions of *Beowulf* on Amazon.com[9] and ranks second on both Barnes & Noble.com[10] and the popular audio-book download site Audible.com.[11] Additionally, perhaps due in part to the popularity of the Heaney audio translation, two new audio versions have recently appeared on the market: one claiming faithfulness to the original,[12] and a second dramatizing the poem.[13] Such audio versions are more than just products of our contemporary age of MP3s and iPods. They also allow for a new critical avenue for looking at the poem.

If it can be granted that the audio version of Heaney's translation represents an important chapter in the history of *Beowulf*, then closer examination of this presentation is appropriate. The recording advertises itself as "unabridged selections,"[14] a somewhat deceptive description, as the recording contains both the removal of large sections and the alteration or omission of 989 lines out of Heaney's original 3182. The cause or thought process behind the omissions remains uncertain to me, not least because I have been unable to get a response on this matter from the BBC, which HighBridge audio says was "the original producer of this program, and thus made all of the production decisions."[15] The purpose of this study, however, is not to discover the motives behind the omissions, nor to explicitly judge the decision to make such omissions. Rather, the point here is to evaluate how the omissions alter the critical understanding and the reception of the poem.

Taken as a whole, the omissions in Heaney's audio *Beowulf* eliminate much of the social, historical, cultural, geographical, and other contexts in which the main action of the poem takes place. They obliterate major themes such as the role of women, the relationship between the Christian and Germanic worlds, and the role of nobility, and they tend to oversimplify and even resolve key ambiguities that often appear when these themes surface in the poem. Thus, these omissions more or less fall in line with the elimination or alteration of themes in other contemporary popular presentations of *Beowulf*, such as those common in movies and comic books. In particular, the omitted lines or passages tend to deal with what are commonly known as the "digressions" of *Beowulf*, the side stories that introduce characters and conflicts not directly related to the three encounters with monsters, give a glimpse into the dynamic world where those encounters take place, and provide insight about the nature of the primary characters. Without these omitted lines and passages, this audio version of the poem presents an altered tale in a less populated, less complete world.

The chart included in the appendix at the end of my paper lists the 103 alterations – omissions and otherwise – in Heaney's audio *Beowulf*, as compared to the 2000 textual edition of his translation. I have characterized the omissions as follows: "A" represents secondary characters; "B" represents especially violent scenes or the repetition of a violent scene; "C" represents fratricide; "D" represents scenes revealing aspects of social relations; "E" represents particularly pessimistic passages; "F" represents feuds, particularly involving the Swedes; and "G" represents minor revisions (in the appendix, types A–F are placed in bold text to distinguish them more clearly from type G). Many of the omissions span multiple categories. How these different types of omission contribute to the overall de-contextualization of the poem will be discussed in greater detail below. Throughout this study, numbers indicate entries on the chart.

To begin the discussion of the ramifications of these omissions, let us take a look at the consequences of eliminating side characters. Some of these omissions may seem rather insignificant in and of themselves, such as the removal in #34 of a scene in which Wealhþeow sits with her sons, Hreðric and Hroðmund. But the result of this ostensibly minor change is to take away some interesting aspects of the Beowulfian world. For example, in this case we may lose sight of the interesting naming convention used by the Danes wherein the names of the sons seem to be derived from that of the father – in this case, Hroðgar. Indeed, the strangeness of names in general helps create a sense of the world in which *Beowulf* operates. Other, more prominent, characters are either eliminated entirely or relegated to a virtually unnoticeable role. One striking example is the virtual elimination of the rather major character Hunferð,[16] as in #12 and #47, which will be dealt with in more detail in connection with the fratricide omissions.

Minor characters in *Beowulf* tend both to illuminate some aspect of a major character and to give insight into the context of the poem's main actions. One example of this phenomenon occurs in #19. The morning after the defeat of Grendel, Hroðgar's "traditional singer deeply schooled / in the lore of the past, linked a new theme / to a strict metre" (59),[17] recounting the tales of first Sigemund, then Heremod. In the printed edition, Heaney actually calls attention to this passage by "a slight quickening of the pace and shortening of the metrical rein," as he himself notes in his introduction to the poem.[18] This "poem within a poem," as Heaney calls it,[19] first recounts Sigemund's triumph over the dragon and his ensuing fame, then the decline of King Heremod as a result of betrayal and of his becoming burdensome to his people.

This set of stories, however, certainly serves the poem as more than a way of passing the time between the appearances of monsters. At minimum, the passage foreshadows Beowulf's fight with the dragon as a parallel to Sigemund's fight with the dragon. Furthermore, as M. S. Griffin has observed, "This narrative sequence invites us to contextualize Beowulf's first great exploit in a broader frame."[20] Exploring this frame, Griffin deals with the problematic relationship between Beowulf and Sigemund. On the one hand, Beowulf is like Sigemund, and therefore a part of the heroic tradition. On the other hand, he is unlike Sigemund, and therefore "the less clear is Beowulf's place in the great heroic tradition but the more freed he is from the stain of heathendom."[21] Through the story of Sigemund, we are able to see the degree to which Beowulf is a part of one of the poem's most significant cultural contexts – the Germanic heroic tradition. Similarly, the Heremod story provides much insight by illustrating the difficulty of remaining prominent within that tradition; King Heremod's betrayal and demise accentuate the prowess Beowulf would have needed to possess during his fifty-year reign before facing the dragon. The nature of Beowulf's world is such that great deeds of heroism must be performed over and over again throughout a lifetime.

An omitted passage whose inclusion makes a perhaps more subtle contribution to the poem is #59, the tale of Mod Þryðo, the cruel queen who would kill a man who dared to look at her but was later turned virtuous by marriage. Interpretations of this passage have varied widely, creating an ambiguity about Mod Þryðo that may reflect ambiguity in the poem as a whole. The immediate effect of this passage is to highlight the character of Hygd, Hygelac's queen. This passage, however, has been fecund ground for interpretation. Marijane Osborn, for one, has taken such highlighting to the next level and interpreted Hygd as having chosen to author her life based on reflecting upon Mod Þryðo's life. Osborn says, "She has apparently rejected the first part of the narrative and adopted the second as a paradigm for her personal narrative, her constructed self."[22] Whether or not Mod Þryðo's changed state leads to a conscious choice on the part of Hygd, the poet has, by telling the story of Mod Þryðo, granted us additional insight into Hygd. Looking at Mod Þryðo another way, Christopher Fee has argued that this seemingly minor character actually provides even greater insight into the landscape of the poem. He links the transformation of Mod Þryðo upon being given away to the general theme of the transformational power of treasure-giving found throughout the poem.[23] Helen Damico makes another connection, linking Mod Þryðo to Grendel's mother, illustrating that the figure of feminine cruelty can exist both in the wild world of the *mere* and the refined world of the court.[24] Damico goes on to claim that Mod Þryðo exemplifies the archetypal "progression of the fierce war-demon to gold-adorned queen."[25] In a unique and intriguing argument, Mary Dockray-Miller has suggested that Mod Þryðo remains a subversive force even after her marriage because she "not only disrupts the masculine symbolic order [by killing men before her marriage] but continues to rebel against it even after her disappearance from her own story"[26] in "choosing to be a peace-maker as the ultimate opposition to society."[27] One might also see Mod Þryðo's transformation as an allegory for the Christian conversion of the Germanic people, in that violence has been transformed into peace by the introduction of Offa, who would in this case stand in as a type for Christ. Finally, my own initial impression upon considering Mod Þryðo is to view both her initial violence and ultimate submission as two different kinds of vice. They have been introduced to illustrate the potential for ignoble action that would have been present to Hygd, and to the nobility in general, in order to underscore the virtuous decision to neither abuse power nor totally abdicate it through submission. In any case, my purpose in bringing up this range of interpretations for Mod Þryðo is to illustrate the fertility of this passage in evaluating several contexts of the poem, including the status of women, the role of nobility, the theme of gift-giving, and the role of the Germanic and Christian cultural contexts. The omission of the Mod Þryðo episode, an episode that has earned the description "truly Beowulfian,"[28] unravels part of the fabric that constitutes the Beowulfian world.

The Mod Þryðo episode is also rather brutal, which leads to the second type of omitted passage: those dealing with particularly violent scenes. Whether it be the comparison of Grendel's mother to an Amazon warrior having ruptured the helmet of a foe (#42), or the description of Beowulf beheading the corpse of Grendel (#51), these particularly gory scenes help relate the Beowulfian world. Additionally, in the case of the beheading example, *Beowulf* is linked thematically to its manuscript neighbor *Judith.*

Violence might also be linked to the essential relationship between the poem and its audience. In a psychoanalytic study of violence in *Beowulf,* Janet Thormann argues not only that the "the perpetuation of violence provides the momentum of *Beowulf*'s narrative"[29] but also that the violence in *Beowulf* is a source of enjoyment as violence in the poem supports the law and therefore appeals to the regulatory function of the superego.[30] Or, to put it another way, the violence that appears throughout the poem, and in several of the omissions, relates directly to the legal context of the poem's world. Even the retaliation of Grendel's mother fits into the concept of *wergild.*

One particular type of violence in *Beowulf* that deserves special consideration, and its own category in this analysis, is fratricide. Virtually every reference to fratricide in the poem has been omitted, including several references to Hunferð's fratricide (#12, #31), the foreshadowing of either fratricide or internal feuding plaguing the Danes (#21), the accidental killing of one of Hreðel's sons at the hand of another (#71), and Beowulf's assertion that he had never murdered a kinsman (#83).

The theme of fratricide links together the two most important contexts that set the background for *Beowulf*: the Germanic tradition and the emerging religion of Christianity. On the Germanic side, fratricide represents the ultimate violation of a society held together by ties of kinship, where loyalty to one's immediate kin supersedes other considerations. The problematic nature of fratricide in this warrior culture comes to the fore when Beowulf recounts the story of Hreðel's son Haeðcyn killing Hreðel's other son Herebeald (#71). The fratricide causes a breakdown in a governing principle of the culture, the *wergild,* because "That offense was beyond redress, a wrongfooting / of the heart's affections; for who could avenge / the prince's life or pay his death-price?" (165). To make right a killing, value or revenge must be exacted by the kin of the slain from the perpetrator, but the system has no mechanism for dealing with a killing when the perpetrator and the kin are the same. Similarly, fratricide represents an absolute incongruity with the principles of Christianity. The Christian call to "love your neighbor as yourself,"[31] and the Christian message in general, would make fratricide particularly heinous. Additionally, the Biblical tradition of Cain, who committed the Bible's first murder, a fratricide, sets the background for evil as portrayed in the poem. (Interestingly, references to Cain are left largely intact in the audio version, including references to his fratricide. Without the other references to fratricide, however, the references to Cain's crime do not make much sense.) In a study of the influence of the Cain story in *Beowulf*, David Williams says that "fratricide is determinate of history."[32] Insofar as fratricide is both a Germanic and Christian abomination, the constant repetition of references to fratricide in the poem forges a unity between the two seemingly incongruous background cultures that so strongly inform the world of the poem. Indeed, Beowulf's death-utterance, "the Ruler of mankind / need never blame me when the breath leaves my body / for murder of kinsmen" (185), seems both a call for the loving embrace of the Christian God *ece Drihten* and the acceptance of his Germanic forbears. Consequently, the absence of these references to fratricide eliminates the strongest connection between the Germanic and Christian cultural contexts of the poem.

The character Hunferð links together fratricide and the other types of omissions already discussed with other social considerations in the poem. In connection with the theme of fratricide, the Hunferð episode (particularly #12, but also #21 and #47) makes manifest the intersection of Germanic and Christian themes in the poem, and the episode has been interpreted as an argument for the primacy of both. The Christian understanding of Hunferð largely relies on linking his fratricide to both Cain and Grendel. G. C. Britton makes this point, saying "Grendel is of Cain's kin: that section of mankind destined because of their rejection of God to be of the devil's party in hell. And Hunferð, the fratricide, belongs most clearly to that party."[33] Along similar lines, Williams argues that Hunferð "can be taken as a kind of Cain."[34] What we see in Hunferð is the manifestation of Cain's sin in a corollary fashion to the manifestation of Cain through Grendel. (Additionally, the fratricide of Cain can be seen as manifested through the dragon, for, as Williams points out, dragons are linked to fratricide in the Christian tradition.[35]) Grendel is the manifestation of sin that exists outside of society, whereas Hunferð is the manifestation of it in society. In order to succeed as a Christian hero, Beowulf must overcome not only the enemy without but also the enemy within. Beowulf's means of overcoming this internal foe, however, draw on Germanic sensibility. F. H. Whitman points out that the tone of the episode "helps establish the Germanic warlord roots of the poem," rather than participating in a Christian tradition of discourse.[36] That mode of discourse is known as the "flyting". Carol J. Clover defines "flyting" by saying, "Most flytings consist of boasts and insults in varying proportions with an admixture of threats, curses, and woes,"[37] or, more directly, "the oral equivalent of war."[38] The flyting, however, should not be understood as some low-brow banter between drunkards. A. P. Church claims that "the flyting is not a crude exchange of wit but an expected convention of heroic society."[39] This exchange of boasts and insults, then, would have been familiar to a Germanic audience and exemplifies the social operation of that society. The Germanic sensibility embedded in the flyting, combined with the Christian interpretation of the episode, produces an interesting synergy: a Christian problem is confronted and overcome by Germanic means. This synergy lies at the core of the world of *Beowulf*, both in the original and in Heaney's textual translation, but is absent in the audio version.

The Hunferð episode also illustrates an important aspect of Beowulf's social interaction with the Danes of Herot. The challenge from Hunferð forces Beowulf to assert himself as capable of accepting the task at hand. "If Beowulf were allowed to proceed in his quest," Church argues, "it would have involved the proud Danes' symbolic surrender,"[40] and, through the assertion, Beowulf "established himself as a credible hero."[41] He avoids giving the impression that he is the early medieval equivalent of a rock star: one coming from far away yet already known, accepted, and loved. Lacking the Hunferð episode makes the Beowulf of Heaney's audio *Beowulf* appear as such: accepted as the hero of Herot with no heroic deeds to establish his worth. Why would this man have been accepted in Herot without his boast? Similarly omitted is Beowulf's first boast, #8, when he describes his slaying of beasts and enemies to avenge the Geats. Adrien Bonjour describes this boast as "giving a first illustration of his uncommon strength and to give at the same time a sort of justification for Beowulf's arrival at the Danish court."[42] The notion that Beowulf needs to provide justification for his arrival receives little treatment in Heaney's audio version, and in fact his arrival seems more a matter of fact than something requiring merit. This is not the case in the world of the poem, where the need for justification at arrival suggests the possibility that Beowulf might not have been welcomed to Herot, and without his boast, might have been slain on the shore by the watchman Wulfgar (a character also omitted in #6).

Other pessimistic passages, particularly those that suggest the possibility of failure, constitute the next type of omission in the present study. A striking passage early in the poem (#9) has Beowulf suggesting what will happen if he should fail to defeat Grendel. "If Grendel wins, it will be a gruesome day; / he will glut himself on the Geats in the war-hall" (31). The passages suggest the possibility of the fall of Herot, the Danes, and the Geats. In fact, with its elegiac mood, the poem is dotted with such suggestions of future and immediate falls from greatness. This mood suggests another, perhaps more reflective, aspect of the characters in the Beowulfian world, and the omission of such passages make victory seem more assured and less the result of human action. Moreover, it renders the final sorrow of Beowulf's funeral a non sequitur.

Some of the most excellent and memorable passages in *Beowulf* can be found in such omissions, and their exclusion from Heaney's audio version is therefore all the more lamentable. For instance, the listener never hears about the cursed journey of the Brosings' neck chain (#37), which brings ill-fate to all who win it in war, ending finally with Hygelac when he falls. Additionally, we miss "Hroðgar's Sermon" (#55), as it is commonly called, where Hroðgar warns Beowulf about the limitations of greatness and the dangers of pride. Elaine Tuttle Hansen says of this passage, "Hroðgar's parental instruction provides a pivotal scene in which joy is tempered and elevated by the certain knowledge of grief to be endured."[43] The key is the elevation: Beowulf's victories ring hollow without the possibility of defeat; joy is accentuated in a world where there is the possibility of sorrow; and the omission of such sorrow is no small detraction from the presence of authentic joy.

The most significant omission in Heaney's audio version comes amid a passage that fits into all six of the major categories of this study, #71. The passage begins with the fratricide involving the sons of Hreðel already introduced above, but then shifts to the sorrowful comparison of Hreðel to a man who must endure the sight of his son swinging from the gallows, and a life with that son's absence. The "Father's Lament," as it has become known, exposes the sorrowful and reflective side of the Beowulfian world like no other passage. Ironically, the poetry of the translation is amongst Heaney's best:

> The wisdom of age is worthless to him.
> Morning after morning, he wakes to remember
> that his child is gone; he has no interest
> in living on until another heir
> is born in the hall, now that his first-born
> has entered death's dominion forever.
> He gazes sorrowfully at his son's dwelling
> the banquet hall bereft of all delight,
> the windswept hearthstone; the horsemen are sleeping,
> the warriors under ground; what was is no more.
> No tunes from the harp, no cheer raised in the yard.
> Alone with his longing, he lies down on his bed
> and sings a lament; everything seems too large,
> the steadings and the fields. (166–67)

This passage is perhaps even more poignant when one considers that the lines are uttered by Beowulf himself, shortly before his death-battle with the dragon. It positions his final triumph and fall in a world of lament and reflection, where the potential for failure is all too real and the chance to triumph is anything but assured. Here, Beowulf is human. Without such reflection, Beowulf appears as a merely fantastic hero fighting battles without authentic consequence, and this narrow presentation is perhaps what informs the contemporary common understanding of the medieval hero.

One of the many references to the ongoing conflict between the Swedes and the Geats which have been omitted from the audio translation immediately follows the "Father's Lament." Throughout the second half of the poem, this historically verifiable conflict emerges through the course of Beowulf's life after leaving Herot: from Hygelac's wars, to Beowulf's forging a temporary peace, to the foreshadowing of the Geats' future destruction at the hands of the Swedes.

More than any of the other types of omission, the absence of passages regarding the feud with the Swedes strips away the immediate backdrop for Beowulf's life and eliminates an important context of his actions. David Day, who also points out that Hroðgar's aid to Ecgþeow in the feud against the Wylfings (#10) sets the background for Beowulf's offer of help against Grendel,[44] asserts that the feud with the Swedes sets the tone for the conflict with the dragon.[45] Thus, as the stories of Sigemund or Mod Þryðo give additional insight into the characters of Beowulf or Hygd, the references to feuds between actual people enlighten the conflicts with the monsters. Furthermore, a rather interesting article by R. T. Farrell in the *Saga Book of the Viking Society of Northern Research* treats in detail the Geat–Swede feud, asserting that the poem "deals almost exclusively with Scandinavian affairs, the relations of Geat, Dane, and Swede, in the troubled times of the late migration period."[46] Regardless of whether there are other historical conflicts being addressed in *Beowulf*, the Swede conflict provides the historical material out of which *Beowulf* emerges, allowing the reader to put the poem in a real place during a real time. This is impossible when these passages are omitted.

Finally, I would like to touch briefly on the minor alterations and omissions. Though they bear little impact on the thesis of the present study, they warrant some comment. It might seem rather inconsequential on the surface whether "*breost-hord þurhbræc*" is translated as "broke out from the breast-cage" or "heaved out from the coffers of the heart" (#85) or even more so whether "*Beowulf maþelode, bearn Ecgþeowes*" becomes "Beowulf, son of Ecgþeow, said" or "Beowulf, son of Ecgþeow, declared" (#14). I have included these passages in the appendix not only to provide a thorough catalogue of omissions and alterations but also because such small changes are suggestive of both the nature of translation and the oral presentation of poetry. Taking for granted the often debated assertion that *Beowulf* was orally performed before it was written down, hearing the poet Heaney orally perform his translation suggests the subtle shifts that might take place in the oral tradition. While it is difficult to discuss the nature of an oral tradition from within a hyper-literate culture such as ours, particularly without additional research, it stands to reason that a small shift from "said" to "declared" would be easy enough to make from performance to performance. Additionally, slight alterations in translations such as the move from "breast-cage" to "coffers of the heart" suggest the possibility of further analysis of the choices of translators and how they affect the critical understanding of the poem.

In closing, I would like to point out that J. R. R. Tolkien's foundational "*Beowulf:* The Monsters and the Critics" has relevance in the context of this study.[47] As many have acknowledged, Tolkien instigated a movement in modern Beowulfian literary scholarship by his refutation of the claim that *Beowulf*'s "weakness lies in placing the unimportant things at the centre and the important on the outer edges."[48] His analysis made it clear to those who have followed in his footsteps as literary scholars of *Beowulf* that the poem is more than a repository of historical data to satisfy curiosity in reconstructing past events that have otherwise been covered over by time. Indeed, over-turning the previous trend of critical study allows the conflicts with Grendel, with Grendel's mother, and with the dragon to come to the fore, as Tolkien asserts that, in fact, "the particular is on the outer edge, the essential is in the centre."[49] Reading Tolkien's essay might lead one to the notion that a presentation of *Beowulf* like Heaney's audio version and other contemporary presentations are the logical conclusion of what Tolkien began: the historical and contextual elements on the outer edges of *Beowulf* had been placed in the center by historicist scholars before Tolkien; they were pushed back to the margins by Tolkien and those who have followed; and they have now been eradicated entirely. To do so, however, devalues the "particular" that Tolkien suggests is the role of these outer episodes. Tolkien says, "The author has used an instinctive historical sense – a part indeed of the ancient English temper (and not unconnected with its reputed melancholy), of which *Beowulf* is the supreme expression; but he has used it with a poetical and not an historical object."[50] The point here is that these side episodes are not extraneous to the poetry, but rather a part of what makes the poetry what it is. The audio version of Heaney's translation of *Beowulf* is certainly beautiful to the ear and full of the many poetic flourishes that characterize the translation (a translation that even in the printed version is not immune to contro-versy). But, because of the omissions, it lacks that which makes it English, locates it in Scandinavia, places it in the Germanic and early Christian traditions, and allows it to exist in some real place populated by real people, however fictionalized and rendered fantastic by monsters and dragons.

APPENDIX

Item	Line #	Time	Description	Type
1	63	3:43	"to" changed to "for"	G
2	177	10:01	"that the killer of souls might come to their aid" changed to "that the killer of souls would come to their aid"	G
3	352–355	19:57	Wulfgar declares that he will go and ask Hroðgar, to whom he gives praise about Beowulf's coming, and return with a reply.	A
4	357–359	20:03	A description of Wulfgar standing courteously before Hroðgar before addressing him.	A, D
5	374–377	20:56	Hroðgar speaks of knowing that Ecgþeow married Hreðel's daughter.	A, D
6	388–389a	21:32	Hroðgar adds that Wulfgar should tell Beowulf and his men that they are welcomed to Denmark.	A
7	397–398	21:57	Beowulf and his men are told by Wulfgar to leave behind their shields and spears before having an audience with Hroðgar.	A, B
8	419–426	23:10	Beowulf recounts, rather graphically, his prowess in destroying beasts and enemies for the Geats.	B
9	442–454	24:02	Beowulf describes the gory scene that will ensue should Grendel win the fight, and says his corpse should be returned to Hygelac.	B, E
10	459–476a	24:20	Hroðgar describes the conditions of his oath of allegiance to Ecgþeow, and mentions his humiliation in needing aid now.	A, D, F
11	480–488	24:33	Hroðgar describes the unsuccessful attempts made by his men to defeat Grendel and the gory results of those episodes.	B, E

Item	Line #	Time	Description	Type
12	499–606	25:10	Hunferð, envious of Beowulf, challenges Beowulf, chiding him for his experience with Breca, and predicts Beowulf will lose against Grendel. Beowulf rebukes Hunferð, claiming he must be drunk, then recounts the tale of the swimming contest and slaughter of nine sea-monsters. Beowulf brings up Hunferð's killing of kin, and blames his lack of courage for Grendel's success and lack of fear. He then boasts of ensuing victory.	A, B, C
13	616–622a	25:44	When Wealhþeow is distributing mead, the lines are omitted wherein she first brings the drink to Hroðgar, who drinks it down as the men cheer before she continues to distribute to the others. The alteration makes it appear that all are given the mead equally, rather than with recognition for rank.	D
14	631	26:16	"Beowulf, son of Ecgþeow, said:" changed to "Beowulf, son of Ecgþeow, declared:"	G
15	665	28:21	"his queen and bedmate. The King of Glory" changed to "his queen and his bedmate. The King of Heaven"	G
16	707	30:41	"God disallowed it" changed to "The Lord forbade it"	G
17	796	35:45	"as best as they could with their ancestral blades" changed to "as best as they could with ancestral blades"	G
18	810	36:30	"and had given offence also to God" changed to "and given offence also to God" (The auxiliary verb "had" also appears early in the sentence with the other half of the compound verb.)	G
19	873b–916	40:04	The bard recounts the story of Sigemund, including the slaying of a dragon and Sigemund's fame. Heremod, burdensome to his friends, is contrasted with Beowulf.	A
20	944	41:41	"labour" changed to "labours"	G

Item	Line #	Time	Description	Type
21	956–1019	42:22	Beowulf laments that Grendel did not die in the hall for all to see. Hunferð is silent as the men examine the damage to Herot, which is ordered to be repaired. Hroðgar calls another meeting in the hall. Essentially, this omission groups together two separate celebrations, decreasing the amount of festivity and time between the Grendel and Grendel's mother episodes. Also notably omitted here: "The Shielding nation / was not yet familiar with feud and betrayal."	A, B, C, D
22	1068	45:14	"the" changed to "that"	G
23	1070–1071a	45:20	"Hildeburh had little cause to credit the Jutes:" changed to "And his sister Hildeburh suffered cruelly."	G
24	1073	45:30	"She, bereft and blameless" omitted.	G
25	1075	45:35	"She, the woman in shock, waylaid by grief" changed to "She in shock, waylaid by grief"	G
26	1090	46:25	"should" changed to "would"	G
27	1100b	47:00	"Their own ring-giver, after all was dead and gone" changed to "Their own ring-giver was dead and gone"	G
28	1104–1107	47:06	During the lay of Finsburg, the bard recounts that a Frisian who stirred up bad blood would be punished with death.	B
29	1142b–1145	49:16	Hengest is presented with the sword Dazzle-the-Duel by Hunlafing.	A
30	1147b–1150a	49:22	Guðlaf and Oslaf return to Friesland. The omission of #29 and #30 eliminate the efficient causes of the slaughter of Finn.	A
31	1161–1167	50:05	Wealhþeow sits between Hroðgar and Hunferð. Hunferð's fratricide is again referred to, as is the possibility of future strife in Herot.	A, C
32	1167	50:08	"The queen spoke:" changed to "The queen spoke to Hroðgar:" This addition is necessary given the omission of #31.	G

Item	Line #	Time	Description	Type
33	1179–1186	50:46	Wealhþeow discusses the possibility of Hroðgar's death, and indicates that he should be replaced by Hroðulf.	A, B, D, E
34	1188	50:52	Wealhþeow sits with Hreðric and Hroðmund.	A
35	1192	51:06	"a wealth of wrought gold" changed to "a wealth of gold"	G
36	1193	51:07	"graciously bestowed" changed to "given to the hero"	G
37	1198–1214	51:21	The hoard given by Wealhþeow is compared to the Brosings' neck-chain. The lineage of the neck chain is recounted, culminating in the death of Hygelac at the hands of the Frisians. Also, the Danes applaud the gift-giving.	A, D
38	1215	51:22	"Wealhþeow" replaced with "the queen," appropriate given that, with the omission of #37, it is clear to whom "the queen" refers.	G
39	1243	53:09	"above" changed to "over"	G
40	1267b–1276a	54:34	When discussing the bringing forth of Grendel as a result of Cain's fratricide, Grendel's death at the hands of Beowulf is quickly recounted, and Beowulf's success is very directly linked to God's aid.	B, C
41	1280	54:52	"earls who would soon endure a great reversal" changed to "earls who would soon know a great reversal"	G
42	1282a–1287	54:57	Grendel's mother is compared to an Amazon warrior bloodily rupturing a helmet.	B
43	1288	55:00	"hard-honed swords" changed to "hard-honed blades"	G
44	1341–1344	58:06	The account of Æschere's having "died in battle" is qualified by revealing that it is common for thanes to anguish at the loss of a ring-giver, and by implication, possibly embellish the death.	D
45	1435	63:32	"the seasoned shaft stuck deep in his flank" changed to "the seasoned shaft went in deep in his flank"	G

Item	Line #	Time	Description	Type
46	1453	64:39	"adorned it with boar-shapes" changed to "embellished it with boar-shapes"	G
47	1465–1472	65:20	After Hunferð loans Hrunting to Beowulf, he can hardly remember his earlier rant, and his reputation is tarnished on account of his inability to follow after Grendel's mother.	A, D
48	1494	:07 (CD2)	"without more ado" changed to "without further ado"	G
49	1497–1517	:17	Beowulf is grabbed by Grendel's mother and dragged into her lair. With the omission, he seems almost to take her by surprise.	B
50	1543	1:43	"The sure-footed fighter felt daunted" changed to "The sure-footed fighter felt suddenly daunted"	G
51	1570–1623	3:07	After killing Grendel's mother, Beowulf discovers and beheads the corpse of Grendel. Hroðgar and his men on land despair for Beowulf, and all abandon except for the Geats. The sword of the Jotuns melts, Beowulf discovers treasures, and he returns to the surface.	B
52	1640–1641	4:01	The Geats return to Herot, bearing the head of Grendel.	B
53	1659–1668	4:32	Beowulf describes the failure of Hrunting, the discovery of the Jotun sword, his victory stroke, and the sword's melting.	B
54	1677	5:05	"the gold hilt" changed to "the golden hilt"	G
55	1687–1784	5:35	Hroðgar examines the sword's hilt. The engraving of the first war and the flood is described. Hroðgar praises Beowulf, again contrasting him with Heremod, specifically referencing Heremod's killing of comrades. Hroðgar praises God and describes how man falls from God's grace, admonishing Beowulf not to give into pride himself. (Often called "Hroðgar's Sermon.")	A, D, E
56	1785–1786	5:35	Beowulf sits before Hroðgar.	D

Item	Line #	Time	Description	Type
57	1868	10:22	"sail with those gifts" changed to "to sail with those gifts"	G
58	1889	11:38	"the young men" changed to "those young men"	G
59	1925–1962	13:39	**Hygd is praised, and contrasted to Mod Þryðo. Mod Þryðo's cruelty is recounted, as is her transformation upon her marriage to Offa.**	A, B, D
60	2003	15:52	"he visited destruction" changed to "he had visited destruction"	G
61	2081	20:13	"he was bloated and furious" changed to "he was bloated and dangerous"	G
62	2117	22:11	"suddenly" changed to "with sudden dispatch"	G
63	2143	23:37	"gifts in abundance" changed to "multitude of gifts"	G
64	2154a–2162	24:30	**Beowulf tells Hygelac that the gear he had just presented had been presented by Hroðgar and that it had belonged to Heorogar.**	D
65	2216	27:30	"He had handled" changed to "He handled"	G
66	2234	28:23	"somebody now forgotten" changed to "some forgotten person"	G
67	2235	28:27	"buried the riches of a high borne race" changed to "deposited the whole rich inheritance of a high-borne race"	G
68	2236	28:30	"this ancient cache" changed to "that ancient cache"	G
69	2238–2240	28:36	"only one left to tell their tale, the last one of their line, could look forward to nothing but the same fate for himself" changed to "one surviving witness of their fate, the last veteran could envisage only the same fate for himself"	G

Item	Line #	Time	Description	Type
70	2345–2416	34:59	Beowulf disregards the dragon's threat. The poet recounts Beowulf's escape via a solo sea voyage from the battle with the Frisians that had taken Hygelac, his denial of Hygd's offer of the throne, Heardred's death at the hands of the Swedes, Beowulf's ascension to the throne, and the befriending of Eadgils to end the feud. Beowulf sets out with twelve men, including the thief, to find the dragon.	A, D, F
71	2425–2510	35:29	Beowulf recounts his own childhood, including the death of Hygelac's brother at the hand of his other brother. Hreðel's loss is compared to that of a man seeing his son die at the gallows ("The Father's Lament"). Beowulf describes the feud with the Swedes in greater detail, and declares he will continue to fight until he dies.	A, B, C, D, E, F
72	2515	35:52	"abandon his earth-fort" changed to "abandon his fort"	G
73	2552	38:07	"Under grey stone" changed to "Under the grey stone"	G
74	2561	38.38	"viciously turned on the king" changed to "vehemently turned on the king"	G
75	2592–2630	40:24	Beowulf's men break ranks as Beowulf fights the dragon. Wiglaf's father, Weohstan, is recalled, including his bestowal of a breastplate on Wiglaf.	A
76	2637	40:47	"those swords" changed to "these swords"	G
77	2638b–2646a	40:53	Wiglaf points out to the men that Beowulf had picked them out specifically because of their prowess.	D
78	2658	41:30	"Should he alone be left exposed to fall in battle?" changed to "Why should he alone be left exposed to fall in battle?"	G
79	2706	44:27	"They had killed the enemy, courage quelled his life;" changed to "They had killed the enemy, their courage quelled his life;"	G

Item	Line #	Time	Description	Type
80	2716	45:09	"struggled toward a seat on the rampart" changed to "proceeded towards the seat on the rampart"	G
81	2736	46:21	"I took what came" replaced with "I stood my ground and took what came"	G
82	2737	46:22	"cared for and stood by things in my keeping" changed to "cared for things in my keeping"	G
83	2740–2743	46:35	**Dying, Beowulf says God will never judge him for having slain kinsmen.**	**C**
84	2773–2779a	48:21	**A "certain man" plunders the dragon's hoard after the dragon has been slain.**	**A**
85	2792	49:07	"broke out from the king's breast-cage" changed to "heaved up from the coffers of the king's heart"	G
86	2812	50:28	"telling him to use it and the warshirt and the gilded helmet well" changed to "telling him to use it and the warshirt and the gilded helmet"	G
87	2816	50:44	Beowulf's final words changed from "Now I must follow them" to "Now I must follow."	G
88	2826b–2830a	51:20	**Repetition of the fact that the dragon is in fact dead and that he had been killed by the sword.**	**B**
89	2837–2842a	51:41	**The poet points out that few would have been strong and brave enough to hold out against the dragon.**	**B**
90	2863–2872	52:52	**Wiglaf admonishes the men, claiming any bestowal of gifts on them by Beowulf was a waste. This beginning of the speech is replaced with, "He upbraided the battle-dodgers, saying […]"**	**D**
91	2877	53:12	"There was little I could do" changed to "I could do little"	G
92	2890–2891	53:59	"A warrior will sooner die than live a life of shame" changed to "A warrior will die sooner than live a life of shame"	G
93	2918	55:31	"his war-gear was laid low" changed to "his war-gear was brought low"	G
94	2927	56:03	"first attacked" changed to "attacked first"	G

Item	Line #	Time	Description	Type
95	2930a–2932	56:15	**Ongenþeow the Swede saves his wife.**	**A, F**
96	2934–2999	56:24	**Ongenþeow besieges the Geats, who are relieved by Hygelac. The Swedes are routed, and Ongenþeow is killed by Eofor. Ongenþeow is looted. Hygelac awards his daughter to Eofor.**	**A, B, D, F**
97	3021	57:44	"high spirits quenched" changed to "his spirits quenched"	G
98	3058–3075	60:00	**The treasure is described as having brought about nothing good. Beowulf is described as being unable to know his exact end, as any warrior. The nobles declare the treasure to be accursed. The poet describes Beowulf's gaze on the gold as not selfish.**	**D, E**
99	3080	60:16	"the prince we loved" changed to "the lord we loved"	G
100	3081	60:21	"vex the custodian" changed to "aggravate the keeper"	G
101	3104	61:47	"take you close" changed to "bring you close"	G
102	3120	62:48	"Next" changed to "then"	G
103	3136	63:37	"the prince on his bier, borne to Hronesness" changed to "the prince on his bier was borne to Hronesness"	G

Types of omissions:

A: References to secondary characters
B: Especially violent scenes or the repetition of a violent scene
C: References to fratricide
D: Scenes revealing aspects of social relations
E: Particularly pessimistic passages
F: References to feuds, particularly involving the Swedes
G: Minor revisions
(Types A–F are placed in bold text to distinguish them more clearly from type G)

NOTES

1. I am indebted to Professors Paul G. Remley and Míceál F. Vaughan of the University of Washington for helping me prepare this study: Dr. Remley for his encouragement and assistance with the initial formulation, and Dr. Vaughan for working with me during the revision process.

2. Daniel Donoghue, "The Philologer Poet: Seamus Heaney and the Translation of *Beowulf*," *Harvard Review* (2000) (repr. in Daniel Donoghue, ed., and Seamus Heaney, trans., *Beowulf, a Verse Translation. Norton Critical Edition* [New York: W. W. Norton & Company, 2002], 237–47 [239]).

3. John Keats, "On First Looking into Chapman's Homer," in *Selected Poems and Letters*, ed. Douglas Bush (Boston: Houghton Mifflin, 1959), 18.

4. University of Oxford, "English at Oxford: Beyond Beowulf," *Annual Review 1999/2000* (2001) <http://www.ox.ac.uk/publicaffairs/pubs/annualreview/ar00/01.shtml> (accessed 10 February 2007).

5. Gareth Hinds, *The Collected Beowulf* (Cambridge, MA: The Comic.com, 2003).

6. *Beowulf and Grendel*, dir. Sturla Gunnarsson (Anchor Bay, 2006).

7. IMDB. *Beowulf (2007)* and *Beowulf: Prince of the Geats* <http://www.imdb.com/title/tt0442933> <http://www. imdb.com/title/tt0455348/> (accessed 31 October 2007). I should add that at the time of completion of this study, I had not yet had the opportunity to see either film and am bringing them up only to indicate the current popularity of the poem.

8. Dianne Glasier, "RE: Question about item 1–56511–427–2, Beowulf trans. Seamus Heaney" (e-mail: 25 October 2006).

9. Amazon.com. "Amazon.com: Beowulf audio," <http://www.amazon.com/s/ref=nb_ss_gw/105–3278509–0438001?url=search-alias%3Daps&field-keywords=beowulf+audio> (accessed 31 October 2007).

10. Barnes & Noble. "Barnes & Noble.com – Book Search: Beowulf," <http://search.barnesandnoble.com/booksearch/results.asp?SRT=S&z=y&FMT=A%2CCD&SZE=10&WRD=beowulf&Go%21.x=22&Go%21.y=13> (accessed 31 October 2007).

11. Audible.com. "Search Results: Beowulf," <http://www.audible.com/adbl/site/enSearch/ searchResults.jsp?D=beowulf&Ntt=beowulf&Dx=mode%2bmatchallpartial&Ntk=S_Keywords&Ntx=mode%2bmatchallpartial&N=0&BV_UseBVCookie=yes&Ns=P_Total_Sold|1> (accessed 31 October 2007).

12. Crawford Logan, *Beowulf* [Audiobook] (Naxos Audiobooks Ltd., 2006).

13. Dick Ringler, *Beowulf: The Complete Story*, prod. Norman Gilliland (audiobook) (Madison: University of Wisconsin Press, 2006).

14. Seamus Heaney, "Beowulf: The Original BBC Recording" (audiobook) (HighBridge Company, 2000).

15. Dianne Glasier, "RE: Question about item 1–56511–427–2, Beowulf trans. Seamus Heaney" (e-mail: 25 October 2006).

16. Except when quoting directly from Heaney, I have chosen to restore the manuscript spelling to "Hunferð". For more on the justification for this spelling, see: M. F. Vaughan, "A Reconsideration of 'Unferð'," *Neuphilologische Mitteilungen* 77 (1976): 32–48. I have likewise elected to use the Old English characters æ, þ, and ð, except when quoting.

17. *Beowulf*, trans. Seamus Heaney (New York: W. W. Norton & Company, 2000). Please note that the page number(s) for quotations from this edition are given parenthetically in my main text after the quote.

18. Seamus Heaney, "Introduction," in *Beowulf*, trans. Seamus Heaney (New York: W. W. Norton & Company, 2000), xiii.

19. Heaney, "Introduction," xiii.

20. M. S. Griffin, "Some Difficulties in *Beowulf*, lines 874–902: Sigemund Reconsidered," *Anglo-Saxon England* 24 (1995): 11–41 (11).

21. Griffin, "Some Difficulties," 39.

22. Marijane Osborn, " 'The Wealth They Left Us': Two Women Author Themselves through Other's Lives in *Beowulf*," *Philological Quarterly* 78 (1999): 49–76 (56).

23. Christopher Fee, " 'Beag' and 'Beaghroden' in *Beowulf*," *Neuphilologische Mitteilungen* 97 (1996): 285–94 (286).

24. Helen Damico, *Beowulf's Wealhþeow and the Valkyrie Tradition* (Madison: University of Wisconsin Press, 1984), 47.

25. Damico, *Beowulf's Wealhþeow*, 49.

26. Mary Dockray-Miller, "The Masculine Queen of *Beowulf*," *Women & Language* 21.2 (1998): 31–38 (35).

27. Dockray-Miller, "The Masculine Queen of *Beowulf*," 36.

28. Adrien Bonjour, *The Digressions in "Beowulf"* (Oxford: Basil Blackwell, 1950), 55.

29. Janet Thormann, "Beowulf and the Enjoyment of Violence," *Literature and Psychology* 43 (1997): 65–73 (67).

30. Thormann, "Beowulf and the Enjoyment of Violence," 72.

31. *New American Bible* (New York: Catholic Book Publishing Company, 1991), Matthew 22.39.

32. David Williams, *Cain and Beowulf – A Study in Secular Allegory* (Toronto: University of Toronto Press, 1982), 21.

33. G. C. Britton, "Unferth, Grendel, and the Christian Meaning of *Beowulf*," *Neophilologische Mitteilungen* 72 (1971): 246–50 (249).

34. Williams, *Cain and Beowulf*, 87.

35. Williams, *Cain and Beowulf*, 36–37.

36. F. H. Whitman, "The Kingly Nature of Beowulf," *Neophilogus* 61 (1977): 277–86 (278).

37. Carol J. Clover, "The Germanic Context of the Unferþ Episode," *Speculum* 55.3 (1980): 444–68 (453).

38. Clover, "The Germanic Context," 452.

39. A. P. Church, "Beowulf's '*ane ben*' and the Rhetorical Context of the Hunferþ Episode," *Rhetorica* 18 (2000): 49–78 (60).

40. Church, "Beowulf's '*ane ben*'," 65.

41. Church, "Beowulf's '*ane ben*'," 67.

42. Bonjour, *The Digressions in "Beowulf"*, 13.

43. Elaine Tuttle Hansen, "Hrothgar's 'Sermon' in *Beowulf* as Paternal Wisdom," *Anglo-Saxon England* 10 (1982): 53–67 (58).

44. David Day, "Defining the Feud in *Beowulf*," *Philological Quarterly* 78 (1999): 77–95 (78).

45. Day, "Defining the Feud in *Beowulf*," 81.

46. R. T. Farrell, "Beowulf, Swedes and Geats," *Saga Book of the Viking Society of Northern Research* 18 (1972): 225–86 (282).

47. J. R. R. Tolkien, "*Beowulf*: The Monsters and the Critics," *Proceedings of the British Academy* (1936) (repr. in Donoghue, ed., *Beowulf, a Verse Translation*, 103–30).

48. Tolkien, "*Beowulf*: The Monsters and the Critics," 103.

49. Tolkien, "*Beowulf*: The Monsters and the Critics," 115.

50. Tolkien, "*Beowulf*: The Monsters and the Critics," 105.

The King's Phantom:
Staging Majesty in Bale's *Kynge Johan*

Thea Cervone

Thomas Cromwell's accounts for September 1539 show an entry for "Balle and his fellows," who were to be paid 40s for performing a play at St. Stephen's beside Canterbury.[1] The play is not named, but it is almost certainly *Kynge Johan*, the most well-known dramatic work of the Reformer John Bale (1495–1563). Though "Bilious Bale," as he was known at the time, became a member of the Carmelite order in 1507, he converted to the Reformist movement in 1533 and within six years composed this attack on the supposed evils and hypocrisies of the Church. In it, he suggests that the papacy aligned itself with England's "traitors" – namely, its lawyers, aristocrats, and proponents of private wealth – and had its spies poison King John. He suffuses a historical drama with contemporary propaganda that surely appealed to his guest of honor at St. Stephen's – none other than Cromwell himself.

In doing so, Bale also develops the character Imperyall Majestie as a remedy to the suffering of King Johan and his subjects, not to mention their heirs. The exact circumstances in which this figure was conceived are not known, for early drafts of the play do not survive, and there is not much evidence for when or how often it was revised. But as we shall see, the figure apparently descends from medieval saint plays, hagiography, and *exempla*, as well as English folk traditions that revolve around ghosts and revenants (the risen dead). He represents the survival of kingship even after the physical death of the king, and he allows Bale to overcome Johan's martyrdom. Through Imperyall Majestie, the playwright is able to chastise the villains, fulfill Johan's sworn obligation to his country, and punish Sedycyon, who doubles as

Johan's poisoner, Stephen Langton. That is, Bale is able to correct the injustices supposedly visited upon John and to suggest that the king's heirs, as well as their subjects, should be free of such treachery.[2]

Bale is not able to do so, however, without carefully adapting his sources.[3] In revising them, he reveals an important relationship between his Reformist beliefs and the medieval texts he uses to construct his arguments. As a monk, Bale had been a chronicler and bibliographer. Moreover, he had worked for many years on a history of the Carmelite House as well as a catalogue of its libraries. Thus, it should come as no surprise that his departures from the past are characterized by a tendency to assert a new sense of authority over existing ideas. But this meant that he had to employ material that he ultimately opposed, a paradox recalling Larry Scanlon's important discussion of how *exempla* influenced late medieval literature: "From the beginning Christianity has been marked by a double insistence: that it bespeaks a Spirit which transcends all material circumstance, but that its believers have to make that Spirit manifest in the very materiality it transcends."[4] And though Bale's scholarly and doctrinal expertise allowed him to readily appropriate material that had originally been used for very different ends, the irony of skillfully and authoritatively employing that which he despised seems to have left him a cynic.

Bale's work reflects his revisionist attitude toward English history. He was especially affected by the idea that the Church had always sought to undermine English kings. King John's forced submission is Bale's primary example, but his stance in this regard can also be seen in his condemnation of St. Dunstan, whom Bale portrays as having overreached his place in attempting to influence Kings Edwyn and Edgar.[5] From Bale's perspective, the British Isles had been alone in preserving the truth of Christianity, and he saw the Church and its representatives as meddlers.[6] His figure of Imperyall Majestie therefore represents not only a practical solution to a limited literary, theological, and political problem from the past, but also an ideological response to a much broader, more enduring, and more recent threat to the Royal Supremacy.

Like many other sixteenth-century writers, Bale was preoccupied by continually identifying, explaining, and justifying the historical place of the movement in which he participated.[7] Indeed, in his *Actes of the English Votaryes* (1546) he suggests that a moral agenda lies behind all of his works on the past, as he says, "It is the nature always of an historye to declare the goodnesse and malice of times by the divers actes of men, to the wanting of others, which I in my writings have decreed to follow."[8] And he did not hesitate to shape the historical context of his didactic and exemplary material to his evangelical mission as he sought to redefine the historical role of the Roman Church and replace it with the Royal Supremacy.[9] Yet, in accord with sixteenth-century views on historiography, he portrays himself not as a mere propagandist, much less a prophet, but as a historian with a duty to the truth, for he presents his "vision" as not only dramatic but also deliberate and academic.

This interpretation of himself and of his sources is anchored in a much wider connection between, on the one hand, dramatic interpretation of contemporary events in the 1530s and, on the other hand, earlier ideas concerning commemoration and memory. According to Benjamin Griffin, much of this connection depends on what he calls "the energies of the Mass,"[10] particularly as they are manifested in Thomas Cranmer's belief that the sacrifice at the heart of the Mass is commemorated, not recreated.[11] From that perspective, change occurs in the thought process of the believer rather than in the substance of the Eucharist. And when that view was driven underground in Bale's time, these "energies" may have found new expression in what Griffin calls a "Renaissance Drama of the past."[12] For example, in *Kynge Johan*, Imperyall Majestie is perhaps most appropriately seen as commemorating, not recreating, the dead monarch for whom the play is named. Thus, Imperyall Majestie serves as a sixteenth-century figure who speaks in support of Reformist doctrine, and his inclusion in the play is presumably part of Bale's efforts to win his audiences over to the Reformist cause.[13]

However, Imperyall Majestie's contemporaneous relevance does not automatically mean he should be identified specifically and solely with Henry VIII, as W. T. Davies supposes,[14] for in addition to embodying the memory of Johan, Imperyall Majestie represents all other English monarchs, including Henry VIII. Indeed, he helps promote such a successful reconciliation of, on the one hand, kingship as a living concept and, on the other hand, Bale's views of historical and contemporary events that twenty years later the play needed only minor revisions to include Elizabeth I.

This reconciliation was absolutely vital to the success and mission of the play, for the work was highly vulnerable to the rapidly changing circumstances of Henrician England,[15] particularly in terms of official views of Purgatory and other matters pertaining to the relationship between the living and the dead. Henrician policies favored the Royal Supremacy over Reformed doctrine with regard to Purgatory, but Cromwell still wielded tremendous power during the 1530s when *Kynge Johan* was composed, and while the king had not yet suppressed Purgatory, Cromwell had condemned it. Bale was therefore saddled with the task of pleasing both his patron and his king on a topic that for both traditionalists and progressives had become something of a shibboleth, as Keith Thomas has described it.[16]

Bale's solution to this dilemma seems to reflect the stated beliefs of John Frith, a Reformer who, in the 1530s, wrote extensive exchanges with Thomas More and John Rastell on the concept of Purgatory.[17] In a refutation of More, Frith accuses the Church of using Purgatory to exploit commoners and argues that Purgatory conflicts with Scripture. He calls his opponents "miscreauntes" who "have ever for the most parte thought and beleved that after the bodyes are deceased the soules of such as were neyther deed lye dampned wretches for ever [...]."[18] And Bale seems to have extended this position to the legends of revenants and ghosts, for these figures were said to roam the earth and are often the subject of vivid stories in which they return from the dead to deliver messages from Purgatory.

Bale thus confronted a highly entrenched system of beliefs, for early modern England had a long history of legends about ghosts and revenants. In the most common formula, these figures appear a few days after their deaths. They bring warnings for the living about Purgatory, appeal for masses to be sung for their benefit, and sometimes bring warnings of events to come.[19] The time frame for their appearances generally revolves around liturgical rites for the dead.[20] For instance, one *exemplum* includes the story of a scholar who appears soon after his death to a friend and says that he, the dead scholar, has been saved because he always prepared himself well for Communion.[21] In another story an observant monk is pursued by a dead man who has risen from his bier to ask him and other Christians to pray for him.[22] And, in a particularly dramatic example, a man recites the *De Profundis* for Christian souls, who subsequently rise from the dead with spades in hand to help him fight his enemies.[23]

In both the folk tradition and *exempla*, the Church functions as a regulatory institution for the sake of the apparition and thereby defines the latter. But in *Kynge Johan* Bale attempts to replace the Church with the Crown in characterizing the ghost/revenant. If he is seen as successful, he will have created an abstract figure that transcends traditional ideas to reflect upon the new function fulfilled by the Crown. But if he is seen as having failed, his audience may be tempted to see Imperyall Majestie as merely a revenant or ghost returning to reinforce traditional doctrines. Since that would presumably be intolerable to a Reformist like Bale, it may explain why he removes several key components of the apparition tale and makes Imperyall Majestie both intangibly allegorical and undeniably sixteenth-century. For example, in contrast to conventional ghosts and revenants, Imperyall Majestie says nothing about Purgatory or masses; he does not appear in relation to Kynge Johan's dead body, such as near his tomb or at some future site for his commemoration; and he does not appear at a character's bedside or in a dream.[24] Thus, Bale gives us a rare glimpse of his own artistry, for rather than choosing one type of story as a model, he adapts elements from various traditions. He shapes his sources around his agenda and presents a figure that is suggestive of a ghost or revenant but functions as neither.[25]

This required some fancy footwork, but it was probably easier than completely overturning the ghost and revenant traditions, for they were strong as well as enduring. Even those who fully accepted Reformed doctrine may have found it difficult to completely ignore local tales about gossamer shapes in cemeteries or troops of long-dead Saxon warriors roaming the fields after dark.[26] And traditions ran particularly deep in rural areas, where the beliefs of the populace could not be continuously monitored.[27] Indeed, despite many efforts to transform rustic attitudes toward the dead, English Reformers were never able to banish the cultural presence of what Robert Scribner calls the "untimely dead," which would certainly seem to include poisoned kings.[28] Thus, Bale was probably quite wise to deflect and co-opt, rather than to completely oppose or deny, the saint and revenant traditions.

Of course, central to his appropriation of them was his preservation of the traditional methods by which sightings of apparitions were transmitted. Medieval ghosts/revenants and saints often appear to a host of witnesses, which frequently include institutional intermediaries like scribes, preachers, and aristocrats.[29] More than a distinct supernatural event, the medieval apparition tale is what the modern scholar Jean-Claude Schmitt calls "[...] a cultural object that was developed socially depending on its circulation."[30] Bearing witness is therefore the key to successful transmission of the medieval apparition tale because it helps the tale develop as it circulates. Especially important are the scribes and clerics who interpret the tale for didactic purposes. Indeed, according to William of Newburgh (1136?–1198?) and Caesarius of Heisterbach (c. 1180–c. 1240), both of whose books Bale collected,[31] the monk–scribe is responsible for the interpretation of local folklore and tales for the sake of the laity.[32] And with *Kynge Johan* Bale appears to be engaging in this traditional monastic activity. As he transmits and interprets Imperyall Majestie's message, he controls folkloric absorption by promoting Reformist doctrine in its place. Imperyall Majestie replaces the ghost and saint at once in a play that bears a familiar pattern: the king dies; a short time passes; and then an apparition enters with a didactic message. Bale changes the message but not the method, and the Carmelite/chronicler becomes the preacher/playwright.

Yet despite Bale's effective use of traditional forms of storytelling and literary expression, he does not seem to have liked fables, especially those that have no biblical precedent.[33] Of the Church's tolerance for fables, he says, "It is sonner sayde than proved. Of lykleyhode ye are some prothonotary of Rome, that ye wold your wurdes to be beleved without reasonable proves."[34] And, in fact, though Imperyall Majestie may be phenomenal, he resists being perceived as a *fabulous* construction. He appears alongside Verity as if he himself were in fact an allegorical truth. And he appears there as if he arrived of his own accord via the will of God. In being neither summoned by prayer nor conjured, he preserves a sense of regal dignity, of a royal reality that balances the mystique of conceptual, spiritual kingship and resists his being perceived as too ghostly, too saintly, or too miraculous for the play's agenda.

Of course, even though Bale condemns fables, he accepts rumors, stories, and the stuff of legend. His *Actes of the English Votaryes*, for example, is rife with tales of corruption, sexual exploits, greed, and sorcery on the part of the clergy in England.[35] Thus, his writing often differs from that of other sixteenth-century authors who tackled the same subjects. For instance, with regard to King John, John Foxe, who shared Bale's Protestant zeal, did not accept that the monarch had been poisoned, and he did not include such information in his massive Protestant pseudo-hagiography *Acts and Monuments* (1563). And though Shakespeare's play *King John* (1596–97) portrays the title character as having been exploited by Rome, the playwright is cautious with legends that gloss over the monarch's possible villainy in the death of Prince Arthur. Indeed, Shakespeare has John not only order the death of Prince Arthur as a means to rid himself of a competitor for the throne,[36] but also express regret after the boy's apparent death and blame that death on Hubert, the man to whom he gave the execution order.[37] That is, in contrast to Bale, who accepts popular legends that whitewash John and attributes the latter's failures to Catholic attacks upon his kingship, Shakespeare rejects these notions and depicts an inconstant and paranoid monarch nearly over-whelmed by the curse of power.

As perhaps the key component of Bale's whitewashing, Imperyall Majestie is an early but by no means isolated example of Bale's overall attempt to recreate the concept of the saint and to empower it, and we can perhaps gain insight to Bale's motives in these efforts by looking at one of his later pieces on the subject. In 1546, he composed a commentary on the examination of Anne Askew, who was burned at the stake with three others in that year. Although this commentary was composed approximately eight years after *Kynge Johan* was written, it probably stems from the same beliefs as that play when it comes to the concept of adapted sainthood for those of the Reformed faith. In the commentary, Bale says "Of his own chosen martyrs Christ looketh for none other miracle but that only they persevere faithful to the end [...] for that worthy victory of the synneful worlde, standeth in the inuyncyblenesse of faythe, and not in miracles and wonders as those waverynge wittes suppose."[38] Bale compares Askew to an early Christian martyr here but encourages a reverence of her memory through her testament alone, without including miracles. He therefore goes on to compare her to St. Blandina, whose martyrdom is characterized not by miraculous events but by the fortitude of the martyr herself.[39] He retells the story of Blandina's martyrdom, attrib-uting her physical strength under torture to her spiritual strength, and then immediately compares Blandina to Askew, saying, "Blandina never fainted in torment: no more did Anne Askew in spirit, when she was so terribly racked of Wrisley the chancellor, and Riche, that the strings of her arms and eyes were perished."[40] Moreover, concerning

Askew's spiritual fortitude, Bale says, "Blandina upon the scaffold boldly reprehended the pagan priests of their error: so did Anne Askew, when she was fast tied to the stake, with stomach rebuke that blasphemous apostate Shaxton with the bishops' and priests' generation, for their manifest maintanance of idolatry."[41]

In comparing Askew to Blandina, Bale makes an important distinction: he has his reader witness Askew's testament rather than the torture of her body. This distinction essentially redefines martyrdom. As Peter Happe notes, Bale takes the position that if the Catholic saints were to be disregarded, Protestant saints would need to be created, but they would need to be free from the concepts of material and ritual phenomena that accompany them.[42] Happe says, "The essential difference was that any Christian who witnessed his faith could be seen as a saint."[43] Any man or woman of faith could perform the act of witnessing with the same credibility as a saint, and Bale gives Askew precisely this kind of credibility as he comments upon her own account of her death sentence. As she is sentenced she forgives her enemies and prays that they might see the truth, to which Bale asks, "If these be not the fruits of a true believer, what other fruits can we ask?" And he punctuates that question with the words "A very saint" in the margin next to it.[44] He canonizes Askew through a process much like that enfolding Imperyall Majestie, as the audience of *Kynge Johan* witnesses the latter witnessing the truths of the play. Although Imperyall Majestie is not a man and therefore cannot technically be a saint, Bale has this conceptual incarnation of kingship bear credible witness and therefore suggest aspects of sainthood while keeping the concept well away from both King John and Henry VIII.

As a part of Bale's tendency to invert the purpose of past methods, this depiction of Imperyall Majestie allows the playwright to condemn the saint tradition even as he uses it. The villain Sedycyon presumes that he is already a saint while being carried off to be executed on the orders of Imperyall Majestie:

> *Sed.* Some man tell the pope, I besyche ye with all my harte,
> How I am ordered for takynge the churches parte,
> That I maye be put in the holye letanye
> With Thomas Beckett, for I thynke I am as wurthye.
> Praye to me with candels, for I am a saynt alreadye.
> O blessed saynt Partryck, I see the, I verylye![45]

To which, Imperyall Majestie responds:

> *I.Maj.* I see by thys wretche there hath bene muche faulte in ye;
> Shewe your selues hereafter more sober and wyse to be.[46]

The character Clergye then disavows the Church's hagiographic tradition in a speech that reveals more of Bale's great cynicism for the figure of the Catholic saint:[47]

> *Cler.* A saynt they can make of the most knaue thys daye lyuynge,
> Helpynge their market. And to promote the thynge
> He shall do miracles. But he that blemish their glorye
> Shall be sent to helle without anye remedye.[48]

Bale's portrayal of Imperyall Majestie as a pseudo-saint helps balance the depiction of the character as a pseudo-revenant, and the need to do so becomes especially apparent as Imperyall Majestie refers to King John in the third person, thereby separating himself from the dead king:

> *I.Maj.* And how do they lyke the customs they haue vsed
> With our predecessours, whom they haue so abused,
> Specyally kynge Iohan? Thynke they they haue done well?[49]

Bale evidently knew that what he said about John reflects upon Henry VIII and that Imperyall Majestie, therefore, could not represent John too directly, for there would have been great danger in representing the current monarch at one such thin remove from a deceased figure, regardless of how saintly the latter may be. Indeed, this important point is suggested by Verity, who argues that the Crown equally represents all men who wear it.[50] Thus, Bale locates Imperyall Majestie between the saint and ghost/revenant traditions without settling on either one and seems at times to define this figure more by what he is not than what he is.

Bale particularly favors characterizing Imperyall Majestie in opposition to the hagiographic tradition, apart from such adaptations of the latter as he used in describing Anne Askew, and akin to his inversion of some aspects of the ghost/revenant tradition. Saint plays had been suppressed under Henry VIII, but, as Eamon Duffy asserts, the king's subjects may have responded only with an outward show of

obedience,[51] for we know that there were three or more stagings of
such plays at Braintree, Essex, in the 1530s and 40s;[52] the Digby Mary
Magdalene procession was not suppressed until five years after it had
been reinstated in 1533;[53] and a Becket play was performed very near
the composition date for *Kynge Johan* and just before Henry VIII's
1537–38 ban.[54] Indeed, as a man of radical beliefs, Bale may have
been impatient with what Duffy calls "the grudging fulfillment of the
will of the Crown."[55] In any case, he appears to have built *Kynge Johan*
on suspicions that, though audiences appeared to be obedient, they
remained unconverted,[56] for his new, Protestant version of sainthood
preserves key traditional elements of the Catholic saint play, particularly the essential relationship between the apparition and its
witnesses. For example, as in many saint plays, the central figure, too,
is martyred and appears after death, whereupon Divine Justice is
administered and the guilty are punished. And like a Catholic saint,
Imperyall Majestie clarifies the nature of the Word as he appears after
death.[57] He serves as a testament to faith.

Yet, these elements serve to argue *against* Kynge Johan's sainthood
because he is kept distinct from Imperyall Majestie. At the play's end,
the latter deals with the play's villains and makes the play's important
moral points, while Kynge Johan is still very much dead. Neither
figure is explicitly doubled, as is, for example, Usurpid Powre with
The Pope, and Imperyall Majestie cannot be seen as either a full incarnation of Kynge Johan or a traditional saint figure.

Of course, in transcending these categories, Imperyall Majestie
also transcends time and links Bale's Reformist agenda, the genre of
saints' lives, and the ghost/revenant tradition. Through the figure of
Imperyall Majestie, Bale uses an established historiographical method
to present an innovative Reformist view of a past figure.[58] Per the
play's timeline, Imperyall Majestie appears soon after Kynge Johan's
death, but the audience soon discovers that Imperyall Majestie refracts
thirteenth-century issues surrounding Kynge Johan's death through
Henrician concerns. Although Imperyall Majestie addresses characters
that supposedly exist in the play's theme year of 1216, he speaks rather
prophetically (if not cryptically) about England's destiny and future
under Henry VIII. After Bale made additions to the play for a possible
1559 performance, this diachronic relevance is made even more
explicit as, upon Imperyall Majestie's exit, Nobylyte refers to Elizabeth
I in his own final speech, saying:

Nob. Englande hath a queen – Thankes to the lorde above –
Whych maye be a lyghte to other princes all
For the godly wayes whome she doth dayly move
To hir liege people, through Gods wurde specyall.
She is that Angell as saynte Iohan doth hym call,[59]
That with the lordes seale doth marke out hys trye servauntes,
Pryntynge in their hartes hys holy wourdes and Covenauntes.[60]

The converted Nobylyte thus joins Imperyall Majestie standing both inside and outside chronological time, bearing witness to Reformist (and Elizabethan) truths, for as Benjamin Griffin rightly points out, "In this play the historical subject is chosen for its analogical relation to the present time, rather than for any current topicalities of these historical figures themselves."[61] Imperyall Majestie is relevant precisely because he exists outside the time span of the play and outside the human figure of Kynge Johan. That is, he exists for the sake of Henry VIII's England, not King John's.[62]

As Imperyall Majestie appears as an agent of Divine Justice to negate Kynge Johan's vow to the Pope and fulfill Kynge Johan's vow to protect Engelonde, he also reinterprets the situation according to Reformist truths.[63] This act fits with Bruce Gordon and Peter Marshall's observation that in medieval historical writing and saints' lives, "chronology was of little importance because to date an event was to condemn it to the past and lose its importance for the present."[64] Thus, Bale comments on Henrician England via not only an analogue to a figure from its medieval past but also a method borrowed from that same era. He refuses to locate Imperyall Majestie in the body of either King John or Henry VIII and thereby doubly asserts that Imperyall Majestie is timeless, that he exists via the Divine Right of Kings and the Royal Supremacy. Indeed, in having Imperyall Majestie hover between the ghost/revenant and saint traditions as an apparition with a continual relationship between himself and the living, Bale encourages his audience to perceive Royal Supremacy as a mystical but real presence in their lives. Since Imperyall Majestie transcends historical time, he leaves King John behind as a phantom precursor, and this is precisely the way kingship works: each monarch is, in effect, an allegory for kingship who stands as a living symbol of the monarchs who came before.

Because Bale's convictions are central to his work, it is difficult to determine the degree and importance of artfulness in *Kynge Johan*. He makes quite an artful turn in drawing upon various literary and folk traditions to construct Imperyall Majestie, yet these efforts serve almost exclusively to complement Bale's political agenda and have not been seen to greatly enhance the enjoyment of the play. Indeed, they have not, to my knowledge, made even a dent in such assessments as W. T. Davies' remark that "It must be confessed [...] [Bale] is more important than readable."[65] But, of course, it is not clear to what extent, if any, Bale wished to entertain his audience, and it is likely that his careful reinterpretation of sources that he had collected before his conversion was intended above all to promote his profound understanding of progressivism. Rather than discarding works that had been condemned by Reformists and/or were antithetical to the movement, he asserted a new sense of authority over what he saw as old, but not necessarily irrelevant or hostile, ideas. And regardless of his interest in artfulness, he created in Imperyall Majestie a character that, despite its problems, proved both enduring and compelling, a character that, even as it is defined more often by what it is not than what it is, hovers like a true phantom between the medieval past and the Renaissance present, between reality and allegory, effectively anchoring the Reformist agenda of Bale's time in the storied politics of England's past.

NOTES

1. Great Britain Public Record Office, *Letters and Papers, Foreign and Domestic, of the Reign of Henry VIII*, ed. J. Gairdner & R. H. Brodie, 21 vols. (London: Longman, Green, Longman & Roberts, 1862–1910; repr. London: Vaduz, Kraus Repr., 1965–76), 14:2, item 782.

2. As noted by Bruce Gordon and Peter Marshall, Bale is evidently striving to express the reality of his own experience as a man with a complex history and a complex present. See their "Introduction: Placing the Dead in Late Medieval and Early Modern Europe," in Bruce Gordon and Peter Marshall, ed., *The Place of the Dead: Death and Remembrance in Late Medieval and Early Modern Europe* (New York and Cambridge: Cambridge University Press, 2000), 1–16 (4).

3. As Peter Happe states, Bale treats his sources as "poetic and historical inheritances." See Happe's "Protestant Adaptation of the Saint Play," in

Clifford Davidson, ed., *The Saint Play in Medieval Europe* (Kalamazoo, MI: Medieval Institute Publications, 1986), 225.

4. Larry Scanlon, *Narrative, Authority, and Power: The Medieval Exemplum and the Chaucerian Tradition* (Cambridge: Cambridge University Press, 1994), 46.

5. Both cases reflect upon what Bale sees as Dunstan's persecution of married clergy and his interference with the privileged sexual practices of the king. See John Bale, *Actes of the English Votaryes* (London: John Tysdale, 1560), R.v. Note that Helen Parish describes Bale's attitude towards Dunstan as revolving around the belief that "it was not the place of the bishop to seek to dictate morality to the king: a salutary warning perhaps to any of Bale's contemporaries who might have hoped to trouble the conscience of Henry VIII." See her "Impudent and Abhominable Fictions: Rewriting Saints' Lives in the English Reformation," *Sixteenth Century Journal* 23/1 (2001): 45–65 (64).

6. Peter Happe, *John Bale* (Amherst: University of Massachusetts Press, 1996), 30.

7. Gordon and Marshall, *Introduction*, 2.

8. Bale, *Actes of the English Votaryes*, d,v.

9. One of the most radical nearly contemporaneous parallels for such an approach is John Leland's *Assertio Inclytissimi Arturii Regis Britanniae* (1544), which, in claiming that England had always been an empire in its own right because of Arthur's establishment of Camelot, builds on Geoffrey of Monmouth's *History of the Kings of Britain* and amounts to one piece of historical revisionism drawing upon an earlier one to justify itself.

10. Benjamin Griffin, "The Birth of the History Play: Saint, Sacrifice, and Reformation," *Studies in English Literature, 1500–1900* 39/2 (Spring 1999): 217–37 (218).

11. Griffin, "Birth of the History Play," 218.

12. Griffin, "Birth of the History Play," 218.

13. Benjamin Griffin, *Playing the Past: Approaches to English Historical Drama, 1385–1600* (Cambridge: D. S. Brewer, 2001), 45. Griffin adds that saint plays also possess a latent "energy" that is expressed dramatically in Reformation drama.

14. W(illiam) T(wiston) Davies, *A Bibliography of John Bale*, Oxford Bibliographic Society Proceedings and Papers, vol. 5, pt. 4 (Oxford: Oxford University Press, 1940), 212.

15. As Gordon and Marshall note on page 6 of their *Introduction*, "Protestant history-making […] varied greatly depending upon the particular circumstances in which it was being nurtured."

16. Keith Thomas, *Religion and the Decline of Magic: Studies in Popular Beliefs in Sixteenth and Seventeenth Century England* (New York: Oxford University Press, 1997), 703–04.

17. Bale's attitude toward Purgatory is well-documented throughout his work; his autograph remarks against the doctrine in a manuscript of *Piers Plowman* are particularly compelling. See *The Piers Plowman Electronic Archive 6: San Marino, Huntington Library MS 128*, ed. Michael Calabrese, Hoyt N. Duggan, and Thorlac Turville-Petre (New York: Medieval Academy of America, and D. S. Brewer, forthcoming).

18. John Frith, *Disputacyon of Purgatorye* (Marburg, s.n.: 1531), lxxxvi.

19. As found in Peter the Venerable, *The Book of Miracles*, vol. 189 in *Patrologiae Cursus Completus, Series Latina*, ed. J. P. Migne, 221 vols. (Paris, s.n.: 1844–1906 [1854]); Gregory the Great, *The Dialogues of St. Gregory*, ed. and trans. Odo John Zimmerman (New York: Fathers of the Church, Inc., 1959); and Bede, *Ecclesiastical History of the English People*, ed. and trans. J. McLure and R. Collins (Oxford: Oxford University Press, 1994).

20. Jean-Claude Schmitt, *Ghosts in the Middle Ages: The Living and the Dead in Medieval Society*, trans. Teresa Lavender Fagan (1994; trans. Chicago: University of Chicago Press, 1998), 172.

21. Harry Leigh Douglas Ward and J. A. Herbert, ed., *Catalogue of Romances in the Department of Manuscripts in the British Museum*, 3 vols. (London: British Museum, 1910), 3:595, no. 145.

22. Caesarius of Heisterbach, *Caesarii Heisterbacensis Monachi Ordinis Cisterciensis Dialogus Miraculorum*, ed. J. Strange, 2 vols. (Cologne, Bonn, and Brussels: H. Lempertz and Co., 1851), 2:16.

23. Ward and Herbert, *Catalogue of Romances*, 3:383, no. 160; 3:449, no. 45; 3:469, no. 45; 3:488, no. 108; 3:494, no. 194; 3:519, no. 7; 3:546, no. 81; 3:548, no. 109; 3:561, no. 24; 3:600, no. 25.

24. One of the most well-known examples of such an appearance is the visitation by the dead Sir Gawain to King Arthur at his bedside (or in a dream) just before the battle against Mordred. It is found in many versions of the Arthurian legend, and Bale was very familiar with this tradition. The most contemporary example in Bale's world was Sir Thomas Malory's *Le morte Darthur*, which received attention from Leland about the same time Bale wrote *Kynge Johan*. Moreover, Malory's work is known for its adaptation of the Arthurian legend to include fifteenth-century politics. Sir Thomas Malory, *Le morte Darthur*, ed. Stephen H. A. Shepherd (New York: W. W. Norton & Company, 2004), 683.

25. Interestingly, Bale may have found a precedent in Gervase of Tilbury (c. 1150–c. 1228). In *Otia Imperialia* Gervase expresses interest in *admiratio*, a wonderment for something new, or rare, which happens as an extension of God's will. Bale had, in fact, catalogued *Otia Imperialia*, which, in its dedication to Otto IV of Brunswick, claims to transmit a message to the Emperor from the ghost of William of Beaucaire. See Gervase of Tilbury,

Otia Imperialia: Recreation for an Emperor, ed. and trans. S. E. Banks and J. W. Binns (Oxford: Clarendon Press, 2002), Part III, Cap. CIII.

26. One major example comes from Rudolphus Glaber and tells of an army of wraiths that stalk their former battlefield. See his *The Five Books of Histories* (Oxford: Oxford University Press, 1989), Book V, Cap I. In England there were many such tales surrounding ancient battlefields.

27. Peter Marshall, *Beliefs and the Dead in Reformation England* (New York: Oxford University Press, 2002), 232–33.

28. R. Scribner, "Elements of Popular Belief," in *Handbook of European History 1400–1600*, 2 vols. (Leiden, E. J. Brill & Co., 1994–95), 1:237.

29. This is in contrast to the present-day ghost/revenant tradition in which a single witness views the apparition and then transmits the story to others.

30. Schmitt, *Ghosts in the Middle Ages*, 186.

31. Caesarius of Heisterbach, *Dialogos Miraculorum* (Cologne: Johann Koelhoff the Elder, 1481), and William of Newburgh, *Historia Rerum Anglicarum* (Antwerp: William Silvi, 1567). Both collections contain a host of ghost stories that bear a didactic message and employ the Church as a regulating entity.

32. Schmitt, *Ghosts in the Middle Ages*, 147.

33. Strangely, Bale accepts the fable of Merlin's origins and uses it to argue against the legitimacy of the origins of Sts. Patrick, Asaph, and Ditrice. Later, he uses the example of Merlin again, this time to justify English kingship as the inheritance of Brutus. Here, Bale is cleverly expedient when it comes to the role of Arthurian lore in Reformist argument. Bale, *The apology of Iohan Bale agaynste a ranke papyste* (London: [S. Mierdman for] Iohan Day, 1550), 20, 50.

34. Bale, *Apology*, xcii.

35. In one of many examples from the *Actes*, Bale accuses the Catholic clergy of using sorcery to turn one dissenter in favor of clerical marriage into an eel (lx). Similar stories appear in various forms in many, if not most, of Bale's prose works.

36. William Shakespeare, *King John*, ed. Claire Mceachern (New York, Penguin Books, 2000), III.3.56–66.

37. Shakespeare, *King John*, IV.2.203–06. Arthur does not in fact die until act IV, scene 3 (1–10), when he falls from a wall as he attempts to escape his prison.

38. John Bale, *The First Examinacyon of Anne Askew, Lately Martyred in Smithfield, by the Romysh Popes Upholders, with the Elucydacyon of Johan Bale* (Marburg: D. van der Straten, 1546), 5. Bale's statement must be taken with a grain of salt, as he had catalogued and studied volumes of saints' lives in which miracles abound. Despite statements like these, Bale was not

delusional; he acted in accord with the idea that if an entire belief system were to be taken from the hands of the Roman Church, radical reinterpretations of ancient ideas would be necessary.

39. Bale avoids a comparison with, for example, St. Lucy (on whom Bale had written a poem before his conversion), whose body refused to die no matter how badly she was tortured. Even as boiling oil and tar were poured on her, and even as a sword was pushed through her throat, Lucy remained physically unharmed and died peacefully when the Sacrament was brought to her. The poem is found in BL MS Harley 1819, fols. 157v–163r, along with poems on various other saints. The Life of St. Lucy is found in Jacobus de Voragine, *The Golden Legend, or, Lives of the Saints, as Englished by William Caxton*, 7 vols. (London: J. M. Dent & Sons, 1900–31), 2:59.

40. Bale, *First Examinacyon*, 8v.

41. Bale, *First Examinacyon*, 8v.

42. Happe, *John Bale*, 13.

43. Happe, *John Bale*, 13.

44. John Bale, *The latter examinacyon of Anne Askew: latelye martyred in Smythfelde by the wycked Synagoge of Antichrist* (Marburg: D. van der Straten, 1547), 227 and marginal note.

45. Bale, *Kynge Johan*, 2586–92.

46. Bale, *Kynge Johan*, 2293–94.

47. For Bale, Sts. Guthlac, Ditrice, and Patrick are frauds whose legends have deceived the English people. He condemns their legends in *Actes of the English Votaryes*, 19–20, where he claims, amid a lengthy condemnation of the clerical vow of celibacy, that St. Patrick had been the illegitimate son of a nun.

48. Bale, *Kynge Johan*, 2660–63.

49. Bale, *Kynge Johan*, 2321–23.

50. Bale, *Kynge Johan*, 2234–39.

51. Eamon Duffy, *The Stripping of the Altars* (New Haven, CT: Yale University Press, 1992), 479. Note that Duffy is referring in large part to towns in East Anglia, where Bale had grown up. And note that Duffy says about many regions (among them East Anglia) that, "[…] in certain areas there pervaded a 'determined traditionalism'." In "Birth of the History Play," Benjamin Griffin states on page 22 that saint plays filled "a cultural niche" that expressed a relationship with saints that the English people apparently needed.

52. Philip Morant, *The History and Antiquities of the County of Essex*, 2 vols. (London: Printed for T. Osborne, J. Whiston, S. Baker, L. Davis, C. Reymers, and B. White, 1768), 2:399.

53. Rev. William Hudson and John Cottingham Tingey, ed., *The Records of the City of Norwich*, 2 vols. (Norwich: Jarrold & Sons, Ltd, 1906–10), 2:cxxxv.

54. James M. Gibson, ed., *Records of Early English Drama* (London: The British Library, 2002). Bale sees King John as a martyr and national hero, but he does not view King John as a replacement for Becket. Bale despised the Becket tradition in concurrence with what Griffin calls "Henry's war on Becket" (*Birth of the History Play*, 236 n. 60). Bale wishes to replace both King John and Becket with Imperyall Majestie. Bale's own play about Becket, called *De Traditione Thomae Becketi* (or *De Thomae Becketi Imposturis*), is no longer extant. See Peter Happe, "Dramatic Images of Kingship in Heywood and Bale," *Studies in English Literature, 1500–1900* 39 (1999): 8–9.

55. Duffy, *Stripping of the Altars*, 480.

56. Bale had a personal history with saint plays, for he had been brought up in East Anglia, which was well-known for its saint and cycle plays. In fact, in *John Bale* (5), Peter Happe calls East Anglia a "dramatic culture," with centers in Bury St. Edmunds, Norwich, Chelmsford, and Cambridge. Moreover, when Bale became a Carmelite monk, he traveled to places on the Continent where his brethren had an interest in drama. For example, he visited Carmelite houses in the Low Countries in 1522–23 and probably came into contact with plays that were, as Happe supposes in *John Bale* (3), "[…] still largely Catholic in orientation."

57. Interestingly, upon Imperyall Majestie's entrance at l. 2317, he is immediately recognized by all parties without being introduced. Such recognition is common (but not exclusive) in saint tales (At times the visiting saint is immediately recognized, especially if he or she appears soon after death. At other times another saint, or perhaps the Virgin, who provides the introduction, accompanies the saint.) and also in the folk revenant tradition (In medieval ghost tales, the ghost is either immediately recognized by the witnessing parties, or provides his or her own introduction. Medieval ghosts rarely appear out of a context that identifies them, in contrast with present-day ghost stories in which apparitions are either completely unidentified, or are identified through the investigation of human parties.). Imperyall Majestie needs no introduction, unlike his companion Verity, who requires one: "I am Veritas, that com hither yow to blame / For castynge away of our most lawfull kynge" (ll. 2282–83). The play's villains require a formal introduction to Truth, but Imperyall Majestie is someone they should, and indeed do, already know.

58. His effort is perhaps evidenced by an interesting (and indeed strange) contemporary event: in 1538, barely a year before the first performance of the play, The Privy Council "cited Becket to appear before them to answer charges of having disturbed the realm; when he (or a representative) failed to appear, judgment was given against him." See F. J. Levy, *Tudor Historical Thought* (San Marino, CA: Huntington Library Publications,

1967), 85–86, paraphrasing David Wilkins, *Concilia Magnae Brittaniae et Hiberniae*, 4 vols. (London: R. Gosling, F. Gyles, T. Woodward, and C. Davis, 1737), 3:835–36. In this case, the Privy Council demanded that the saint translate himself chronologically to answer the "charges" against him in a later historical period, when attitudes toward him, and toward the religion he practiced, were changing.

59. A reference not to the dead King Johan but to St. John the Apostle.

60. Bale, *Kynge Johan*, 2671–77.

61. Griffin, "Birth of the History Play," 227.

62. Bale visited the tomb of King John at Worcester in 1529. The tomb had been opened, and Bale took the opportunity to view the body of the king. It was, of course, utterly decomposed, and yet it retained enough stately demeanor to inspire Bale to write a poem about it. Interestingly, that poem was scribbled into the margin of a copy of Trevet's *History of the Angevin Kings*. Nicholas Trevet, *Annales Regum Angliae*, Parker Library, Corpus Christi College, Cambridge MS 152 fol. 48. After Bale's conversion, he was still inspired, but this time by the living memory of the Royal Supremacy rather than by a regal corpse.

63. Bale explains in his *Apology* (lxxxiii) how one oath can be fulfilled by negating another. He says to his enemies, the Papists: "Yea if all thynges must be persolved, that hath bene promised in papisme, than must king Johans most iniuriouse & hurtful vowe, be also fulfilled in al hys successours, kings of thys realme, to the utter destruccion of the same both wayes whiche the eternall God forbbyd. For al these were false promises to God, made with a solemne deliberacion, as ye say by diffynicion, your unchaste vowes are."

64. Gordon and Marshall, *Introduction*, 8.

65. Davies, *Bibliography of John Bale*, 201.

Rodelinda Goes Opera:
The Lombard Queen's Journey
from Medieval Backstage to
Händel's "dramma per musica"[1]

Werner Wunderlich

Georg Friedrich Händel (1685–1759) composed forty operas, most of which belong to the quite formal and heroic genre of *opere serie*.[2] These *dramme per musica*, as they are often called in their own libretti, catered to the political needs and aesthetic expectations of their aristocratic audiences, for they revolve around characters from the upper ranks of society.[3] That is to say, they bring erotic impulses and the duties of … virtue into conflict with the dynamic intrigues of state actions, allow for the glorification of wisdom, responsibility, and modesty as the ideals of enlightened absolute monarchy, and exploit the dramaturgical concept of the proportional fall, the belief that the abrupt demise of a protagonist, as well as the vicissitudes of his or her life, affect the audience in direct relationship to his or her social prominence.

Opere serie particularly favor literary and historical figures who were renowned for having exhibited extraordinary virtue in difficult circumstances. Composers combed the past in search of protagonists who could unleash passionate arias that would morally edify the public as those figures endure severe trials and enjoy great triumphs. Of course, the composers often turned for such protagonists to the history and myths of Antiquity, but they did not entirely skip the Middle Ages, for at least a dozen *opere serie* by Händel, and many more by his contemporaries, were set during that period. Indeed, the

Lombards alone gave rise not only to Händel's *Rodelinda, Regina de' Longobardi* (1725) but also to Gian Domenico Partenio's *Il Flavio Cuniberto* (1682), which was composed with Matteo Noris's libretto and features Rodelinda's son as its titular hero; Agostino Steffani's *Tassilone* (1709), whose title refers to the Duke of Bavaria, Tassilo III, and which praises the fidelity of his wife, Gismonda, who was the daughter of a Lombard king, Desiderius; Girolamo Polani's *Berengario, Rè d'Italia* (1710) and Pietro Torri's *Adelaide* (1722), both of which join Händel's *Ottone* (1723) in revolving around Adelheid, the widow of an Italian king supposedly murdered by a fictitious Lombard king, Berengar II, who held Adelheid prisoner as he sought to force her to marry his son Adalbert (in 951 she married Otto I instead, elevating him to "Rex Francorum et Langobardorum" and forcing Berengar a year later to swear an oath of loyalty to Otto in return for receiving Italy as a fiefdom); and another opera by Händel, *Flavio, Rè d' Longobardi* (1723), which presents Berengar as the titular hero and ruler of Britannia.[4] Evidently, Händel and his contemporaries found the conflict-driven history of the Lombards to be a highly suitable source for characters and circumstances around which they could build *opere serie*.

Of course, that is not to say these composers were particularly concerned with the characters as historical figures or with conveying the original contexts of the figures as fully as possible. Indeed, as we shall see in the case of *Rodelinda*, the composers often ignore inconvenient facts, favor much later accounts over earlier ones (even when giving direct evidence of knowing the latter), and freely embellish early sources on those occasions when they do indeed pull on them. Moreover, with *Rodelinda* and many other *opere serie*, they seem to favor figures who were so obscure in the early sources that they were known for little more than having survived difficult circumstances. Thus, the medievalism of these composers appears to be largely incidental, to stem not from an interest in the Middle Ages as a unique cultural phenomenon or as a direct parallel to particular seventeenth- or eighteenth-century socio-political scenarios but from a need to satisfy the demands of stereotypical *opere serie*.

That may be suggested above all by the fact that though the "Argomento" of the libretto for Händel's *Rodelinda* claims that its initial background for the opera "agrees with the History of Paolo Diacono,"[5] which is the primary early source on the Lombards,

Rodelinda's centrality to the opera is hardly prefigured by her role in Paul the Deacon's *Historia Langobardorum*.[6] Paul (c. 720/30–796) was a Benedictine monk who spent time at the court of Charlemagne and was, in his day, a well-known poet.[7] In 790 he began composing the *Historia* from older historical sources, such as Gregory of Tours' *Historia Francorum* (before 594), as well as from transmitted sagas, legends, stories, and anecdotes. His text, which was widely copied and disseminated during the Middle Ages, stops abruptly with King Liutprant's death in 744 but not before mentioning Rodelinda three times and celebrating the Lombards as courageous, loyal, and honorable.[8]

The material most relevant to Händel's portrayal of her primarily comes from the fifth and sixth books of Paul's text. After the death of Aripert I in 661, the elder son, Godepert, retained Pavia, and the younger son, Perctarit (Bertarido in Händel's *Rodelinda*), controlled Milan, which led to a bitter rivalry. As part of that rivalry, Godepert sent Garipald (Garibaldo) of Turin to the powerful Duke Grimoald (Grimoaldo) of Beneventum in order to win him as his vassal. In return, Grimoald was supposed to receive Godepert and Perctarit's sister (without name in the *Historia* but known as "Eduige" in Händel's opera) as his wife. But Garipald, a vile schemer, encouraged Grimoald to pursue his plans. Back in Turin, the treasonous manipulator met what Paul treats as a well-deserved fate because a court dwarf, whom Garipald had adorned with horns, decapitated him. Grimoald, however, stabbed Godepert, usurped the throne of Pavia, and married Aripert's daughter in order to legitimize his new dynastic position.

When Perctarit learned of his brother's murder, he hastily fled Milan and made his way to the Avar King of Hungary, leaving behind his wife, Rodelinda, and young son, Cunicpert, whereupon both were banished by Grimoald to Beneventum. After some time, Grimoald reconciled with his brother-in-law, and the latter returned from exile, ready to abdicate his throne if Grimoald would let him live in peace with his wife and child. But when Perctarit's considerable number of adherents reappeared, Grimoald wanted once again to dispatch his rival. So Perctarit fled with the help of his vassal Unulf (Unulfo) to Clotaire III in Frankish Neustria. In the following years, Grimoald strengthened his rule by conquering the Franks and Byzantines, bestowing dukedoms on vassals, passing wise laws, and scrupulously and violently suppressing every act of resistance. Finally, according to Paul, he died painfully in 671 as a result of poisoned medicines.

Three days later, a voice from Heaven supposedly called Perctarit back to his homeland, whereupon he returned to Pavia, drove out Grimoald's son, and was again placed on the throne by the Lombards. Only after he had reascended the crested throne and was sure that he would keep it did he call his wife and son back from Beneventum. They then dutifully returned, and, according to Paul, Rodelinda gave thanks for their happy ending by founding a magnificent church of Our Lady in front of the walls of Pavia. She subsequently disappears from Paul's narrative – and, in fact, from every other early source on the Lombards – though Paul does give a small amount of extra information that is relevant to Händel's opera, as in noting that Perctarit elevated his son, Cunicpert (who, in accord with the title used by the Lombard rulers to underscore the legitimacy of their kingdom, is given the Roman name "Flavius"), to the position of co-ruler around 680.

Not surprisingly, Paul's slim references to Rodelinda had little impact on Renaissance court romances, which were a major source of medievalism for Baroque composers.[9] Händel and his colleagues unabashedly mined works such as Ludovico Ariosto's *Orlando furioso* (1516) and Torquato Tasso's *La Gerusalemme liberata* (1581) for idealized representatives of medieval chivalry. And, like that of many of Händel's contemporaries, his general understanding of the Middle Ages seems to have been heavily influenced by allusions to that era in Renaissance court culture as filtered through those romances. Indeed, many Baroque operas thoroughly resonate with echoes of the grand public spectacles in which fifteenth- and sixteenth-century nobles celebrated themselves as heirs to medieval chivalry. And besides revolving around such "medieval" characters as Rinaldo and Orlando, many Baroque operas are wrapped in Renaissance versions of medieval art, architecture, and music. But for the character Rodelinda and the events specific to her life, Baroque authors initially had to turn to either Paul's text or humanistic historical works, such as Flavius Blondus' *Historiarum ab inclinatione Romanorum* (1483), Antoine du Verdier's *Diverses leçons* (1610), and Erycus Puteanus' *Historiae babaricae* (1614). And that is precisely what Pierre Corneille (1606–84) did for his five-act tragedy *Pertharite, Roi des Lombards*, which had its premiere at the end of 1651.[10]

In seeking material, Corneille went further than many of his contemporaries by looking beyond the overt fiction of earlier writers and consulting works presented as serious scholarship.[11] But, like many authors of the next several generations, he often seems to have chosen subjects not so much for their historical importance as for the ease with which they could be adapted to the demands of Baroque theater. For example, the basic outline of the story behind the tensions between Grimoaldo and Bertarido (Perctarit), particularly its focus on the incompatibility of violent usurpation and dynastic legitimacy, evidently appealed to Corneille for its dramatic potential and its broad parallels to the political contexts of his own time. Through his historical Roman dramas, he had long sought to bring the problems of his era to the stage, as in addressing the political pros and cons of purposive strictness and honorable clemency in the state.[12] Yet, as mentioned above, he also seems to have felt a need both to clarify the themes he saw as most relevant in the narrative he inherited from Paul and from the Renaissance humanists and to make them more moving within the conventions of mid-sixteenth-century French theater.

On a comparatively broad and abstract level, he therefore introduced or underscored dyads of dramatic motifs such as separation and reunification, revenge and forgiveness, love and jealousy, and hate and intrigue. And on a more local and practical level, he built those dyads on alterations he made to the setting, characters, and plot as they had come down to him. For example, though his cast is largely the same as in his sources (except for the christening of Bertarido's and Godepert's previously anonymous sister as "Eduige"), he substantially changes their contexts, personality, and actions. The plot is set not in Pavia but in Milan, two years after Grimoaldo takes the city. In the background of the story, which is told in an introductory dialogue between Rodelinda and Unulphe, Godepert is killed not by Grimoaldo but by his own brother Bertarido, and as Godepert lies mortally wounded he makes Grimoaldo swear to avenge him. The plot then revolves around complex, intertwined love affairs that usually are not even hinted at in Corneille's sources. The malicious Garibaldo, for instance, loves Eduige, who, however, loves Grimoaldo. He, in turn, loves Rodelinda, who, for her part, loves Bertarido. Because the usurper believes the escaped king to be dead, he would like to wed the latter's widow so that he might become the rightful regent of Milan. But the Lombard queen remains steadfast, and in order to make her more compliant,

Grimoaldo threatens to have her son killed, whereupon she counters her blackmailer with political *raison*, as she declares she would rather sacrifice her son immediately and deny Grimoaldo the heir he hoped to have out of the relationship with her. In the third act Bertarido returns unexpectedly (and initially unrecognized), after which Bertarido and Rodelinda fall once again into each other's arms as they exchange mutual vows of fidelity, and Bertarido then kills the villainous interloper Garibaldo. Finally, the remorseful Grimoaldo abdicates in Milan after Eduige assures him of her continuing love for him, whereupon Bertarido generously leaves Pavia to "ce grand Héros" as he concludes that, for the noble display of virtue, only glory can be the one true reward: "Que des hautes vertus la gloire est le seul prix."[13]

Despite Corneille's extensive adaptation of his sources, his play was not a success, and it was pulled from production after only two performances.[14] Evidently, the public did not want to see a king as a coward, particularly one who had only his wife and faithful vassals to thank for his throne. But Corneille's talent for creating "heroic souls," to which Goethe attributed Corneille's general success, made his play an ideal source for *opere serie*.[15] Indeed, its content, motifs, and theme seem to have been tailor-made for a genre devoted to rationalistic belief in the moral contemplation of virtue set against depraved emotions such as anger and hate. Thus, its revised version, which was printed in 1663, gave rise to at least two branches of operatic imitation.

The first branch maintained the importance of Corneille's titular figure, as exemplified by the work of Stefano Ghigi.[16] He provided the libretto for Carlo Francesco Pollarolo's musical score *Flavio Bertarido, Re dei longobardi* (1706). And his libretto was translated by Wendt for Georg Philipp Telemann, whose *Flavius Bertaridus, König der Langobarden* (1729) enjoyed a successful premiere at the oldest German opera house, the *Gänsemarktoper* (Goose Market Opera House) in Hamburg.

The second branch shifted Rodelinda from a wallflower to a heroic titular figure and protagonist, as can be seen in the work of Antonio Salvi (1664–1724), a medical doctor in the service of the Medici as well as an avid librettist for opera performances in the Prince's Villa in Pratolino.[17] Relying in part on the translation of the *Historia Langobardorum* in Emmanuele Tesauro's *Del Regno d'Italia* sotto I Barbari (1663), Salvi wrote a highly successful libretto, *Rodelinda, Regina de' Longobardi*, which had its premiere on 21 September 1710 and amounts to a dramaturgical revision of Corneille's tragedy.[18] Out of five acts he makes three, sending Bertarido on stage already in the first act. He also depicts Bertarido's escape from his dungeon and, in the third act, elevates Garibaldo's death to the high point of the plot. The heavily criticized happy ending of Corneille's work, combined with Grimoaldo's unmotivated u-turn from Rodelina to Eduige, suffice for Salvi – in the tradition of the "clemenza" operas – as the effective *lieto fine*.[19] That is to say, as in works such as Pietro Metastasio's *La clemenza di Tito* (1734), which was set to music at least fifty times and was immortalized in Mozart's KV 621 (1791) for the King of Bohemia's coronation as Leopold II, sovereign clemency presides and, in this case, celebrates Bertarido's reunion with his wife. Of course, most relevant to my paper is the fact that Rodelinda makes considerably more appearances in Salvi's opera than in Corneille's work and is no longer just the "femme de Pertharite [Bertarido]." Rather, she is henceforth at the top of the register and stands in the center of the plot as the "Regina d'Longobardi," whom the unlucky and weak Grimoaldo would like to wed in order to raise his sense of self-worth and strengthen his power. Indeed, in contrast to his own appearance, he is confronted with an actual royal person – an impressive woman who is courageous, decisive, virtuous, deliberate, and willful. Even in the gravest of dangers she is the faithful, loving wife, keeping both a steadfast demeanor and the upper hand. Thus, out of the dim margins of early medieval history, as recorded by Paul, emerges a dramatic titular heroine who is one of the most impressive female figures of Baroque opera.

Yet as great as is Salvi's Rodelinda, she pales beside Händel's version of her. His *Rodelinda, Regina de' Longobardi* had its premiere on 13 February 1725 as a "drama da rappresentarisi nel region teatro di Hay-Market, per La Reale Accademia di Musica" and was revised in 1731 with the addition of some popular melodies from his operas *Tolomeo* (1728) and *Lotario* (1729).[20] Its libretto was adapted from Salvi's *Rodelinda* by Nicolà Francesco Haym (1678–1729), who was a cellist, composer, and stage manager of the Royal Academy of Music at King's Theatre.[21] But as with Haym's libretti for Händel's *Giulio Cesare* (1724) and *Tamerlano* (1724), Haym's work on *Rodelinda* was evidently carried out with Händel's compositional and dramatic requirements in mind.[22] For example, though Haym adheres to the order of events established by Salvi, he abridges long musical recitatives and emphasizes the lyrical power of expression in the arias, as he divides the performances of the titular figure equally among all three acts and increases the number of arias from five to eight. Moreover, he expands the arias from a loud and powerful means of imparting boisterous emotions to occasions on which he establishes dynamic motives that propel the plot and serve as a means of characterization. That is to say, through these solos, Haym elevates Rodelinda's stature and significance as he enhances her psychological believability and hones the dramatic profile of her and of the work as a whole.

He and Händel did so in part by adapting to the vocal bravura, incomparable timbre, and outstanding coloratura of Händel's *primadonna*, Francesca Cuzzoni.[23] In fact, the score goes out of its way to provide her with ample occasions to demonstrate *spianar la voce*, which is the vocal equivalent of "rolling out noodle dough." And she apparently took full advantage of these opportunities, for, according to her contemporaries, she invariably conveyed Rodelinda's emotions with a virtuoso and moving voice.[24] Whether expressing grief, unwavering love, a desire for solace, unshakeable steadfastness, hate for the usurper, contempt for his ambitious political advisor, despair, readiness for sacrifice, relief, and/or joy, she roiled audiences, as she availed herself of the especially sentimental and moving manner in which Haym and Händel framed these states and feelings, as she took advantage of what Johann Mattheson describes in his 1761 German edition of John Mainwaring's biography of Händel as "expression of the particular action, emotion, and sentiment that is introduced at a given point."[25]

Rodelinda's highly diverse emotions are articulated in eight arias that represent exactly how far she has come from Paul's marginal figure, as they underscore her centrality to the passions and plot of the opera (the aria number of the libretto is provided in parentheses):

1 (No. 1) Lament, C minor: "Ho perduto il caro sposo" (I have lost my dear husband)

2 (No. 2) Tirade, G minor: "L'empio rigor del fato" (The cruel harshness of fate)

3 (No. 8) Lament, B minor: "Ombre, piante, urne funeste" (Shades, trees, and tombs of grief)

4 (No. 10) Tirade, E major: "Morrai, sì" (Yes, you will die)

5 (No. 16) Tirade, B flat major: "Spietati, io vi giurai" (Pitiless man, I swore to you)

6 (No. 22) Love aria, G major: "Ritorna, o caro, e dolce mio tesoro" (My dearest, sweetest treasure, come back)

7 (No. 30) Lament, F minor: "Se 'l mio duol non è si forte" (If my grief is not bitter enough)

8 (No. 34) Triumphal aria, G major: "Mio caro caro bene!" (My beloved!)[26]

In these arias nuance and depth of musical expression capture Rodelinda's magnanimity as one who loves and mourns, even as they also represent her carefully considered superior conduct as queen. Moreover, they begin to do so from the very beginning of the play, for in contrast to Corneille and Salvi, whose plots begin with a lengthy dialogue between Rodelinda and Unulfo, Händel has his protagonist stand alone on stage and open the opera with her first aria (I, 1, no. 1). As she laments "I have lost my dear husband and here, alone in my misfortune, my suffering grows worse,"[27] she does not know that he is not only alive but also plotting to rescue her and their son from the clutches of the usurper, Grimoaldo. And with this misunderstanding and mourning, the stage is set for the passions and plot to come.

Indeed, when Grimoaldo surfaces shortly thereafter and reveals the "pure passion" of his "flames of love" (I, 1) while attempting to force his affections upon Rodelinda, the queen's G-minor tirade (I, 1, no. 2) indignantly sends him on his way, as she announces at the top of her voice that "the cruel harshness of fate may make me wretched but not dishonorable."[28] That leads to sharper conflict with her adversary and to more arias in which general themes of love and mourning, as well as hate and wrath, are underscored through the expression of Rodelinda's emotions. For example, still within the first act, she pours out her second aria of lament (I, 7, no. 8) to the elegiac notes of a German flute as, secretly observed by her husband in disguise as a Hun, she declares at his supposed gravestone that even at the price of her own life, she would remain steadfast: "Shades, trees, and tombs of grief, / you would delight my heart [...]."[29] The short opening phrases of this B-minor cavatine gradually coalesce to generate the beautifully sustained flourish at the words "del mio sen," while, in contrast with the more despairing nature of her first aria of lament, this one as a whole shows a more poignant aspect of Rodelinda's grief.

The supposed widow then deals with the devious advisor of the usurper and braves the vile schemer Garibaldo, as she declares in her second aria of fury (I, 8, no. 10), "Yes you will die because your evil head shall be the step upon which I shall tread to attain the throne."[30] And, in fact, as she subsequently agrees to marry Grimoaldo, she demands that he put Garibaldo to death. Moreover, for another wedding present, she insists that Grimoaldo kill her son Flavio in front of her, since she cannot remain mother to the rightful king while being married to the usurper. Of course, through such an act, Grimoaldo would publically reveal himself to be a monstrous tyrant, but there can be little doubt that Rodelinda wants such a revelation, as, boldly confronting him and Garibaldo, she hurls her third aria of fury at them: "Pitiless men, I swore to you that I would visit you with grief and anguish" (II, 3, no. 16).[31]

The opera and Rodelinda's character then take a tender turn, as she learns that her husband might still be alive and as she articulates her unsatisfied and unquenchable longing for him in the Sicilian love aria (II, 6, no. 22): "My dearest, sweetest treasure, come back."[32] But the gentleness of this aria is quickly displaced by great grief, as, in reaction to the supposed passing of Bertarido, she prepares herself in her third aria of lament (III, 4, no. 30) for her own death: "If my grief is not bitter enough, oh God, who in mercy will pierce and stop my heart?"[33]

The sorrow does not last, however, for before Rodelinda can kill herself, Bertarido returns, slays Garibaldo, saves Grimoaldo, and restores the latter to the throne of Milan, all of which leads Rodelinda to sing in her final, triumphal aria (III, 8, no. 34), "My beloved! I have no anguish or pain left in my heart. Seeing your happiness I now feel only love within my heart."[34] The sense of joyful release, for Rodelinda and for the audience, is the greater for her having endured such extremes of emotional experience, as the closing chorus by all of the principles – excepting, of course, the dead villain, Garibaldo – makes clear: "Dopo la notte oscura, / più lucido, più chiaro / più amabile, più caro / ne spunta il sol quaggiù. / Tal dopo ria sventura / figlio d'un bel soffrire, / più stabile giore / nasce della virtù." (III, 6, no. 35: "After the dark night, the sun which shines down on us is clearer, brighter, more delightful, and more precious. After such cruel misfortune, a more sober happiness, child of our suffering, is born of virtue.").

We have clearly come a long way from the historically marginal figure of Rodelinda in the *Historia Langobardorum*, for she is now a protagonist who, as the Baroque ideal of marital love and fidelity, saves both life and throne. And in that transformation lie both a waning interest in the historical figure of the queen and a growing concern for the composer's dramatic needs. Beginning with Corneille and culminating with Händel, Rodelinda's interpreters evidently felt free to depart from the facts presented by Paul and passed on by Renaissance humanists. They enhanced, or at least underscored, her position within Lombard society in accord with the belief that the highs and lows of her life would thereby have a greater impact on the audience; they wrapped her in complicated love affairs and betrayals as a means of multiplying those vicissitudes; they endowed her with great passion and sensitivity as motives for emotional responses to the swings of her fate; and they gave her the determination and resilience not only to endure her many trials but, in the case of Händel's opera, also to ensure a *lieto fine*.

Yet Händel and his fellow composers needed a foundation on which to build these fictions. And that is where works like the *Historia Langobardorum*, as it was filtered through the Renaissance humanists, came in handy. In describing Rodelinda, Paul was vague enough to impose very few limits on the interpretation of her personality and the details of her life. But, at the same time, he presented her in broad contexts that were dramatic and detailed enough to support works that would fulfill the political needs and aesthetic expectations of aristocratic audiences in the seventeenth and eighteenth centuries. And that appears to have been the primary criterion by which Händel and many other composers of *opere serie* selected their protagonists. Rather than comb the past for figures that were depicted in great detail and then accommodating their dramatic structure to those portraits, they sought models that, regardless of the detail with which they were described, were flexible enough to accommodate the demands of stereotypical *opera seria*. Thus, their medievalism was incidental in that, though they may demonstrate awareness that their ultimate sources were medieval, their references to the past were apparently motivated not so much by a particular interest in the Middle Ages as a cultural phenomenon or by a desire to find extensive historical parallels to particular political scenarios of their time as by a desire for more affective, and therefore effective storytelling, for an enhanced *dramma per musica* that commented on both its own time and the past only insofar as it appealed to the aristocratic interests of its audience.

NOTES

1. This is a revised version of the German article "*Die Liebe wächst mit meinem Muthe ...* Die Langobardenkönigin Rodelinda als Opernheldin," in Gudrun Marci-Boehncke and Jörg Riecke, ed., *"Von Mythen und Mären" – Mittelalterliche Kulturgeschichte im Spiegel einer Wissenschaftler-Biographie. Festschrift für Otfrid Ehrismann zum 65. Geburtstag* (Hildesheim, Zurich, and New York: Olms, 2007), 19–32. Also given as a paper at the 42nd International Congress on Medieval Studies, Kalamazoo, Michigan, 12 May 2007. Trans. by Isaac Tubb (University of California, Davis).

2. For more on Händel, begin with Guy A. Marco's bibliography *Opera. A Research and Information Guide*, 2nd ed. (New York and London: Garland, 2001), 185–96. For more on *opere serie*, begin with Marita P. McClymonds' article "Opera seria," in Stanley Sadie, ed., *The New Grove Dictionary of Opera*, 4 vols. (London: Macmillan, 1997), 3:698–707.

3. For more on *dramme per musica*, and their audiences, see Herbert Schneider's and Reinhard Wiesend's handbook *Die Oper im 18. Jahrhundert* (Laaber: Laaber, 2006), 9ff., 59ff.; and the article "Opera seria," in Sadie, ed., *The New Grove Dictionary of Opera*, 1:1242.

4. Note that where spellings for characters, titles, and – in the case of the Lombards/Langobards – groups vary among secondary sources, I have gone with the most common current version, as determined from a range of internet databases. To minimize confusion in comparing Händel's work and its sources, I have also regularized the spelling of such subjects in my discussion of primary sources, regardless of differences in spelling among those sources.

5. See Christoph Gottlieb Wendt's translation for the first German version of the opera, *Rodelinda, Königin in der Lombarday. In einem Sing-Spiele auf dem Hamburgischen Schau-Platze im Jahr 1734 vorgestellt* (Hamburg, 1734), 1.

6. Paulus Diakonus, "Geschichte der Langobarden," *Historia Langobardorum*, ed. Alexander Heine, trans. Otto Abel (Essen: Phaidon, 1986).

7. For more on Paul and his history of the Lombards, begin with Walter Pohl's "Paulus Diaconus und die Historia Langobardorum," in Anton

Scharer and Georg Scheibelreiter, ed., *Historiographie im frühen Mittelalter*, Veröffentlichungen des Institutes für Österreichische Geschichtsforschung 32 (Vienna: Oldenbourg, 1994), 375–405.

8. For more on the Lombards, see Jörg Jarnut, *Geschichte der Langobarden* (Stuttgart: Kohlmeyer, 1982); Neil Christie, *The Lombards: The Ancient Longobards* (Oxford: Oxford University Press, 1995); and Karin Priester, *Geschichte der Langobarden. Gesellschaft, Kultur, Alltagsleben* (Darmstadt: Wissenschaftliche Buchgesellschaft, 2004).

9. For more on how medieval figures found their way into Baroque culture via Renaissance prose and poetry, see Gerhild Scholz-Williams, "Vergegenwärtigung der Vergangenheit: Das Mittelalter im 15. Jahrhundert," in James F. Poag and Gerhild Schoz-Williams, ed., *Das Weiterleben des Mittelalters in der deutschen Literatur* (Königstein/Ts.: Athenäum, 1983), 13–24; and Johannes Janota, "Zur Rezeption mittelalterlicher Literatur zwischen dem 16. und 18. Jahrhundert," in Poag and Schoz-Williams, ed., *Das Weiterleben des Mittelalters*, 37–46. For more information specifically on how the artistic, architectural, and musical reception of the Middle Ages, as reflected in Renaissance court epics, served as décor and theme for Renaissance culture, see Annette Kreutziger-Herr, *Ein Traum vom Mittelalter. Die Wiederentdeckung mittelalterlicher Musik in der Neuzeit* (Cologne: Böhlau, 2003), 208ff.

10. Pierre Corneille, "Pertharite," in *Pierre Corneille. Oeuvres completes*, ed. Georges Couton, 2 vols. (Paris: Gallimard, 1984), 2:713–84.

11. For more on Corneille's sources, begin with Lawrence Melville Riddle, *The Genesis and Sources of Pierre Corneille's Tragedies from "Médée" to "Pertharite"*, The Johns Hopkins Studies in Romance Literatures and Languages 3 (Baltimore, MD: The Johns Hopkins Press, 1926), 181–98.

12. See Susan Read Baker's study *Dissonant harmonies. Drama and ideology in five neglected plays of Pierre Corneille* (Tübingen: Niemeyer, 1990); and Manfred Brauneck's handbook *Die Welt als Bühne. Geschichte des europäischen Theaters* (Stuttgart-Weimar: Metzler, 1996), 219ff., 283ff.

13. Pierre Corneille, "Pertharite," in *Pierre Corneille. Oeuvres completes*, 2:782.

14. For more on the initial reception of *Pertharite*, see George Couton's *Corneille et la Fronde. Théâtre et politique il y a trios siècles* (Clermont-Ferrand: Bussac, 1951), 79ff.

15. Johann Wolfgang von Goethe, 1 April 1827, to his confident Johann Peter Eckermann, in Ernst Beutler, ed., *Gedenkausgabe der Werke, Briefe und Gespräche. Johann Wolfgang Goethe* (Zurich-Stuttgart: Artemis, 1970), 616.

16. For more on Ghigi, see Winton Dean's article "A Handel Tragicomedy," *The Musical Times* 110 (1969): 819–22.

17. For more on Salvi, begin with Francesco Giuntini's article "Salvi, Antonio," in Sadie, ed., *The New Grove Dictionary of Opera*, 4:152.

18. Antonio Salvi, *Rodelinda, Regina de' Longobardi. Dramma per musica. Rappresentato nella villa di Pratolino in Florence* (Florence, 1710). See Francesco Giuntini, *I drammi per musica di Antonio Salvi. Aspetti della "riforma" des libretto nel primo Settecento* (Bologna: Mulino, 1994). Salvi's *Rodelinda* was scored for its premiere by Giacomo Antonio Perti, the "maestro di cappella" of San Pietro and San Petronio in Bologna. Later, Salvi's libretto was repeatedly set to music: in 1724 by a Lucca native, Giovanni Antonio Canuti; in 1725 by an anonymous composer under the title *L'amor costante*; in 1727, with the misleading title *Il Bertarido, re dei Longobardi*, by the Venetian Giuseppe Boniventi; in 1731 by Boniventi's countryman Bartolomeo Coran; and in 1732 by an anonymous composer of operas. In 1741, Carl Heinrich Graun, the court composer for Frederick II, premiered in Berlin *Rodelinde, Königinn der Langobarden, ein Singespiel [...] auf der neuen Königlichen Hofschaubühne auf Befehl Sr. Königl. Majest. von Preußen* ([Giovanni Gualdberto Bottarelli and Johann Christoph Rost]: *Rodelinda Regina de Longobardi. Dramma per musica. Da rappresentarsi nel nuovo Regio Teatro della Corta. Per ordine della Sacra Maestà Il Re di Prussia/ Rodelinde Königinn der Longobarden. Ein Singespiel welches auf der neuen Königlichen Hoffschaubühne auf Befehl Sr. Königl. Majest. Von Preußen soll vorgestellt werden* [Berlin, 1741]). The Dresden High Finance Secretary, Johann Christoph Rost, was the author of the text. This was translated from the Salvi and Haym revisions, respectively, stemming from the librettist Giovanni Gualdberto Bottarelli.

19. See Werner Wunderlich, "Tradition and Reception of Roman Imperial Ethics in the Opera *La clemenza di Tito*," *The Comparatist* 25 (2001): 5–21.

20. For the original version, see *Rodelinda. An Opera as it was Perform'd at the Kings Theatre. Compos'd by Mr Handel* (London: Cluer, 1725).

21. For more on Haym, begin with Lowell Lindgren's article "Haym, Nicola Francesco," in Sadie, ed., *The New Grove Dictionary of Opera*, 2:680–81.

22. See Emile Dahnk-Baroffio, "Nicola Hayms Anteil an Händels Rodelinde-Libretto," *Die Musikforschung* 7 (1954): 295–300.

23. For more on Cuzzoni, see Winton Dean and C. Vitali, "Cuzzoni, Francesca," in Laura Macy, ed., <http:/ www.grovemusic.com>.

24. See the remarks of the English music historian Charles Burney cited on page 18 in Werner Wunderlich's article "... *das übrige bleibt erdichtet* oder Wie eine Opernkönigin Gestalt annimmt," in Hella Bartnig, ed., *Programmbuch zur Münchner Erstauffürung* Rodelinda, Regina de'Langobardi *von Georg Friedrich Händel* (Munich: Bavarian State Opera,

Season 2002/03), which is based on Charles Burney's *General History of Music from the Earliest Ages to the Present Period (1789)*, ed. Frank Mercer (New York: Dover, 1957).

25. Bernhard Paumgartner, ed., *John Mainwaring. G[eorg] F[riedrich] Händel, nach Johann Matthesons deutscher Ausgabe von 1761 mit anderen Dokumten* (Zurich: Atlantis, 1947), 130: "Ausdrückung der besonderen Handlung, Leidenschaft und Empfindung, die da vorgestellt wird."

26. "Rodelinda. Regina de' Longobardi," in Ellen T. Harris, ed., *The Librettos of Handel's Operas*, 13 vols. (New York: Garland, 1989), 4:211–95.

27. "Ho perduto il caro Sposo / E quì sola alle sventure / Vie più cresce mio penar."

28. "L'empio rigor del Fato / Vile non potrà farmi, / Se misera mi fe."

29. "Ombre, piante, urne funeste / Voi sareste / Le delizie del mio sen [...]."

30. "Morrai, sì; l'empia tua testa / Già m'appresta / Un gradin per gire al trono."

31. "Spietati, io vi giurai: / Se al mio figlio il cor donai, / Di serbavi e duolo e affano."

32. "Ritorno, o caro, e dolce mio tesoro."

33. "Se 'l mio duol non è si forte, chi trafigge, o Dio!"

34. "Mio caro caro bene! / Non ho più affanni / e pene al cor!"

Ring of the Nibelung and the Nibelungenlied: Wagner's Ambiguous Relationship to a Source

Edward R. Haymes

Richard Wagner never much liked the *Nibelungenlied*, a Middle High German epic from around 1200 that was responsible for a certain level of nationalistic madness in Germany in the early nineteenth century. I can sympathize. When I first read the epic I was tremendously disappointed. Where were all the gods, dwarves, giants, and other mythical creatures and events that give Wagner's *Ring* its special glamour? The epic is grounded in a fictional world that reflects the politics and social concerns of its own times, the beginning of the thirteenth century. The opening chapter, for example, is a relatively pedestrian description of the main court offices and their holders among the Burgundians in Worms on the Rhine. It concludes with a dream that afflicts the young princess Kriemhild and its interpretation as the prophecy of her eventual marriage to a doomed hero. Not a dwarf or a giant in sight. They do appear later, but they play very minor roles on the whole, and the heathen gods naturally are banned from the Christian world of the poem. The best the poet can do with the Huns, who are heathen and who play a considerable role in the second, un-Wagnerian part of the epic, is to remark that they sing the mass very differently (Strophe 1851).[1] And yet, as the huge bibliography on the *Nibelungenlied* testifies, it remains an endlessly fascinating work.

The nationalistic fervor that surrounded the *Nibelungenlied* in the early nineteenth century, however, had little to do with its actual qualities. By the end of the Middle Ages, the work seems to have passed out of favor and never made it into print during the early days of printed books. The poem was discovered in the middle of the eighteenth century and published in an edition that seems to have raised the ire of Frederick the Great of Prussia, who wrote that the whole work was not worth "a shot of powder."[2] The poem came into its own during the patriotic surge of the Napoleonic Wars and was printed in numerous editions (some more translations than editions). Friedrich Heinrich von der Hagen (1780–1856) – who coincidentally held the first professorship in *Germanistik* anywhere – published numerous editions of the work, each one claiming to represent "the original text."[3] There was even a special edition of the translation by August Zeune to be carried in the knapsacks of patriotic German soldiers fighting Napoleon.[4] The *Nibelungenlied* was seen as a German epic to hold up against the great ancient Greek and Roman works that had played such an important role in the essentially classical education virtually all cultured Germans had experienced. It was no accident that it was soon referred to widely as the "Teutsche Ilias", the German *Iliad*, using the archaizing spelling of "deutsch" to drive home its point.[5] Many writers – including Wagner – referred to it simply as "Die Nibelungen",[6] and there was considerable pressure on composers to produce a "Nibelungen"-opera during the 1840s.

There is no question that Wagner knew the *Nibelungenlied* well. Most scholars have chosen to ignore this fact in the light of his remarks in *Eine Mitteilung an meine Freunde*. These fall in the middle of a discussion of Wagner's rejection of historical drama in favor of myth, which he understood as the product of the *Volk*, the whole people. He chose to ignore the fact that the Icelandic Eddas and sagas he selected as his main sources were – at least in their written form – somewhat younger than the *Nibelungenlied* itself. However, he felt that the myth behind them was much older and that they represented the myth better than did the Middle High German epic:[7]

> Even if the figure of Siegfried had always attracted me, it first really enchanted me when, freed of all later costuming, I was successful in seeing it in its purest human appearance before me. Only now did I recognize the possibility of making him the hero of a drama; something that had never occurred to me as long as I knew him only from the medieval *Nibelungenlied*.[8]

The Scandinavian materials were appropriated quite early to the German nationalistic project. Von der Hagen had already published translations of them beginning in 1813. Most scholars were happy to include these stories and figures in their picture of a mythic past for the Germanic peoples. The most important works for this were written down in Iceland in the thirteenth century. Snorri Sturluson (1178–1241), one of the greatest scholars of his time, assembled the stories of the Germanic gods and heroes as sources for poetic expressions in a book which he called *Edda*.[9] Some time later an unknown Icelander wrote down what were probably the only remaining songs of the pagan past known to him. Beginning in the seventeenth century, scholars associated this collection with Snorri's work and called it *Edda* as well. Since its songs are generally considered to be older than Snorri's, it is often referred to as the *Elder Edda*.[10] Another Icelander decided to retell the stories found in these songs in prose and add to them stories he knew about Sigmundr and his ancestry in a saga known as *The Saga of the Volsungs*.[11] At about the same time, an unknown writer working in Norway collected stories associated with the Gothic king Theoderic the Great, probably of North German origin, and wrote them down in Norse prose around the middle of the thirteenth century.[12] This collection, generally known as the *Saga of Thidrek of Bern* was included in the Old Norse library von der Hagen translated into German.

Since Wagner played down the importance of the *Nibelungenlied* in the formation of his version of the Nibelung legend, most scholars have followed his lead and minimized their treatment of it as well. Even Elizabeth Magee, who has presented us with the most exhaustive study of Wagner's use of his sources, pays the epic little heed.[13] Árni Björnsson is determined that we should never attribute things that are specifically Icelandic to a generalized North or to a more generalized "Germanic" past. In demonstrating his point he analyzes at great length the debt Wagner owed to Icelandic sources.[14] These scholars leave little doubt that the first three operas of the *Ring* – *Das Rheingold*, *Die Walküre*, and *Siegfried* – are largely derived from Scandinavian sources. It would carry us too far afield to discuss this well-traveled road. Suffice it to say that the notion of the cursed ring is present in both the *Poetic Edda* and the *Saga of the Volsungs*, although it never plays the pivotal role it does in Wagner. The building of the fortress is derived from Snorri's *Edda*. The love story of *Die Walküre* is derived largely from the *Saga of the Volsungs*, while the conclusion of the same opera is expanded hugely from some clues in a song of the *Poetic Edda*. Most of *Siegfried* is once again derived from the *Poetic Edda* songs and the *Saga of the Volsungs*. The role of the gods is also heavily influenced by their position in Greek drama, but that is also an entirely different area of study.[15] Wagner derived other notions for his *Ring* from various sources, such as Jacob Grimm's massive *Deutsche Mythologie* or the collection of *Kinder- und Hausmärchen* by the brothers Grimm, but we cannot really ignore the influence of the "teutsche Ilias" both on the early libretto for *Siegfrieds Tod* (2:167–226) and on the final text of *Der Ring des Nibelungen* (5:199–268; 6:1–256), mainly in *Götterdämmerung*. We will treat the differences between these two texts later.

A major problem in all this is that Wagner was a great synthesizer. He combined the different versions of "the Nibelung legend" he knew into a single version he felt was truer to the original mythic spirit of the legend than were any of the surviving medieval texts and turned it into a scenario for a drama in the early fall of 1848. Although some details he added later are missing, this scenario tells most of the story we later find in the *Ring*, even though he only intended to use the conclusion of the story on the stage. In this synthesis of story elements from all available sources he was following the syncretic example of men such as Wilhelm Grimm[16] and Franz Joseph Mone,[17] who each presented a synthesis of the surviving versions of Germanic heroic legend in the hope of bringing the modern reader closer to that myth. Wagner chose to ignore the fact that the *Nibelungenlied* is incompatible in important ways with the Icelandic poetry and prose he preferred, and he saw all of these works as evidence of a single Nibelung myth. In doing this he was, if anything, just as "medieval" as his sources. Those who choose to excoriate Wagner for his failure to represent accurately the medieval versions ignore the fact that the medieval authors, particularly the anonymous poet of the *Nibelungenlied*, did exactly the same. They took an existing legend and re-expressed it in the language and social structure of their own times. The *Nibelungenlied* assumes the social structure of 1200, not of 436 (the historical time when the Gibichung kings met their deaths), as the basis for its highly political version of the story. Siegfried and Kriemhild engage in a very modern "courtly love" relationship that would have had no meaning even fifty years earlier. The problematic situation of Hagen as vassal was somewhat older, but it too is a product of its times. Wagner simply made similar use of ancient stories to explore political, philosophical, and psychological matters appropriate to the middle of the nineteenth century. The connection between Wagner's work and the politics of his time has been a central theme of Wagner scholarship since at least George Bernard Shaw's famous *The Perfect Wagnerite*, first published in 1898.[18]

We do not know when Wagner first read the epic, but his Dresden library included three editions and a translation.[19] He apparently tried to read the Middle High German text as well as the translations by von der Hagen and Simrock. In his famous 1856 letter to Franz Müller in Weimar, he mentions the edition by Karl Lachmann (1793–1851) as well as Lachmann's studies on the epic, but he does not mention the translations.[20] Perhaps he was hiding the fact that he needed the translations, but their language made a definite impression on Wagner as he was preparing his own versions of the legend for the operatic stage. While still in Dresden in the fall of 1848, Wagner wrote the scenario mentioned above and the libretto for a single opera on the Nibelung theme, *Siegfrieds Tod*. The scenario on the "Nibelungen-Mythos" shows that Wagner had worked out his version of the Nibelung story even before writing a single opera on the subject. He expanded his project backwards during his exile years in Switzerland (after 1850) and eventually produced a text by early 1863 that was recognizably our *Ring*.[21] I have included an outline of the plot of the first three dramas of the Ring as an appendix. The following discussion follows the plot of *Siegfrieds Tod* and *Götterdämmerung* closely, so there is no need to outline its plot there.

The names used in *Siegfrieds Tod* and in *Der Ring des Nibelungen* are generally the German forms, even in those places where the Icelandic texts govern the events. Some of these are derived from the *Nibelungenlied* itself, although most of them reflect what the nineteenth century thought to be the "real" names. For example "Siegfried" is the form of the name universally adopted in Germany, although we occasionally run into forms such as "Sigfrid." The Middle High German text of the *Nibelungenlied* uses the contracted form "Sîfrid," but the circumflex accent in the first syllable indicates a contraction and the usual assumption is that the first syllable was originally "Sigi." The variant spellings do not affect the meaning of the syllable. "Sieg" or "Sigi" means "victory" no matter where it occurs.

The name "Siegmund" has been adjusted to fit with Wagner's spelling of his son's name. The most common forms in nineteenth-century Germany were "Sigmund" (as in Freud) or even "Sigismund." Wagner followed the *Nibelungenlied* in calling Siegfried's mother "Sieglinde," using the same spelling of the opening syllable he had used with the father's name. The names in the *Nibelungenlied* are "Sigemunt" and "Sigelint," but, of course, they are not twins as their Icelandic models had been.

The spelling "Wotan" is Wagner's invention. The most common spelling for the German god, one Wagner had used in both *Lohengrin* and his sketches for the *Ring*, was "Wodan." Jacob Grimm lists all the different spellings he knows,[22] but Wagner's spelling is new, being a combination of "Wodan," which was the north German form, and "Wuotan," which came from the south. The Norse version is, of course, "Óðinn." "Brünnhilde" is Wagner's own spelling, built (like "Isolde") on the dative of the medieval form of the name found in the *Nibelungenlied* – "Prünhilt" (the initial "p" here is the result of a south German dialect tendency to unvoice consonants). The Old Norse version of the name was "Brynhild[r]" and the (Latinized) Gothic form found in Gregory of Tours is "Brunichildis." It is possible that Wagner spelled the name in this fashion to emphasize its roots in "Brünne" (Byrnie, i.e., upper-body chain mail) and "Hild" (battle).

Wagner chose the Norse "Guðrún" in a German form, "Gutrune," for the final text of the *Ring*, although he used a transitional form, "Gudrune," in *Siegfrieds Tod*. He probably adopted the final spelling in order to facilitate Siegfried's pun on "gute Runen" (good runes) that appears in both *Siegfrieds Tod* and *Götterdämmerung*. Siegfried's queen in the *Nibelungenlied* is "Kriemhild" (spelled "Chriemhilt" in most manuscripts), which is probably related to the Norse "Grimhild[r]." Wagner follows the *Völsungasaga* in assigning this name to the mother of the Gibichungs. Gunther's name remains relatively unchanged from the Middle High German, although the name appears as "Gunnar" in Old Norse. The *Nibelungenlied* usually uses a three-syllable form of the name "Hagene," but by the nineteenth century the name had established itself as "Hagen." The Norse version was "Högni." Gibiche, although his name does occur in several later texts and in one manuscript of the *Nibelungenlied*, appears in the thirteenth-century epic as "Dancrat." We have no way of knowing how this name entered the legend. The name "Alberich" is derived from the *Nibelungenlied* as well, although its bearer is a very different kind of dwarf than the Icelandic Andvari, who had cursed the ring when the god Loki took it from him.

It has already been remarked that Wagner built his *Ring* backwards: that is, that he wrote each of the three operas leading up to the final one as an explanation of what went after. This relatively mechanical view of things ignores the fact that Wagner radically changed the conclusion of his *Ring* and thus its entire message in the process of this revision. In *Siegfrieds Tod*, Siegfried's death leads to a restoration of the gods and their power, while the *Ring* follows the gods from the establishment of their power through the building of the castle Valhalla to their end. This change reflects both Wagner's changed circumstances and his changed attitudes. When he started the project and wrote his original drama, he was restlessly chafing at the limitations of his position as Royal Kapellmeister in Dresden, while flirting with revolutionary politics and anarchy. When he returned to his project, he was a fugitive in Switzerland with a price on his head, having seen his revolutionary project collapse in Dresden in the spring of 1849. One could argue that the change in Siegfried's role represents the development of Wagner from a relatively optimistic revolutionary to the disappointed pessimist portrayed in the Wotan of *Die Walküre* who only wishes for "das Ende." The ground was thoroughly prepared for both Schopenhauer's pessimism, which Wagner was soon to adopt enthusiastically, and the new vision of Siegfried's sacrifice as the catalyst that brings about the end of the gods.

The change in the overall goal of the myth has no parallel in any medieval source and can be sought primarily in Wagner's own psyche.[23] He reflects this clearly in the changes he wrote into the opening scene of what had been *Siegfrieds Tod*. In order to emphasize the importance of Siegfried's role in the Nibelung myth, Wagner chose the Norns, the Three Fates of Norse mythology. In *Siegfrieds Tod* these three merely tell events of the past that are important for the understanding of what follows. When Wagner changed the significance of Siegfried's murder, he also changed the meaning of this scene. In the original version the Norns tell pivotal events in the past: Alberich's theft of the gold and his making a ring from it; the gods' fortress paid for with the ring; Siegfried's killing of the dragon and his awakening of Brünnhilde; and finally a reference to Wotan's exchange of an eye for wisdom at the Norns' spring. Each of these episodes (except for the last) is allowed to extend into the future with a brief text that foreshadows the tragic drama about to unfold. During this scene the Norns protect the rope of Fate that "binds the world." In the revision in *Götterdämmerung*, the Norns concentrate on the events that lead to the gods' downfall: Wotan's cutting a branch from the World Ash Tree for his spear; the contracts cut in the shaft; and Siegfried's shattering of the spear. Only toward the end of the scene do we get a mention of Alberich's theft of the gold. This last is over-shadowed by the breaking of the rope, marking the end of Fate and the "twilight of the gods."

The second scene, in which Brünnhilde sends Siegfried forth to new deeds, was inserted in response to advice from a friend that Wagner show Siegfried and Brünnhilde as a happy couple before things begin to unravel in *Götterdämmerung*. In the course of this fare-well scene, Siegfried gives the ring to Brünnhilde. This scene is preserved almost unchanged in *Götterdämmerung*. Following an orchestral passage depicting Siegfried's descent to the Rhine, we find ourselves in the hall of the Gibichungs, with Gibich's offspring – Gunther and Gutrune – and their half-brother Hagen in a scene derived largely from Siegfried's arrival in Worms in the *Nibelungenlied*. Wagner obtained the idea of Hagen as a half-brother, whose father was a supernatural being, from the *Þiðrekssaga*, but he then simplified this notion and made it more telling by making him the son of the evil genius of the *Ring*, Alberich.

Hagen's role as Siegfried's main adversary is prefigured in the *Nibelungenlied*, a role he does not play in the Icelandic versions. In fact he argues against killing Sigurd in both the *Fragment of a Sigurd Lay* and in the *Volsungasaga*. In the German epic, on the other hand, he is already mentioned by a concerned Sigemunt as an obstacle to Siegfried's expressed plan to woo the Burgundian princess Kriemhild:

> If there were no one else than Hagen the warrior,
> who can arrogantly show his prowess,
> So that I greatly fear that it would bring us harm
> If we were to woo that most noble maiden. (54)

> Ob ez ander niemen wære   wan Hagene der degen
> der kan mit übermüete   der hôhverte pflegen,
> daz ich des sêre fürhte   ez müg' uns werden leit,
> ob wir werben wellen   die vil hêrlîchen meit.

In spite of parental warnings, Siegfried decides to set out on his own, accompanied in the epic by eleven other knights, to win Kriemhild.

Although he is not an immediate member of the royal family as he is in the Icelandic sources and in the *Ring*, Hagen's position as main counselor to Gunther is also established in the *Nibelungenlied*. When Siegfried arrives in Worms, it is Hagen who, like his counterpart in *Siegfrieds Tod* and *Götterdämmerung*, prepares Gunther and his court with a carefully prepared version of his past. Although the *Nibelungenlied* establishes a courtly upbringing for Siegfried that is totally at variance with the wild youth in the woods we know from the Norse sources and from the later German *Lied vom Hürnen Seyfrid*, Hagen tells us about a youth that is much closer to the traditional one. In Hagen's narration he is reported to have killed a dragon and bathed in its blood, becoming invulnerable. He is also reported to have gained a great treasure from the brothers Schilbung and Nibelung, whom he agreed to help divide their inherited treasure. Siegfried was unable to reach an equitable division and simply killed the two brothers and took the treasure for himself. The "fee" the Nibelung brothers had offered Siegfried was the sword Balmung. Wagner used this name in his original draft, *Siegfrieds Tod*, but he changed it to his own invention, "Nothung," in the final *Ring* poem. After killing the brothers, Siegfried leaves the dwarf Alberich in charge of the defense of the land of the Nibelungs and the treasure. The *Nibelungenlied* is the only medieval text that divides the killing of the dragon from the winning of the treasure.

The *Tarnhelm* is derived from what is probably a misreading of the language of the *Nibelungenlied*. Among the treasures Siegfried wins from the Nibelung brothers is a *tarnkappe* or a *tarnhût*. Many early readers of the poem read both of these terms as referring to some kind of headgear. The *kappe* of the first word, however, is the same etymon (i.e., it shares an etymological ancestor) as the English word "cape" and the *hût* of the second word is actually a word denoting the pelt of an animal, related to the English word "hide." The garment was a cape or cloak that made its wearer invisible, a more or less logical notion. Wagner made a further change by making it into a helmet, usually represented by a piece of chain mail on stage. In order to reach this form he may have combined the *tarnkappe* with the "helmet of terror," the *ægishjálmr* of the *Völsungasaga*, but there is no indication that this device could make anyone invisible. It serves only to terrify enemies. In the *Völsungasaga* Sigurðr found the *ægishjálmr* among the treasures he won by killing Fáfnir and Reginn. Wagner also combines the ability to make the wearer invisible from the *Nibelungenlied* with the frequent shape-shifting episodes in the Norse sources to produce a new device of power that, in combination with the ring, allows the wearer to change his shape, to disappear, or to travel great distances. In the *Nibelungenlied*, Siegfried uses the *tarn-kappe* to help Gunther win his bride Brünhild.

Wagner reflects the arrival scene in the *Nibelungenlied* by having Hagen introduce Siegfried and give information about his past even before he has been sighted. There is no source for this in the Norse poems or prose. Like the Hagen of the epic, the operatic Hagen provides only the information he wishes his hearers to have, leaving out the crucial fact of his relationship to Brünnhilde.

After Hagen's bloodthirsty introduction of the hero in the Nibelung epic, he simply recommends that Gunther and his court give Siegfried a polite welcome. Siegfried responds to the welcome by challenging Gunther to single combat with their respective kingdoms as a winner-take-all prize for the victor. Gunther's brothers are able to mollify Siegfried and convince him to join their court as the hero remembers that he is there to woo the princess Kriemhild. Ironically, the formulas of politeness used by the Burgundians to establish peace grant him metaphorically all that he had sought to gain in reality by force:

> The lord of the land spoke: "Everything we have –
> If you can honorably deign to accept it – let it be subject to you
> And let it be divided with you, persons and property."
> Lord Siegfried then became a little softer in his mood. (127)

> Dô sprach der wirt des landes   "allez daz wir hân,
> geruochet irs nâch êren,   daz sî iu undertân,
> unt sî mit iu geteilet   lîp unde guot."
> dô wart der herre Sîvrit   ein lützel sanfter gemuot.

In *Siegfrieds Tod* Wagner reduces Siegfried's challenge and the Burgundians' peacemaking to a single sentence: "nun ficht mit mir – oder sei mein Freund!" (6:191), a line that survives unchanged in the text of *Götterdämmerung*. The *Nibelungenlied* is the only source for this challenge. In the Norse versions Siegfried's arrival is only

important because of the potion of forgetfulness he receives at that
point. Siegfried's concern about his inability to offer lands and
peoples in return for Gunther's blood-brotherhood may also echo the
political implications of the scene in the *Nibelungenlied*, as such
concerns are totally lacking in the other sources Wagner used. Wagner
concludes the exchange with an echo of the politeness formula cited
above:

> Greet happily, O Hero,
> The hall of my father:
> Wherever you go,
> Whatever you see,
> Consider that your own:
> Yours is my heritage:
> Land and peoples –
> Let my body support my oath!
> I give you myself as your vassal.

> Begrüße froh, o Held,
> die Halle meines Vaters;
> wohin du schreitest,
> was du sieh'st,
> das achte nun dein Eigen:
> dein ist mein Erbe,
> Land und Leute –
> hilf, mein Leib, meinem Eide!
> mich selbst geb' ich zum Mann. (6:192)

After Siegfried has established himself at court (in the epic) by
spending a full year there without seeing the object of his quest,
matters are changed when Gunther and his brothers are challenged by
Saxon and Danish armies. Siegfried takes over the leadership of the
defense and easily defeats the enemies. As a reward he is allowed to see
the princess Kriemhild. The courtly ceremony in which they meet is
quite operatic in its magnificence, but Wagner wisely chose to omit it.
In the epic it has the function of emphasizing the courtly elements of
the relationship between Siegfried and Kriemhild. After this episode
Gunther hears of a fabulous bride in a faraway land, and Siegfried is
asked to help to woo her. He agrees to do this if Gunther will wed his
sister to him upon successful completion of the wooing expedition.

Wagner included this bargain in both versions of his opera. After tasting the draught of forgetfulness (a motif from the Icelandic versions), Siegfried is filled with passion for Gutrune. He agrees to use his powers to win Brünnhilde, whom he has forgotten, for Gunther. Hagen settles down to watch the hall of the Gibichungs, secure in his knowledge that Siegfried is following his plan. Siegfried uses the Tarnhelm to change into Gunther's shape and forces himself in this shape upon Brünnhilde, since Gunther is unable to win her for himself. He announces that the sword Nothung will guard his honor after Brünnhild has been sent off to her chamber to await him.

There is no indication in the *Nibelungenlied* that Siegfried has ever met Brünhild before, and the fact that they recognize each other has no more significance than the fact that Hagen recognizes Siegfried upon the latter's arrival in Worms. Many scholars have sought clues to a previous meeting between Siegfried and Brünhild in the text, but there is really nothing there. The Norse sources all include a meeting and even a betrothal between the two, and it is only natural for Wagner and others to assume that this is the "real" shape of the myth. It is important for our understanding of the *Nibelungenlied*, however, to realize that any previous knowledge of Brünhild is lacking here and not to read into her words or actions anything that is not there.

Upon their arrival in Iceland/Isenstein, Siegfried claims to be Gunther's vassal. In order to demonstrate this, he takes his place behind Gunther in line as they appear before the princess. This jostling for place in line is reflected in the final scene of the second act in *Siegfrieds Tod*, but it did not make it into *Götterdämmerung*. He then uses the *tarnkappe* to allow Gunther to win the games required to gain the bride: throwing a giant stone; leaping a great distance; and throwing a spear. The opponent in all of these games is the princess Brünhild herself, a woman of great physical power as long as she retains her virginity. Siegfried aids Gunther by physically carrying him through the games while doing the stone throwing, the leaping, and the spear throwing himself. Fortunately, we are told, the *tarnkappe* provides not only invisibility, but also the strength of twelve men. Later Siegfried uses the powers of the *tarnkappe* to help Gunther overcome his unwilling bride and take her virginity, making her no stronger than other women. The *Nibelungenlied* is very specific that Siegfried subdued the bride but did not carry out the sexual act. This he leaves to Gunther. These details become important in the oath scene later in the epic.

Another episode of the *Nibelungenlied* that finds its way into the text of *Götterdämmerung* takes place between the winning of Brünhild in Iceland and the marriage in Worms. Gunther and Hagen send Siegfried back to Kriemhild to report their success and to order them to prepare the reception for the new queen. There is an important scene in which Siegfried plays messenger to Kriemhild and her ladies and in which he demands a messenger's reward, something that would normally only be given to a messenger of lower status. Siegfried engages in a fiction of lowered status as a part of his courtly-love game with Kriemhild. Wagner retains specific reference both to Siegfried's role as messenger ("Heiß' mich willkommen, Gibichskind! / Ein guter Bote bin ich dir," 6:213) and to his demand for a messenger's reward in *Siegfrieds Tod* ("So sagt dem Boten Dank!" 6:215), both lines of which survive into the final version of *Götterdämmerung*. Gutrune does not react to either line, leaving them as strange relics of Wagner's sources.

In the *Nibelungenlied* Siegfried took along Brünhild's ring and belt as trophies after the bridal-night episode and foolishly gave them to his wife, Kriemhild. We are not told what he said about them. She later uses them in a very public dispute with Brünhild over the relative merits of their husbands. In this dispute she claims that Siegfried had taken Brünhild's virginity and that, if Brünhild maintained Siegfried was a vassal, then she, Brünhild, was a vassal's tart. The claim that Siegfried had had improper relations with Brünhild brings us back into the plot Wagner has assembled. Here the claim is much simpler. Brünnhilde claims that Siegfried is her husband, which is true, and that he had taken sexual advantage of her during the night he spent at her side as Gunther, which is not. As in the *Nibelungenlied*, a ring plays a major role in both *Siegfrieds Tod* and *Götterdämmerung*. In both the operas and their source, it is the ring Siegfried had taken from Brünhild on his night with her in the guise of Gunther. Of course, Wagner has identified it with the cursed ring of Alberich, a quite different ring in his sources, and thus magnified its importance. In both the *Nibelungenlied* and Wagner's texts, the ring is used as evidence of improper relations between Siegfried and Brünhild/Brünnhilde.

In the *Nibelungenlied* Siegfried is called upon to swear an oath to silence the accusation arising out of the "battle of the queens" described above. The men of the court are called upon to form a ring, a detail Wagner uses, and Siegfried raises his hand to swear the oath. It is unclear from the text whether Siegfried actually swears the oath or whether his readiness to do so is considered sufficient for Gunther, who has no interest in having Siegfried's knowledge spread abroad:

> Siegfried the very bold raised his hand for the oath.
> The powerful king [Gunther] then spoke: "I know so well
> Of your great innocence. I will release you
> From what my sister has accused you; that you have never done
>   it." (860)

> Sîfrit der vil küene   zem eide bôt die hant.
> dô sprach der künich rîche   "mir ist sô wol bekant
> iuwer grôz unschulde;   ich wil iuch ledic lân,
> des iuch mîn swester zîhet,   daz ir des niene habt getân."

We should also remember that in the epic Siegfried was due to swear only that he had never boasted of such a deed, not that he had not performed it.

Wagner kept the accusation, put it in his new context, and then refashioned the oath into a wonderful piece of theater while following his source quite closely. We have to admire Wagner's ability to simplify and contract the versions in all the sources to what we find in both *Siegfrieds Tod* and *Götterdämmerung*. It is also a stroke of genius to simplify the claims and counter-claims to the single point: had Siegfried taken advantage of his night in Gunther's shape beside Brünnhilde? Both Siegfried and Brünnhilde swear on the weapon that will eventually be used to kill him.

Brünnhilde's betrayal of Siegfried in the operas is fashioned after the somewhat contrived betrayal of Siegfried in the *Nibelungenlied*. There it is Kriemhild (i.e., Wagner's Gutrune) who is tricked into becoming complicit in Siegfried's death. Gunther and Hagen claim that the Danes and Saxons have renewed their attack, and as they prepare to go to meet the enemy, Hagen goes to Kriemhild to discover the location of Siegfried's vulnerable spot, claiming that he needs to know where it is in order to protect him there in the heat of battle. Kriemhild tells him of the linden leaf that fell between his shoulder blades when he was bathing in the dragon's blood, leaving a vulnerable spot and agrees to sew a little cross on his garments there, so Hagen will know exactly where it is. The false war is called off, and a hunt is planned instead. The poet of the Middle High German epic never explains why Siegfried would wear his war clothing on a hunt, but the little cross is clearly visible in the murder scene.

Wagner allows Brünnhilde rather than Kriemhild/Gutrune to carry out this "betrayal," and she gives Hagen the critical information, knowing full well that he plans to use it to kill Siegfried. Wagner has also eliminated the messy bath in dragon's blood that hardened the hero's skin. Instead of that, Brünnhilde tells Hagen that she had magically protected him with spells everywhere but in the back, because she knew that he would never turn his back on an enemy.

The scene in which Hagen and Gunther plan Siegfried's murder is present in some form in most of the versions of the story, but Brünnhilde's role in *Götterdämmerung* is most closely related to that in the *Nibelungenlied*, where she is not actually present, but where Hagen has promised to avenge the wrong done to her:

> He asked what was the matter, he found her weeping.
> She told him the story and he promised on the spot
> That it would be paid for by Kriemhilde's husband
> Or for that reason he would never be happy again. (864)

> Er vrâgte, waz ir wære,   weinende er si vant.
> dô sagte si im diu mære   er lobt' ir sâ zehant,
> daz ez erarnen müese   der Kriemhilde man
> oder er wolde nimmer   dar umbe vrœlîch gestân.

He then goes on to force the issue on an unwilling Gunther. As has often been pointed out, the *Nibelungenlied* does not provide a cogent reason for the murder of Siegfried. All of the reasons suggested in the massive interpretive literature to this point rest on interpretations of Hagen's character that are not really made explicit in the epic. Wagner lets Hagen play the same role in *Siegfrieds Tod* and *Götterdämmerung* but with plenty of motivation. He is the actual driving force behind the decision to kill Siegfried. As he points out to Gunther:

> No brain can help, no hand can help you.
> Only Siegfried's death can help you.

> Dir hilft kein Hirn. Dir hilft keine Hand.
> Dir hilft nur Siegfrieds Tod. (6:230)

In the original text of *Siegfrieds Tod*, this would have been the point when the title of the opera was sung on the stage, attracting attention to itself. Brünnhilde provides him with the means, and Gunther agrees to the plan, after being assured that Gutrune will not be told the truth about the killing.

After referring to vengeance for the wrong done to Brünhild in the *Nibelungenlied*, Hagen further whets Gunther's desire for Siegfried's death by depicting the power that would become his if Siegfried's possessions should come to him:

> except that Hagen
> advised again and again Gunther the warrior
> [that] if Siegfried no longer lived there would be subject to him
> many kingdoms. The hero began to grieve for this. (870)

> niwan daz Hagene
> geriet in allen zîten   Gvnther dem degene,
> ob Sîfrit niht enlebte,   sô wurde im undertân
> vil der künege lande.   der helt des trûren began.

In Wagner's *Ring*, we find Hagen using the same argument but tying it directly to the power of the ring itself:

> Great power will be given you
> If you gain the Ring from him.

> Ungeheure Macht wird dir
> Gewinnst du von ihm den Ring. (6:231)

The scene with the Rhine Daughters at the beginning of the Third Act stands in a complex relationship to the *Nibelungenlied*. As Magee has pointed out, the Rhine Daughters are essentially Wagner's invention, although there were some influences that led to this. One of the clearest predecessors is a scene from the *Nibelungenlied*. However, two major differences have led many to discount this scene as an influence on Wagner. The first is that the hero in question is Hagen, not Siegfried. The second is that the mermaids are in a backwater of the Danube, not of the Rhine. In an episode that has no parallel in Wagner's *Ring*, as most of the figures who would take part have been killed off in the *denouement* of *Götterdämmerung*, Gunther and Hagen are leading the Burgundians east to accept an invitation from Kriemhild's second husband, who is none other than Attila (the Hun), known in Middle High German as Etzel. When the Burgundians arrive at the Danube, the river is swollen, and there is no ferry in sight. Hagen sets out to find a ferry to cross the river and encounters two mermaids swimming in a backwater of the river. He takes their clothes to force them to give him information. They first tell him that the Burgundians will come to Etzel's land. When he returns their clothing, they tell him that the Burgundians will all die there if they go. They should turn back immediately, or only the king's chaplain will return to Worms alive. Hagen scoffs at their warning, but they give him further warning about the lords of Bavaria, a land they must traverse, saying that the Bavarians will also attack them. Finally they tell him how to find and deceive the ferryman so that he will take them across. Hagen finds the ferryman, kills him, and begins the job of setting his 20,000 men across the river. On the last trip he throws the king's chaplain overboard. The poor man cannot swim, but he is miraculously borne up by the water and washes ashore on the other side, where he can return to Worms alive. Hagen sees this as a confirmation of the mermaids' prophecy and destroys the boat after this last crossing, knowing they will not be returning.

Wagner retains the dire prophecies of the mermaids, but he addresses them to Siegfried instead of Hagen. Their warning gives him a last chance to avoid losing his life, which he tosses from him with a symbolic clod of dirt. In *Siegfried's Death* Wagner had not yet decided on all aspects of the role of the mermaids, nor does he give them names, simply referring to them as three "Wasserfrauen" ("Water-Women") and then numbering them like the Norns in the opening scene. In the epic they have the names of "Hadeburc" and "Sigelint" (nothing is made of the latter name's identity with that of Siegfried's mother). Wagner gave them names in *Das Rheingold* and carried these forward to the scene in *Götterdämmerung*, befitting their greatly increased importance in the cycle. At the end of their fruitless altercation with Siegfried, they decide to turn to Brünnhilde in the hope of receiving the ring after his death. Gutrune twice refers to Brünnhilde's going down to the Rhine, and Brünnhilde refers to their advice in her final scene:

Wise sisters of the depths!
The fire that burns me,
Let it cleanse the Ring of its curse:
You will melt it down and protect
It pure, the radiant gold of the Rhine,
Which was stolen from you to great misfortune!

weise Schwestern der Wassertiefe!
Das Feuer, das mich verbrennt,
rein'ge den Ring vom Fluch:
ihr löset ihn auf und lauter bewahrt
das strahlende Gold des Rhein's,
das zum Unheil euch geraubt! (2:227)

This is the text from *Siegfrieds Tod*, and it was little changed when it was revised for *Götterdämmerung*, becoming one of the few passages from this final scene to survive the revision.

In the Middle High German epic, Siegfried is very successful in his hunting, bringing back much booty for the hunters' dinner. In addition he catches a live bear and releases it into the midst of the party, causing great uproar until the beast is driven out of the camp. Siegfried then catches up with it and kills it, bringing it back to add to the huge stores of meat he has already provided. As the hunters eat their supper, Siegfried asks for wine. It has, he is informed, been sent to the wrong place. Hagen suggests a nearby spring to slake their thirst. Hagen and Siegfried strip off their weapons and engage in a foot race to the spring. Siegfried waits to allow Gunther to drink first. Then when Siegfried is drinking, Hagen strikes him through the little cross Kriemhild has sewn on his garment with his spear. Siegfried tries to strike back, but his strength leaves him. He dies, expressing concern for his wife.

Wagner has made judicious use of this material. The bear episode has been transported to the first act of *Siegfried*, where the young hero releases a bear into Mime's cave in order to watch his discomfort. Wagner's bear is allowed to survive and return to the forest.

Wagner also adopts the hunting camp as a location for the murder in both *Siegfrieds Tod* and *Götterdämmerung*. Unlike his medieval model, Wagner's Siegfried spends his time talking to the Rhine Daughters and ends up with no game at all. Wagner eliminates the missing wine in favor of letting Siegfried upbraid Gunther for failing to drink. Hagen also uses the wine to pass Siegfried an antidote for the potion that had caused him to forget the past. When Siegfried is in the middle of the story that would have cleared his name once and for all, Hagen thrusts his spear into the hero's back. In *Siegfrieds Tod* Siegfried attempts to crush Hagen with his shield, echoing a similar attempt in the *Nibelungenlied*, but he is unable to carry out the attack. Gunther and the men act surprised, but Hagen insists that he is only avenging perjury. Siegfried, mortally wounded, finishes his tale of the awakening of Brünnhilde and dies.

The murder scene is one that required extensive revision when Wagner moved from his original conception in *Siegfrieds Tod* to the final version in *Götterdämmerung*. In *Siegfrieds Tod* the dying Siegfried is overcome by a vision of Brünnhilde as a Valkyrie leading him to Valhalla. As this no longer holds true in the later version, Siegfried has a vision of the reawakened Brünnhilde greeting him as he dies.

Wagner builds Gutrune's scene of fearful anticipation from elements suggested by the *Nibelungenlied*, as the Icelandic versions with their murder in the bedchamber in her presence had no place for this. Kriemhild's immediate apprehension of the truth is replaced here by a dull expectation of catastrophe. Gutrune fears Brünnhilde, but she also seeks her company in this loneliest of moments. In the epic, Gunther and his men decide to hide Hagen's deed and to claim that robbers had killed Siegfried. They bring the body back to the castle and leave it in a passageway near Kriemhild's chamber. Kriemhild realizes as soon as she hears that there is a knight's body there that it is Siegfried. She remembers her conversation with Hagen in which she had told him of Siegfried's vulnerable spot. She correctly surmises that "ez hât gerâten Prünnhilt, daz ez hât Hagene getân" (Prünhilt plotted it so that Hagen has done it [1010,4]) even before she sees the corpse. She runs to Sigemunt, who is in Worms with her, and he laments that he cannot think of revenge in his old age. He also has too small a force there to think of attacking the Burgundians. When Kriemhild confronts her brothers, she repeats her accusation of Hagen, but Gunther insists that robbers had killed him and that Hagen had not done it. Twenty years later, at Etzel's court, Hagen finally admits the deed before Kriemhild, although the narrator lets us know that it is public knowledge that he had killed Siegfried, "the strongest of all warriors." In a very dramatic, almost operatic confrontation in the *Nibelungenlied* in which Hagen refuses to rise to acknowledge

Kriemhild the queen, she renews her accusation. Hagen responds truculently: "ich binz aber Hagene der Sîfriden sluoc" (It was I, Hagen, who slew Siegfried [1790,2]).

When Hagen brings Siegfried's corpse onto the stage in the operatic versions, he first claims that the hero has been slain by a wild boar, which is an echo of a monitory dream Kriemhild reported to Siegfried before the hunt in the epic. In her dream Kriemhild saw how two wild boars had torn her beloved to pieces. This dream is also recalled by Wagner in Gutrune's line "Schlimme Träume störten mir den Schlaf" (Evil dreams disturbed my sleep [6:247]). In the opera Gutrune turns her rage on all the men until Gunther says that it is Hagen who was the wild boar. Hagen echoes his model in the epic in his defiant admission of the deed: "Ich, Hagen, schlug ihn zu Tod" (I, Hagen, struck him dead [6:249]), but we do not have to wait twenty years for the admission.[24] There is perhaps a final echo of the epic at the moment in which Hagen attempts to take the ring from Siegfried's dead hand. His hand rises against Hagen, and all present are shocked and frightened. At this point Brünnhilde arrives and takes charge. In the epic, when Hagen approaches the dead body at the funeral, the wounds begin to bleed afresh, showing Hagen's guilt to the assembled multitude even though he continues to deny it.

In *Siegfrieds Tod* Brünnhilde prepares to join Siegfried on the funeral pyre. The body itself is borne to the pyre by members of the court singing a dirge. At the end of the opera, Brünnhilde emerges from the fire with Siegfried, whom she leads by the hand to join the gods in Valhalla. The radical change in *Götterdämmerung* alters the tone of this scene. Brünnhilde, who is now arguably the "hero" of the drama, sums everything up in dramatic speeches to Wotan, to Loge (via Wotan's ravens), to the Rhine Daughters, to Grane (her horse), and finally to Siegfried himself. She then rides into the fire, and the rising flames burn not only the hall of the Gibichungs but also Valhalla and the gods. The Rhine Daughters ignore Hagen's final cry and recover the ring while dragging Hagen himself off to drown in the Rhine. The conclusion is highlighted in the gleaming melody played by the strings as the music proceeds towards its dramatic, but serene, close. The secret of Wagner's final concept of the *Ring*'s "message" is contained in those final bars, but it is locked in the music.

Of course, Wagner's concerns were quite different from those moving the poet of the *Nibelungenlied*. The thirteenth-century author set out to explore ethical and political questions of his time using a traditional story to do it. Except for the mermaid scene and an echo of Hagen's watch over the Burgundians in Etzel's hall, there is not much notice in either of his poems of events after Siegfried's funeral. He also rigorously excludes anything having to do with the courtly world in which the Nibelung drama is played out. He is not as radical in his reductionism as he had been in his treatments of the Tristan and Parzival romances from the same period, but it is clear that he is mining the epic for something he considered to be behind it, rather than for its novelties.

The mature Wagner (like many of his contemporaries) considered myth to be the foundation of a nation and thus his search for a truly mythical basis for drama has a strongly nationalistic aspect. As mentioned before, he sought the mythical basis behind a story and considered the actual works of medieval art to be accidents of history; like many of his contemporaries, he felt them to be infected by foreign (mainly French) influences. He referred to Gottfried von Strassburg, who composed *Tristan*, and Wolfram von Eschenbach, who wrote *Parzival*, as being caught up in an age that was, as he said in a letter to Mathilde Wesendonck, "barbaric and completely confused, an age suspended between ancient Christianity and the newer age of nation-states."[25] Unlike many of his contemporaries, Wagner did not idealize the Middle Ages, but rather saw them as a period his national myths had passed through on their way to what he probably would have considered a more nearly definitive form in his dramas. This is ironic in view of the fact that virtually all of Wagner's materials after *Der fliegende Holländer* (1843) are derived in some way from the thirteenth century. Even the sixteenth-century hero of *Die Meistersinger von Nürnberg*, Walther von Stolzing, cites the thirteenth-century poet Walther von der Vogelweide as his teacher.[26] In this we might characterize Wagner as a reluctant medievalist, a medievalist who really did not like the Middle Ages.

A final point passes by so quickly in the *Nibelungenlied* that many do not notice it. There is a model here for the ring itself, but it is not a ring; it is a wand or simply a rod. When the Burgundians bring the treasure to Worms after Siegfried's death, we are told that this item was a part of it:

The wishing rod lay within it, a little rod of gold.
Whoever could have recognized it could have been master
Over all the world [and] over every man.

Der wunsch der lac darunder,   von golde ein rüetelîn
der daz het erkunnet,   der möhte meister sîn
wol in aller werlde   über ietslîchen man. (1124,1–3)

Nothing is ever made of this powerful magic, since no one ever recognizes it, but it is very similar to the magic inhering in Wagner's ring as
described by Wellgunde in *Das Rheingold*:

The wealth of the earth
Would be won
By him who from the Rhinegold
Could make the Ring,
Which would give him limitless power.

Der Welt Erbe
gewänne zu eigen,
wer aus dem Rheingold
schüfe den Ring,
der maaßlose Macht ihm verlieh'. (5:210)

One can imagine the frustrated composer happening upon the stanza
above and seeing it as a key to his understanding of the treasure and its
power. One can only imagine it, though, since Wagner left no reader's
notebook on his reactions to the epic.

Appendix

Plot summaries of *Das Rheingold*,
Die Walküre, and *Siegfried**

Since the plot of *Götterdämmerung* has been discussed extensively in
the body of this essay, I have chosen to summarize only the plots of
the first three dramas in the cycle.

Das Rheingold

After a prelude built entirely on the chord of E-flat, the curtain rises
on a scene in the depths of the Rhine. Three Rhine Daughters (Floss-
hilde, Woglinde, and Wellgunde) swim about enjoying the pre-dawn
peace when they are interrupted by an unattractive dwarf (Alberich)
who tries to seduce each one of them in turn. Their flirtation is interrupted when the rising sun makes the Rhinegold visible. When the
dwarf expresses disdain for the gold, he is told that unlimited power
would come to the one who could form the gold into a ring, but that
the condition for that was to give up love. Alberich immediately
foreswears love and steals the gold, leaving the Rhine Daughters to
swim in the dark. Wotan, the chief of the gods, has ordered a castle
built for him by two giants named "Fasolt" and "Fafner." Wotan's
wife, Fricka, is concerned that Wotan has bargained away her sister,
Freia, in return for the building. Wotan depends on the trickery of
Loge to get him out of the bargain. The other gods, Froh and Donner,
appear to defend Freia. Finally Loge arrives and says that he has found
only one person who was willing to give up "woman's pleasure and
worth" and that was Alberich, who had foresworn love and made the
ring. The giants agree to accept the dwarf's hoard as replacement for
Freia, but they take the goddess along to ensure the bargain. Loge and
Wotan descend to Nibelheim, where Mime, Alberich's brother, has
just finished making a magic helmet, the Tarnhelm, that will allow
Alberich to assume any shape or become invisible. After Alberich
threatens the gods with his new power, they manage to get him to

---

* Synopsis by the author, based on the text of Der Ring des Nibelungen
(5:199–268; 6:1û256). Complete text is also available in Spencer (fn. 7).

demonstrate the Tarnhelm. He first changes himself into a giant serpent to frighten them, and then, in response to Loge's challenge, he changes himself into a toad. The gods grab him and take him bound to the surface. As a condition of his freedom, Alberich is forced to bring up his hoard, and finally he is forced to part with the Tarnhelm and the ring, which he curses, saying it will bring death to anyone who possesses it until it is returned to him. The giants return and make as their condition that the gold completely hide Freia from them. When all the gold is piled up, they still see her hair, and so the Tarnhelm is added to the pile. Finally they see only her bright eye through a chink that can only be filled with the ring, which Wotan is unwilling to part with. The goddess Erda appears from the earth and warns Wotan that the end of the gods approaches and he would do best to avoid the ring. He adds the ring to the treasure. The giants fight over their wealth, and Fafner kills Fasolt, demonstrating the power of Alberich's curse. After the giants leave, the gods prepare to enter their castle, which Wotan calls "Valhalla." The Rhine Daughters mourn the loss of their gold, and the gods enter to mock pomp from the orchestra.

Die Walküre

Siegmund is fleeing through the night after losing his weapons in a battle. He stumbles into a cottage whose major feature is a tree growing through the floor and roof. He is given water by the woman living there. A mysterious connection grows between them as he tells a bit of his story, and she informs him that she is the wife and property of the house owner, a man named "Hunding." Hunding returns, and after questioning Siegmund, who gives his name as "Wehwalt," he discovers that this is the man he had set out to attack. He sends his wife to bed and tells Siegmund he will have to defend himself the next day. Siegmund wonders where he will find the sword his father had promised him in his hour of greatest need. The woman returns and tells him that she has given her husband a drug so that he will sleep deeply and then proceeds to tell him about a weapon that had been stuck in the tree at her wedding by an old man who had come unbidden into the hall. No one had been able to move it an inch. The doors fly open, and the winter storm has turned to spring, a fact that Siegmund celebrates in song. The woman asks for the real name of his father, and he responds "Wälse," and she enthusiastically gives him the name "Siegmund" and identifies herself as Sieglinde, his long-lost twin sister. He draws the sword and names it "Nothung." The two fall into each other's arms as the curtain falls quickly. They do not know that Wälse is none other than Wotan in disguise.

In the second act Wotan instructs his Valkyrie daughter Brünnhilde to aid Siegmund in battle. Brünnhilde withdraws as Fricka arrives to bring Hunding's case as a wronged husband. Fricka convinces Wotan that Siegmund is nothing but an echo, a slave of Wotan's will, and that he will have to fall to avenge the wrong done to the laws of marriage (not to mention incest) if the gods are to continue in their power. Wotan, beaten, agrees to her bargain. When Brünnhilde returns he bares his soul to her, telling her about the deceit involved in the payment for Valhalla and the fact that he has been touched by Alberich's curse, all, of course, from his point of view. He also mentions that Alberich has fathered a son who will soon be born. He concludes his powerful monologue with his wish for the end, an end that will be prepared by Alberich. He countermands his earlier order and sends her to announce death to Siegmund, warning her of the consequences of disobedience. When she goes to announce the death to Siegmund, she is drawn into his love for Sieglinde and agrees to shift her allegiance. Hunding arrives and attacks Siegmund, but, protected by Brünnhilde, Siegmund gains the upper hand. Wotan then appears and shatters Siegmund's sword, whereupon the defenseless Siegmund is slain by Hunding. Wotan regrets the death of Siegmund and kills Hunding before setting out in pursuit of the disobedient Brünnhilde.

At the beginning of the third act, the Valkyries, which translates as "choosers of the slain" and who are Wotan's daughters, are assembling on a mountain peak with their dead heroes. Brünnhilde arrives with Sieglinde on her horse. Sieglinde wishes to die until Brünnhilde tells her that she is pregnant with the greatest hero of the world. She sends Sieglinde off with the fragments of the sword and instructions to name the boy "Siegfried." Wotan arrives in a great rage and, after warning the other Valkyries off, turns to the punishment of Brünnhilde. She is to be banished from the immortals, left in a magic sleep to be awakened by the first man to find her. She will then serve him as his wife. She manages to soften the blow by having Wotan surround the rock with a fire that will prevent all but the bravest from penetrating to her. All references to this hero are sung to the notes of the Siegfried theme. The drama closes as Wotan surrounds the sleeping Brünnhilde with fire and slowly leaves.

Siegfried

The opening takes place in the smithy of Mime, Alberich's brother. Mime has been unable to forge a sword that will be strong enough for his young charge, Siegfried. Siegfried appears with a live bear who terrifies the dwarf. After driving the bear out, Siegfried demands a sword. He shatters the latest attempt, and Mime finally allows him to see the fragments of Nothung, Siegmund's sword, that he has been unable to forge. Siegmund rushes out into the forest after commanding Mime to forge him a sword from the fragments. A wanderer (Wotan in disguise) appears to Mime and proposes a riddle game in which each of them would wager his head on being able to answer three questions. Mime asks questions that call for general knowledge, and the wanderer answers them easily. Then the wanderer asks Mime which race of peoples were loved most by Wotan but were treated badly by him. Mime then shows that he knows a great deal more about the Wälsungs than he had admitted to Siegfried. Then he asks what weapon is necessary to kill Fafner, the dragon (the giant Fafner had used the Tarnhelm to change himself into a dragon to guard the hoard). Mime realizes it is Nothung, the sword. Finally the wanderer asks who will reforge Nothung. Mime cannot answer this question and thus loses his head. The wanderer tells him that "only the one who knows no fear" will be able to reforge the sword, and he says that the one who knows no fear will also take Mime's life. Siegfried returns and – violating all the rules of good smithing – files down the sword and reforges it. While he is at work, Mime brews a potion that is supposed to render Siegfried unconscious after he kills the dragon. The act ends when Siegfried demonstrates the power of his sword by cutting Mime's anvil in two.

At the beginning of the second act, Alberich is waiting for Fafner's killer. Wotan appears and awakens Fafner to allow Alberich a chance to regain the ring by exchanging it for Fafner's life. The dragon replies "I lie here and possess; let me sleep." Wotan withdraws, and Alberich engages in an argument with Mime over the ring, before both withdraw to watch the proceedings. Siegfried enjoys the peaceful beauty of the forest and attempts to communicate with a forest bird by means of a reed. It does not work, so he sounds his horn, which awakens the dragon. Siegfried kills the dragon. Some of the monster's blood gets on his finger and burns him. He puts his finger in his mouth, and when he tastes the blood, he can understand the forest bird. First he is instructed to recover the Tarnhelm and the ring from the hoard, which he does. Then he is warned about Mime, whose speech is also transformed by the dragon's blood so that Siegfried understands his meaning, not what he says. When Mime admits that he intends to kill Siegfried, the boy kills the dwarf. Finally the bird sends Siegfried off to awaken a beautiful maiden on a fire-surrounded rock.

At the beginning of the third act, Wotan awakens Erda in hopes of gaining further information from her. When she realizes that Wotan has separated himself from their daughter Brünnhilde, she realizes that she can no longer help him. Wotan tells her that the Wälsung approaching will pass through the fire and win Brünnhilde and that he has already gained the ring. Erda returns to sleep, and Wotan stands in the way of the approaching Siegfried. He engages in bantering talk until Siegfried tries to pass him, then he bars the way with his spear, telling the boy it had once shattered the sword he carried. Siegfried strikes out and cuts the spear in two, ending Wotan's power. Wotan withdraws, and Siegfried proceeds toward the mountain peak. The final scene is built around the awakening of Brünnhilde and her gradual transformation from the maiden protecting her virginity to the woman who will unite with Siegfried in "glowing love and laughing death."

NOTES

1. All quotes from the *Nibelungenlied* are from *Das Nibelungenlied: Nach der Ausgabe von Karl Bartsch herausgegeben von Helmut de Boor*, 22nd ed. (Wiesbaden: Brockhaus, 1988). All translations are my own and are designed to be literal rather than poetic. I have set down my thoughts on the *Nibelungenlied* in *The Nibelungenlied: History and Interpretation* (Urbana and Champagne: University of Illinois Press, 1986).

2. Quoted in Winder McConnell, *The Nibelungenlied*, TWAS 712 (Boston: Twayne, 1984), xii.

3. The publication history of the *Nibelungenlied* up to and including all of the editions by von der Hagen is discussed in the biography of the

scholar by Eckhard Grunewald, *Friedrich Heinrich von der Hagen 1780–1856*, Studia Linguistica Germanica 23 (Berlin: de Gruyter, 1988), 34ff.

4. An overview of this development can be found in English in McConnell, *The Nibelungenlied*.

5. Otfrid Ehrismann, *Das Nibelungenlied in Deutschland: Studien zur Rezeption des Nibelungenliedes von der Mitte des 18. Jahrhunderts bis zum Ersten Weltkrieg*, Münchener Germanistische Beiträge 14 (Munich: Fink, 1975).

6. Richard Wagner, *Mein Leben*, ed. Martin Gregor-Dellin (Mainz and Munich: Piper-Schott, 1983), 52–53.

7. All references to Wagner's writings are to his *Sämtliche Schriften und Dichtungen*, 16 vols. (Leipzig: Breitkopf und Härtel, n.d. [1911]). Stewart Spencer has a very good translation of the *Ring*, together with the German text, in *Wagner's Ring of the Nibelung: A Companion* (New York: Thames and Hudson, 1993). *Siegfrieds Tod* is available in a translation by William Ashton Ellis in his supplementary volume to *Richard Wagner's Prose Works*, 8 vols. (London: Routledge and Kegan Paul, 1899), 8:1–52.

8. "Hatte mich nun schon längst die herrliche Gestalt des Siegfried angezogen, so entzückte sie mich doch vollends erst, als es mir gelungen war, sie, von aller späteren Umkleidung befreit, in ihrer reinsten menschlichen Erscheinung vor mir zu sehen. Erst jetzt auch erkannte ich die Möglichkeit, ihn zum Helden eines Drama's zu machen, was mir nie eingefallen war, so lange ich ihn nur aus dem mittelalterlichen Nibelungenliede kannte." (4:312).

9. Snorri Sturluson, *Edda*, ed. Anthony Faulkes, 4 vols. (London: Viking Society for Northern Research, 1999). Also in English, translated by Anthony Faulkes (London: Dent, 1987).

10. *Edda: Die Lieder des Codex Regius*, ed. Gustav Neckel and Hans Kuhn, 4th printing (Heidelberg: Winter, 1962). In English in *The Poetic Edda*, trans. Carolyne Larrington, Oxford World's Classics (Oxford: Oxford University Press, 1996).

11. Guðni Jónsson, ed., in *Fornaldar sögur Norðulanda*, 4 vols. (Reykjavík: Islendingasagnaútgafan, 1954), 1:109–218. In English by Jesse Byock, *The Saga of the Volsungs: The Norse Epic of Sigurd the Dragon Slayer* (Berkeley: University of California Press, 1990).

12. Henrik Bertilsen, ed. (Copenhagen: Möller, 1905–11). Translated by Edward R. Haymes in *The Saga of Thidrek of Bern*, Garland Library of Medieval Literature 56B (New York: Garland, 1988).

13. Elizabeth Magee, *Richard Wagner and the Nibelungs* (Oxford: Clarendon Press, 1990).

14. *Niflungahringurinn og Íslenskar bókmenntir* (Reykjavík: Mál og Menning, 2000). In English as *Wagner and the Volsungs: Icelandic Sources of*

the Ring of the Nibelung, trans. Anna Yates and Anthony Faulkes (London: Viking Society for Northern Research, 2003). A somewhat different overview of Wagner's sources can be found in Danielle Buschinger *Le Moyen Age de Richard Wagner* (Amiens: Presse du Centre d'Études Médiévales, 2006).

15. The Greek connection is explored in Michael Ewans, *Wagner and Aeschylus: The "Ring" and the "Oresteia"* (New York: Cambridge University Press, 1982); and M. Owen Lee, *Athena Sings: Wagner and the Greeks* (Toronto: University of Toronto Press, 2003).

16. Wilhelm Grimm, *Die deutsche Heldensage* (Darmstadt: Wissenschatliche Buchgesellschaft, 1957; repr. of 1889 edition, originally published in 1829). I have discussed Wagner's use of these secondary sources in "Richard Wagner and the Altgermanisten," in Reinhold Grimm and Jost Hermand, ed., *Re-Reading Wagner* (Madison: University of Wisconsin Press, 1993), 23–38.

17. Franz Joseph Mone, *Untersuchungen zur Geschichte der teutschen Heldensage* (Quedlinburg and Leipzig: Basse, 1836).

18. George Bernard Shaw, *The Perfect Wagnerite* (London: Constable, 1898).

19. Curt von Westernhagen, *Richard Wagners Dresdener Bibliothek 1842 bis 1849* (Wiesbaden: Brockhaus, 1966), 99.

20. *Der Nibelungen Not mit der Klage*, ed. Karl Lachmann (Berlin: G. Reimer, 1826). Karl Lachmann, *Über die ursprüngliche Gestalt des Gedichts von der Nibelungen Noth* (Berlin: Dummler, 1816). The letter to Müller is quoted by Magee in *Richard Wagner*, 18–19.

21. This process is described by Barry Millington, *Wagner and his Operas* (Oxford: Oxford University Press, 2006), 96. Wagner did not settle on the final names for the dramas until 1856.

22. Jacob Grimm, *Deutsche Mythologie*, 2nd ed., 3 vols. (Wiesbaden: Drei Lilien Verlag, 1992, originally 1844, repr. of 4th ed. 1877), 3:48–61.

23. The only source for the new ideas is perhaps represented in the confusion surrounding the expression *ragna rök* (the doom of the gods) with *ragna rökr* (the twilight of the gods). The German translation of the latter would be *Götterdämmerung*. Scholars generally feel that *ragna rök* is the original term.

24. Cf. the treatment in Wolfgang Golther, *Die sagengeschichtlichen Grundlagen der Ringdichtung Richard Wagners* (Berlin: Verlag der Allgemeinen Musik-Zeitung, 1902), 102.

25. *Tagebuchblätter und Briefe an Mathilde Wesendonk 1853–1871*, ed. R. Sternfeld (Berlin: Deutsche Buchgemeinschaft, n.d.), 185.

26. Cf. Edward R. Haymes, "Two-Storied Medievalism in Wagner's *Die Meistersinger von Nürnberg*," *Studies in Medievalism* 3 (1991): 505–13.

Contributors

THEA CERVONE received her Ph.D. from the University of Illinois at Chicago in 1998. Her field of study is the English Reformation, especially the Tudor use of medieval materials in the Henrician period. She also researches oaths, vows, and covenants in the Tudor era and their roots in medieval legal, customary, and literary traditions. She lectures in medieval and Renaissance literature at the University of Southern California. Her courses focus on the enduring presence of medievalism in contemporary American entertainment, politics, and consumer culture. She is currently researching manuscript materials pertaining to fealty oaths to Henry VIII.

ELIZABETH EMERY is Professor of French at Montclair State University and the author of *Romancing the Cathedral: Gothic Architecture in Fin-de-siècle French Culture* (State University of New York Press, 2001), co-author of *Consuming the Past: The Medieval Revival in Fin-de-siècle France* (Ashgate, 2003), and co-editor of *Medieval Saints in Nineteenth-Century France* (McFarland, 2004). Her essays about medievalism and nineteenth-century French literature have appeared in such publications as *The Oxford Journal of the History of Collecting*, *The Journal of European Studies*, *Prose Studies*, *French Literature Studies*, *The French Review*, *Les Cahiers Naturalistes*, *Excavatio*, and *Modern Language Studies*.

KARL FUGELSO is Associate Professor of Art History at Towson University and Editor of *Studies in Medievalism*. He has published widely on medieval miniatures, Gothic architecture, Renaissance portraiture, nineteenth-century prints, and twentieth-century illustrations. He is currently studying the early fourteenth-century illumination of Musée Condé MS 597, which contains a presentation copy of Dante's *Inferno* and Guido da Pisa's commentary on it.

EDWARD R. HAYMES is Professor in the Department of Modern Languages at Cleveland State University. His Dr. Phil. is from the Friedrich-Alexander-Universität in Erlangen, Germany. His current areas of research are: the *Nibelungenlied*, oral theory, traditional Germanic epic, and Richard Wagner. At present he is working on a study of the earliest stages of *Der Ring des Nibelungen*, including a translation of *Siegfried's Tod*, an early version of *Götterdämmerung*.

EMILY HEADY received her Ph.D. in Victorian Literature from Indiana University and is Associate Professor of English and Director of the University Writing Program at Liberty University. Her work has appeared in *Dickens Studies Annual, Christianity and Literature, Texas Studies in Literature and Language, JNT,* and *Praxis.* She is at work on a book project dealing with the relationship between Victorian realism and religious conversion.

GWENDOLYN A. MORGAN is Professor of Medieval and British Literature and Language at Montana State University. Specializing in Medieval Literature and Contemporary Popular Culture, she has published four books in these areas as well as numerous articles and book chapters. She is also the editor of *The Year's Work in Medievalism,* an annual publication of the International Society for the Study of Medievalism, of which she is a senior officer. Her latest project, currently under way, is the writing of a grammar text for senior high school and university students.

GAIL ORGELFINGER received her Ph.D. from the University of Chicago and is Senior Lecturer in English at the University of Maryland, Baltimore County. Her research focuses on the reception of Joan of Arc in English culture, the subject of a monograph in progress. She is the author of *The Hystorye of Oluyer of Castylle: A New Edition* (Garland) and has published scholarly articles on Carl Theodor Dreyer's film *The Passion of Joan of Arc* and on late medieval chivalric practice. She is currently editing a volume of essays, *J. K. Rowling's Medievalism,* for the Edwin Mellen Press.

NILS HOLGER PETERSEN received his Ph.D. in 1994 and is Associate Professor of Church History and Centre Leader for the *Centre for the Study of the Cultural Heritage of Medieval Rituals* (under the Danish National Research Foundation) at the Theological Faculty, University of Copenhagen. His research concentrates on medieval liturgy and its reception in the modern arts. He is a consultant editor for the forthcoming *Encyclopedia of the Bible and its Reception* (De Gruyter). Together with Dr. Eyolf Østrem he is co-authoring the monograph *Medieval Ritual and Early Modern Music: The Devotional Practice of "Lauda" Singing in Late-Renaissance Italy* (2008).

TOM SHIPPEY is currently Walter J. Ong Chair of Humanities at Saint Louis University. He has published three books on Tolkien, the latest being a collection of papers, *Roots and Branches* (2007). He has also published widely on Old and Middle English, and on the history of philological studies: his books include *The Critical Heritage: "Beowulf"* (1998), and the edited collection *The Shadow-walkers: Jacob Grimm's Mythology of the Monstrous* (2005). A collection of essays on the latter theme – *Constructing Nations,*

Reconstructing Myth, edited by Andrew Wawn – was published in his honor in 2007. Professor Shippey is preparing a further collection, provisionally titled "Forging the Nation(al Epic)."

CLARE A. SIMMONS is Professor of English at The Ohio State University. She is the author of *Reversing the Conquest: History and Myth in Nineteenth-Century British Literature, Eyes Across the Channel: French Revolutions, Party History, and British Writing 1830–1882*, and papers and articles on nineteenth-century British literature and medievalism. The Co-Editor of *Prose Studies*, she also edited the essay collection *Medievalism and the Quest for the "Real" Middle Ages* and Charlotte Mary Yonge's *The Clever Woman of the Family*. Her current project is titled *Popular Medievalism in Britain 1789–1851*.

MARK B. SPENCER is Associate Professor of English and Humanities at Southeastern Oklahoma State University. He holds two doctoral degrees, one in medieval history from the University of Kentucky and the other in comparative literature from the University of Arkansas. A revised version of his first dissertation on late medieval historical writing was published as *Thomas Basin 1412–1490: The History of Charles VII and Louis XI* in 1997, and his current scholarly focus is on modern historical novels set during the Middle Ages and Renaissance. Forthcoming articles include studies of Pär Lagerkvist's *The Dwarf* and George Garrett's *The Death of the Fox*.

M. J. TOSWELL, Associate Professor of English at the University of Western Ontario, works principally on Old English psalm translations and Anglo-Saxon psalters, but her magpie tendency has led to articles on Tacitus, Earle Birney, W. H. Auden; editing for six years the journal *Florilegium*; courses on fantasy literature after Tolkien, Arthurian literature, and neomedievalism; and many byways in administration.

DOUGLAS RYAN VANBENTHUYSEN received his B.A. in literature from The Thomas More College of Liberal Arts and his M.A. in English from Marquette University; he is current working on his Ph.D. in English with a medieval focus at the University of New Mexico. His research interests include Anglo-Saxon poetry, the poetic manuscripts, and old Germanic languages. His dissertation will focus on how the choices made in transcriptions, translations, and other presentations of *Beowulf* (including films, comic books, video games, etc.) influence the critical understanding of the poem. He also has designed and maintains the website for the Medieval Graduate Students in English at UNM: <http://megse.unm.edu/>.

KATHLEEN VERDUIN is Professor of English at Hope College. From 1982 until 1998 she served as Associate Editor of *Studies in Medievalism*. She is at work on a book tracing the nineteenth-century American response to Dante.

WERNER WUNDERLICH is director of the Institute of Media and Communication Management and holds the Media and Culture chair at the University of St Gallen (Switzerland). In 2006 he founded the Competence Centre for Bibliology and established the degree program "Studies in Bibliology." His research interests are the cultural history of media, medieval German literature, and medieval reception, economics and culture, as well as inter-media studies of opera. Together with Ulrich Müller (University of Salzburg) he is the editor of the series "Medieval Myths."

Previously published volumes

Volume I

1. Medievalism in England
Edited by Leslie J. Workman. Spring 1979

2 Medievalism in America
Edited by Leslie J. Workman. Spring 1982

Volume II

1. Twentieth-Century Medievalism
Edited by Jane Chance. Fall 1982

2. Medievalism in France
Edited by Heather Arden. Spring 1983

3. Dante in the Modern World
Edited by Kathleen Verduin. Summer 1983

4. Modern Arthurian Literature
Edited by Veronica M. S. Kennedy and Kathleen Verduin. Fall 1983

Volume III

1. Medievalism in France 1500–1750
Edited by Heather Arden. Fall 1987

2. Architecture and Design
Edited by John R. Zukowsky. Fall 1990

3. Inklings and Others
Edited by Jane Chance. Winter 1991

4. German Medievalism
Edited by Francis G. Gentry. Spring 1991
Note: Volume III, Numbers 3 and 4, are bound together

IV. Medievalism in England
Edited by Leslie Workman. 1992

V. Medievalism in Europe
Edited by Leslie Workman. 1993

VI. Medievalism in North America
Edited by Kathleen Verduin. 1994